PRAISE FOR *THE FORGIVENESS TOUR*

"Susan Shapiro mixes memoir, religion, psychology and journalism to tell amazing stories of forgiveness. The tales, ranging from uplifting to unsettling, are always riveting." —A.J. Jacobs, bestselling author of *The Year of Living Biblically* and *It's All Relative*

"As a popular chronicler of bad habits and poor life decisions, Shapiro has found her best topic yet: how to confront the pain in your life caused by someone you believe owes you an apology. *The Forgiveness Tour*'s wide-ranging tales of true heartache and gripping confrontation show readers how to find what they need to finally heal from what has been hurting them. Smart, witty and inspirational."

—Tom Reiss, Pulitzer Prize author of *The Black Count*

"*The Forgiveness Tour* takes us on journeys to right unforgivable wrongs. Shapiro illuminates how we can heal from those who harmed us most. Powerful, intimate and profound."

—Gabrielle Selz, author of *Unstill Life*

"In her signature quick-witted, compulsively readable voice, Susan Shapiro explores forgiveness with honesty, humor and heart."

—Erin Khar, author of *Strung Out*

"Shapiro holds my eye and ear with urgency, compelling dialogue, and fresh insights into human behavior. I found *The Forgiveness Tour* hard to put down."

—Grace Schulman, author of *Strange Paradise* and *The Marble Bed*

THE
FORGIVENESS
TOUR

THE
FORGIVENESS
TOUR

HOW TO FIND THE PERFECT APOLOGY

SUSAN SHAPIRO

Skyhorse Publishing

Skyhorse Publishing books may be purchased in bulk at special discounts for sales promotion, corporate gifts, fund-raising, or educational purposes. Special editions can also be created to specifications. For details, contact the Special Sales Department, Skyhorse Publishing, 307 West 36th Street, 11th Floor, New York, NY 10018 or info@skyhorsepublishing.com.

Skyhorse® and Skyhorse Publishing® are registered trademarks of Skyhorse Publishing, Inc.®, a Delaware corporation.

Visit our website at www.skyhorsepublishing.com.

10 9 8 7 6 5 4 3 2 1

Library of Congress Cataloging-in-Publication Data is available on file.

Cover design by Eyal Solomon

Print ISBN: 978-1-5107-6271-8
Ebook ISBN: 978-1-5107-6615-0

Printed in the United States of America

TABLE OF CONTENTS

Author's Note: Some names, dates, timelines, settings, and personal characteristics have been changed for literary cohesion and to protect privacy. In several cases, I went back to further interview subjects and added source material to elucidate the story.

Short excerpts of this work have appeared, in slightly different form, in *The New York Times, Longreads, Salon, The Independent, Tablet,* and *The Revealer.*

Dedication: To my father, Jack Shapiro

NOTE TO THE READER

My childhood rabbi once explained that on Yom Kippur, the saddest day of the Jewish calendar, sins made before God in the past year were mercifully erased, but not offenses committed against fellow humans. To come clean, we have to approach those we've wronged, confess our misdeeds, and beg forgiveness. And when someone offers a sincere apology, we're required to forgive. Yet what if the one who hurt you refuses to express any regret?

This question haunted me after the person I trusted most lied to me repeatedly for months on end. Stunned by his betrayal, I could barely eat or sleep. When he wouldn't apologize or explain his ongoing deceit, I vowed we'd never speak again. Yet ghosting him didn't end my distress. I found myself having screaming arguments with him in my mind, reliving our fight in panicked nightmares, even lighting a candle and chanting a secret Yiddish curse to exact revenge. I was losing my dignity and sanity. His inability to acknowledge his mistake or say "I'm sorry" sent me into a tailspin. I couldn't just move on.

As I told friends and colleagues why I was so upset, they revealed their own wounds caused by those who'd let them down without ever explaining or atoning for their sins. Listening to their struggles, often way worse than mine—through wars, alcoholism, divorce, sexual abuse, and death—put my fury into perspective.

"But what happens if they never apologize?" I kept asking. "Is it possible to forgive someone anyway?"

Self-proclaimed forgiveness authorities bombarded pages, screens, and airwaves, offering proof of the infinite benefits of embracing those who'd offended you. They warned about the burdens of not forgiving. These so-called experts claimed that, for your health, you should grant mercy, even to someone completely remorseless. But honestly, how hard was saying two damn words after a major screw-up? Their broad advice to exonerate everyone for everything felt like bullshit.

Donning my reporter's hat, I embarked on what I called "The Forgiveness Tour," asking thirteen people I knew across the nation, "Who owes you an apology? How do you reconnect with someone if they won't say I'm sorry? Would hearing their remorse make it possible for you to forgive?" Further researching the concept of forgiveness, I spoke with gurus from all faiths and backgrounds who painted a more nuanced picture of when someone should be pardoned, and when not.

My odyssey helped me understand how significant apologies were, and how small my saga was. I was intrigued to see that holding a grudge could actually be healthier and that spite could be inspiring. Also that reparations to repair the damage done might have a stronger effect than words of contrition. While I'd never been kosher or kept the Sabbath, my resentment drove me to religious exploration. I became fascinated by ways that wise clergy and scholars from different beliefs decided whether benevolence was called for. What I learned gave me the strength to face the one whose inexplicable actions motivated my quest. Finally speaking with him, I uncovered a heartbreaking secret that blew the lid off all the theories of forgiving.

I hope sharing my story and those of others who suffered much more than I did will push you to pinpoint the most important apology you need and to ask for it directly. Or perhaps, if atonement is not forthcoming, it will help you find ways to heal—and deal—without it. You might be as surprised as I was. Seeing the wreckage caused by unspoken apologies may even inspire you to say "I'm sorry" to someone you hurt.

CHAPTER 1
A BETRAYAL EXPOSED
AUGUST 2010

"Forgiveness is not forgetting. It is letting go of the other person's throat."—novelist William Paul Young

I'd always seen myself as someone compassionate who never held grudges, but that changed the night I turned the corner of West 9th Street and caught Haley leaving *his* brownstone. What the hell was *she* doing *here*? I prayed my eyes were playing tricks and the woman in skinny jeans, heels, and a pink blouse was another tall redhead, not my favorite student. Inching closer, it was her unmistakable auburn hair flapping down her back as she flounced away. I froze, so crushed I couldn't breathe.

Recovering enough to rush inside, I yelled, "I just saw Haley walk out. You've been lying to me!"

"I never lied to you," he insisted, quickly closing his door.

"Don't tell me you're sleeping with her?"

"Of course not." He looked horrified.

This wasn't my lover, cheating with a younger woman. He was the long-term therapist who'd saved me from decades of drugs, alcohol, and self-destruction. I couldn't believe that right before our session, Dr. Winters had met with my protégée, whom I'd loved like a daughter. For the past three years, she'd sat in my classroom, my living room, beside me at literary events, and joined me for speed walking around the park. She was the only person I'd ever asked him not to see, and she'd vowed not to invade my private haven. I felt hoodwinked by both sides.

Just hours before that hot Friday evening in August, Haley had emailed to see if I'd recommend my gynecologist, housekeeper, and literary agent. "Want my husband too?" I'd joked. In the spring, when I'd first sensed she was ransacking my address book and life, I'd asked Dr. Winters what he thought of the eerie *All About Eve* aura.

"She sounds nuts," he'd said.

"That's your clinical assessment?" I asked, adding "Don't be flippant. She's important to me. And she asked for your number so she could see you too."

He'd sworn he wouldn't treat her, brushing off my paranoia.

Now I could barely speak as I realized she'd broken her word. Worse, he'd let her in, giving her the slot directly before mine, then ran late, as if he wanted me to catch her. Perched at the edge of his leather couch, I imagined Haley sitting right where I was, leaning on the embroidered cushions, spilling secrets she'd previously shared only with *me* to *my* confidante. His plush workspace morphed from my relaxing refuge for fifteen years into the creepy *Cabinet of Dr. Caligari*.

"Then why was she here?" I couldn't process her so out of context.

"That woman is not my patient," he insisted.

His technical wordplay sounded like Bill denying Monica. I craved a drink, joint, and cigarette.

So the charming acolyte, who'd reminded me of me, hadn't been harmlessly competitive, as I'd rationalized. She'd ruthlessly conspired to be my replacement—and succeeded. She'd somehow become my rival, whom Dr. Winters preferred. She was twenty years younger, prettier, breezier. At twenty-nine, her youth mocked me. A time machine was suddenly transforming me into a distorted funhouse reflection of myself, like the actor in the Truffaut film shocked by his image in the car window, yelling "I'm so old!" I went from hip urban success story to pathetic middle-aged hair-dyeing wannabe.

On my way to his office that evening, wearing a flowery summer skirt, T-shirt, and sandals instead of my all-black armor, I'd envisioned how proud he'd be when I handed him the signed copy of my first novel, hidden in my purse. After spying Haley, my world twisted darker.

"You're not having an affair with her?" I repeated, recalling she'd recently split with her fiancé.

"No, of course not. I would never touch a patient," Dr. Winters insisted.

"Aha. You just called her your *patient!*" I yelled, all the impulse control he'd taught me flouncing down the street with Haley. "Is she paying to see you? Or not?"

"I am not her *official* therapist," he repeated, sitting down.

"You're arguing semantics with me now?" I yelled. "Really?"

He should have been straight and said, "I need the money," or "I'm sick of your boring issues. I want new blood." I could have handled honesty. If I understood, I'd forgive him anything. I respected his candor. Once, when I asked why he called me his "most taxing patient," he told me: "You have a chronic anxiety level connected to a hyperactive mind that's plugged into an analytic level of consciousness. There's no rest or rhythm. It's all high-pitch. There's a continual idiosyncratic intensity that's exhausting."

Captivated by his weirdly apt description of me, I'd scrawled it down in my notebook and quoted my personalized diagnosis everywhere, like an alibi to get me out of faking normalcy. When I read it to Mom over the phone in Michigan, she said, "Wow. That perfectly describes your father." My conservative dad, who hated my writing, my move back to his old city, and my devotion to therapy, had also been a heavy smoker. We'd bonded over our shared method of self-destruction, which we'd stopped around the same time, although—unlike me—he went cold turkey.

I could only quit with the behavioral cure cultivated by Dr. Winters, the adoptive New York father who "got me." With his short brown hair and glasses, he was nerdily handsome like Dad, but twenty years younger. He dressed fastidiously, in buttoned shirts tucked into khakis and slim ties. At 6 feet and 160 pounds (yes I asked), he was thinner and more diet-obsessed than Dad, or anyone in my family. Perhaps that was why Dr. Winters could help me give up all my bad habits—including the Juicy Fruit gum I'd chewed compulsively post-cigarettes, joints, and vodka. I'd even miraculously lost weight while giving up tobacco. When he advised me to "depend on people, not substances," I told him that a feminist relying on a sexist male like himself was ridiculous.

"To stay clean, you have to trust me," he'd said. A former chain smoker, he confided that his mother was a raging alcoholic who chose booze over him. Softened by the disclosure, I lost my skepticism, anointing him my sage, sponsor, and higher power, though he was only eight years my senior. To battle what he called "the worst nicotine withdrawal in history," he taught me to "suffer well."

While I relinquished my toxic habits, he revamped my existence: pushing Aaron to propose, helping me land more teaching gigs and book deals in my forties, tripling my income. When I was devastated that my dad trashed my memoirs, Dr. Winters said, "He's threatened. He'll come around to seeing how important your work is." He urged me to teach, do charity, "err on the side of generosity." In his office-sanctuary, he was the WASP rabbi I confessed to with religious devotion. "*Everything* is too important to you," he declared. If I felt snubbed, he said, "The slight is never your imagination but then you overreact." Was I overreacting now?

I couldn't ask him or be rational when *he* was the one I was slighted by. What happened when your crisis management strategy became your crisis? With our trust broken, my sobriety and success could unravel, my fierce reliance on him going haywire.

"Don't you think this two-faced mind game is counterproductive?" I tried to breathe.

"I'm not playing mind games. I don't lie." He crossed his legs, ruffled.

"I just can't fucking believe Haley was here," I said, their dual deception unhinging me.

"I don't want to talk about it anymore."

"But you're the one who says 'Always lead the least secretive life!'" It felt like he was violating his mantra, which I'd repeated in my classes and books, like a chanting Moonie. I pictured tossing a chair through his window, shattering glass on his gray carpet, storming out for good. But after fifteen years, I needed an explanation. Plus he'd charge me $200 for the appointment regardless.

"Is this about money?" I demanded, recalling his fee was higher for new patients.

"If you don't like how I run my practice, let's cancel all your sessions," he snapped.

I winced. I had an intense unconventional link with Dr. Winters, but his threat was out of character. I never felt so abandoned or vulnerable, not even when Dad read my *New York Times* essay on my infertility and emailed, "Stop running naked through the streets. You're humiliating our whole family." Getting bamboozled by the head doctor who fixed me was more distressing because it was unexpected. Being trustworthy was his *job*.

Had I been deluded to believe I was important to him? He'd shown me poetry about his abusive mother. He'd shared how distraught he'd been when his Battery Park townhouse was destroyed in the 9/11 attacks. Unlike my real dad, he loved my work. We'd actually taken notes to coauthor a substance abuse guide together in the future. My best friend Claire worried I was caught in some kind of counter-transference I couldn't control. I argued that most addiction therapy was unorthodox and, since overdoses could be fatal, "You can do anything as long as it works." Yet my powerful bond with him convinced me I was special, a colleague he confided in, *his* star protégée, the way Haley was mine.

"You realize you colluded with my student to deceive me?" I asked.

"I hope you can forgive the imaginary crime you envision I've committed," he sneered.

I was stung by his sarcastic non-apology. "I didn't imagine you'd treat the one person you swore you wouldn't. Haley's a former student now in my private writing group. She took a newspaper job I recommended. She's my exercise buddy and good friend..."

"That woman is *not* your friend," he interrupted.

"What the hell does that mean?" Him telling me that Haley had become my enemy poured gasoline onto my heart-flames. His statement was out of line on so many levels, my brain was exploding. "So she was just sitting here, trashing me?" I asked, tangled in an Oedipal tornado that wouldn't stop spinning.

"Susan, what do you want from me?"

"An apology for screwing up, and an end to this disturbing triangle. Can't you just refer her to someone else like you promised?"

"You don't tell me which patients I see," he yelled. "It's my institute. You don't control my baby!"

I'd never heard him raise his voice like that or refer to his practice this way. Now it was official: the person in charge of healing my psyche was crazier than I was.

CHAPTER 2
WHEN AN APOLOGY IS CALLED FOR

"It is easier to forgive an enemy than to forgive a friend."

—William Blake

I stumbled home to my apartment, mumbling to myself, then picked up my landline. "Why did you call Dr. Winters when you said you wouldn't?" I asked Haley.

"I can't fathom what business of yours that is," she replied.

"It wouldn't be, if you hadn't called *my* therapist after I asked you not to. You can't just co-opt my editors, saviors, and existence. That doesn't even work," I told her. "How long have you been seeing him?"

"Since May," she said, quietly.

"So you ask if you could call my shrink, I say no, and you steal him anyway?"

"Sue, I adore you, I'm closer to you than my own relatives. But seeing him has nothing to do with you. I'm quitting the newspaper and your workshop. I can only have one guru. I need to listen to Daniel now."

Using his first name while dumping me—and the editorship I'd recommended—stung.

I'd met Haley in my feature journalism class three years before, her beauty hidden under overalls and a fishing hat. "Your addiction memoir changed my life," she said with a Southern twang as we went around the room to introduce ourselves the first session. "I knew your husband Aaron when I studied at NYU. He's the best professor there."

Man, this chick aced Networking 101. As a forty-six-year-old childless teacher well-known only in my little twelve-block radius, I'd found her comments flattering. The book she cited chronicled my extraordinary treatment with Dr. Winters, the tall, dashing rule-breaker who'd let me explore in print his provocative disclosures about the violent alcoholic mother who hated him. A few critics felt it made his ardent theories credible. Others branded him a renegade for sharing such personal details with a patient. Yet he was the only one to rid me of toxic habits I'd had since I was thirteen. He was my "core pillar," as he called it, along with my husband, a curly-haired Jewish charmer who was only addicted to me.

I'd been jolted by Dr. Winters' part-time move to Arizona the year before. Our twice weekly sessions switched to twice monthly when he'd fly to New York. Aaron took a gig with long hours as a producer on a TV cop drama. Then my father had a heart attack and retired from his fifty years in medicine. I was thankful he made a full recovery. But this gave him more time to trash my career. Having given up my former artistic crowd of stoners and drinkers, I was lonely. "Just when you think you lost everything, you find you have even more to lose," Bob Dylan sang. I was so substance restricted, a friend said, "Hey, let's go out and get some water."

"Take on more classes," Dr. Winters advised. "That way you'll do good in the world."

Teaching weekly essay courses at night was a balm for social isolation, and I sympathized with students chronicling their failures and emptiness. For my assignment on "your most humiliating secret," Haley told how, after a year of real estate hell, she and her fiancé Donald bought her fantasy downtown loft—then he dumped her the day they moved in. She was heartbroken, crashing on classmate's couches. I recognized her hunger to get everything (apartment, love, clips) too quickly, like me. I'd subtitled my method "Instant Gratification Takes Too Long" and indeed her piece immediately saw print. Yet from rough draft to publication, she changed the last line from her breakup to "I finally found my true home."

"Original ending was better," I told her.

"We got back together and you said in nonfiction you can't lie," she told me.

"If you stay in past tense, you're not lying," I said, not one for corny endings.

A week later I bumped into Haley at a Cooper Union reading with Donald, who was tall, with regal bearing. In her miniskirt and heels, with makeup and her long red hair down, she was a bombshell.

"I first saw you at a panel here a year ago," she'd confided in the ladies' room, tinting her lips pinker in the mirror. "The way you showed off about your successful students made me want to study with you. That's why I tracked you down." I was just moderating the panel of big-name literary headliners. To Haley, I was the rock star.

After our six-week class was over, she requested one of my walk-and-talk office hours. As we speed-walked around Washington Square Park, she asked advice on everything from career to marriage to drinking moderately. I urged her to give up alcohol altogether, as well as fantasies of being saved by her off-and-on wealthy fiancé. I divulged sagas of my past self-destruction, as Dr. Winters had with me. I recommended her for a gig as an assistant newspaper editor. She landed the job and was promptly promoted. To thank me, she published the work of a bunch of my current students. I invited her to join the private workshops I ran at home, where she gracefully line edited all of my rough drafts.

When Haley invited me to a big party for her twenty-ninth birthday in May, I promised to attend. My urban frontier days, where dozens of poets crammed into my old 300-square-foot studio for free beer and popcorn, were a far cry from her Lower East Side penthouse duplex with a wrap-around terrace. I looked forward to a late bash I didn't have to plan, finance, or schlep to Brooklyn for.

"Come early," she'd emailed. "I need your eye."

At 9 p.m., I stepped from the elevator into her chic 3,000-square-foot palace. She hugged me, wearing cut-off shorts, high heels, and a glittery top. "Sue! You're here! I'm so psyched you came!" she gushed like I was a dignitary.

I handed her a Strand bag filled with books, crudités, hummus, cheese and crackers.

"Thanks, Jewish mother," she laughed as others she'd hired to help dribbled in to set up.

Haley unwrapped my gift, the books *High Maintenance* and *Little Stalker* by my colleague Jennifer, since Haley loved urban fiction. "And here's a signed galley of my novel like you requested."

"I'm honored. Can't wait to read it. What a rave in *PW*! Is that why you look so lit up?"

I smiled, feeling youthful and festive in my swingy black summer skirt and high sandals. "When I sent the advance reviews to my mom, she said 'Go ahead, tell the whole world you're in therapy.'"

"My mom says that too! 'All you crazy New Yorkers with your therapists.'" Haley mimicked her mother's Alabama twang. "Sue, can I ask you something? Do you really think that without Dr. Winters you wouldn't be sober, published, and married?"

I nodded, sensing something wrong. "Where's Donald?" I glanced up the winding staircase.

"After we had a fight, he jetted off to Belize this morning," she said.

On her birthday? Damn him. The timing made their romantic troubles melodramatic. Then again, my best party at her age was motivated by the loss of my heart to a sociopathic biographer I'd also stupidly moved in with too soon.

"I keep begging Donald to try couples therapy," she said, looking fragile.

"Aaron only tried when *I* walked out on *him*," I told her. "You know what Paula says?" I'd recommended my old therapist, Paula Goode, who Haley was seeing. "Remember 'Love doesn't make you happy. Make yourself happy. Then you'll find love,'" I quoted.

"Last night in bed I was reading Donald the scene in your memoir where Dr. Winters said you're not allowed to criticize your husband. Donald said, 'Now that doctor is smart.' You think it's bad to criticize your guy?" Haley asked, forgetting the whole "Make yourself happy" part.

Picturing her reciting the dialogue between Dr. Winters and me to her fiancé in bed felt too intimate, even for an over-sharer like me.

"Can I call Dr. Winters?" she asked.

I said no, explaining that the patient-therapist relationship was based on confidentiality and transference and that therapists weren't like dentists. There was an unspoken rule not to see the same shrink as your close friend, relative, or teacher. I certainly didn't want to bump into her in his waiting room, my safest harbor, where I ripped off my teacher/author mask. That was why I'd referred her to Paula. "I can recommend another smart male shrink," I offered.

"You're so generous, Sue." She leaned her head on my shoulder. "I won't call Winters. I didn't mean to overstep." Then she asked, "Is the number of the Jungian astrologer you wrote about listed? He has a PhD in clinical psych, right?"

Before I could reiterate that she should try some of the other 20,000 head doctors in the city, she spun off to greet a bunch of guests I recognized. Two students from my last class stepped off the elevator. The girl with a nose ring shouted, "Hey, Prof Sue, what are you doing here?"

"I'm helping her promote her dazzling roman à clef, coming out in August, the month shrinks are away," Haley said, flitting by. "There's a keg, and red and white wine by the bar."

She was a fun hostess, like I'd once been—before I quit alcohol, drugs, and became a workaholic. "My shrink is actually coming to town in August," I clarified.

"So cool about your novel," said Nose Ring, who also had a silver hoop through her lip.

I handed her a postcard for my upcoming reading, wondering if it hurt when she kissed.

By 11 p.m., the space was packed with friends, colleagues, and other students I was schmoozing with. My editor Robert walked in. "Aside from the fact that a newspaper assistant making $200 a week lives in a $5 million loft, notice anything strange?" he asked.

I looked around, clueless.

"Is there anyone here you don't know, Sue?"

"No wonder I'm having a good time," I said.

"Everyone upstairs for a surprise," Haley yelled, guiding the crowd up the winding stairway.

"My back is too old for that staircase," Robert said as we sat on the couch together, catching up.

When Nose Ring came back downstairs, I asked, "What's happening up there?"

"A flame-thrower's eating fire on the roof," she said on her way to the loo.

"We met the flame thrower at a book event I took her to last week," I said. "Funny she didn't mention hiring her."

"That your agent?" Robert pointed. I nodded as he asked, "Sure you trust red-headed Vampira?"

"Of course," I answered.

But at my next Dr. Winters session, I told him, "Haley connected with 100 of my Facebook friends. She sees my old female therapist and wants to call Stargazer—and you. What if she's shrink-stalking me?"

"Don't worry. If she ever called here, I would just recommend a colleague," he'd reassured.

Case closed. Until the August night I learned they'd been shrinking behind my back. After hanging up the phone with her, I emailed Dr. Winters in disbelief. "You've been seeing Haley for *four* months?"

"She's getting smart advice from me," he responded right away. "Let people move on."

They acted like I was crazy to care if he saw her or that they'd double-crossed me. Was I?

That night, I had a nightmare my father was eloping with the daughter

I never had. I couldn't concentrate, sleep, or eat. I lost thirteen pounds over the next thirteen days. Paranoia reigned. "Let's not tell Sue. It's just between us," I pictured Haley whispering. "You shouldn't listen to her. She's not a doctor, she just repeats what I tell her," he'd answer. As daily cyber arguments with Haley and Dr. Winters built, so did my resentment. One Wednesday, when they both ignored my emails, I *really* lost it.

That stormy dawn, as Aaron snored, I broke free of his arms. I sneaked to the living room, opening the windows. The lightning outside mirrored my frenzied mood. I turned on the old rhythm and blues mix tape my first heartbreak made me in high school. I'd never officially hexed anyone before but recalled the time my mother, invoking her maiden name, whispered, "The Goodman women are witches." Sitting on the floor, lights dimmed, I lit a wildflower candle. Groggy and frazzled, I put a double curse on Dr. Winters and Haley. I chanted a Yiddish expression my mother taught me was profane: *Vaksn zolstu vi a tsibele mitn kop in dr'erd*, adding confessional poetry and Edith Piaf, scrawling in my notebook that she needs to stay out of my life and he should hurt as much as I did. Forgetting what my mom's expression meant, I emailed her to ask.

"May your head grow in the ground like an onion," she wrote back.

Eight hours later, Haley emailed she was on a plane to Europe. My curse had chased her bad juju away from my city. Next Dr. Winters responded that he'd been bedridden, in pain from kidney stones; he could barely move. I felt wildly powerful. Then I was petrified she'd die in a crash and my Semitic spell would kill him. Sleep deprived, my sanity was slipping.

"Sorry you're sick," I typed, freaked out, imagining Dr. Winters doing daily phone sessions from the hospital long-distance with Haley, where they kept insulting me:

"You should see the sucky first drafts Sue brings to the group," Haley would tell him.

"You should have seen her while she was drinking and smoking," Dr. Winters would confide.

Aaron woke to find me sobbing at my desk. "Step away from your computer," he commanded, imitating the voice of a policeman from his TV show. He read the email chain.

"Remember the nickname I gave Haley the first time I met her, when she acted like she'd been my best NYU student and I had no idea who she was?" he asked. "Crazypants."

Patting my head, he said, "It's time we lose Haley and Dr. Winters altogether."

I told Haley not to call me again. Insisting I break off all communication with Dr. Winters, Aaron left a phone message on his machine instructing him not to contact me anymore. That provoked an incendiary email: "So your husband speaks for you now?"

For the first time in fifteen years, I did not respond.

* * *

My mind kept trying to solve the infuriating enigma of my head doctor and Haley. It seemed an important sign when I heard a message from Moshe Pindrus, an Orthodox rabbi friend in Israel. He knew how wise Dr. Winters could be. Moshe had phoned me after reading a review of my addiction memoir in *The Jerusalem Post*. Needing help to stop smoking, he asked if he could do a few long-distance sessions with Dr. Winters. I'd had no trouble giving this stranger the number for Skyping from afar with my shrink, who soon became his elixir too. We met a year later when he visited Brooklyn. Calling Moshe back, I blurted out everything that had happened.

"In your religious view, are there actions that are unpardonable?" I asked.

"None," Moshe said. "If one properly repents, The Talmud says you can be forgiven anything."

"What if you leave the fold?" I wanted to know.

"In Judaism, if you return to the faith and truly regret your past sins, you'll be forgiven."

Aha! There's the rub. "But what if there are no regrets or atoning?"

"When a person has wronged another, he must obtain forgiveness from the one he hurt first, before God will pardon the sinner," Moshe replied. "But according to the letter of the Jewish law, as long as you have informed the offending party of your grievance, you are under no obligation to forgive him until he apologizes. You should not remain silent and despise him."

"You don't think I have a right to be pissed off?" I was confused.

"Not me. That's Samuel 13:22," he said. "'He is commanded to make the matter known and ask him, 'Why did you do this to me? Why did you wrong me regarding that matter?' You shall surely admonish him.'"

"I admonished him," I said. "So you're saying more admonishment?"

"That was Leviticus 19:17," he clarified.

A bearded grandfather with a quick wit, Moshe often spoke in Hebrew bible quotes—that is, when he wasn't showing me pictures of his dozens of offspring, asking questions about nicotine withdrawal, or soliciting tips for dropping weight post-tobacco.

"Yes, keep admonishing," he advised.

I emailed Dr. Winters the question: "Don't head doctors take the Hippocratic Oath to do no harm?"

Within hours he responded, "Things are not always as you see them."

Wondering what that meant, I sifted through our past correspondence. When Aaron went to L.A. on business, I stayed up twenty hours straight, reading thousands of emails from Dr. Winters over the years. I came across the notes I'd taken for the addiction proposal we'd worked on, fascinated by the medical records he'd shared of (nameless) patients he helped get off alcohol, drug, and food dependencies. Forgetting to sleep, I printed out pages, scrawling comments in the margins, starring important passages, as if I could do therapy by osmosis. I was overjoyed I could use all of his methods to soothe me without needing him.

By Friday, I was a mess. Desperate not to relapse, I tried all of Dr. Winters' coping techniques that I'd underlined: I journaled. Drank green tea. Took deep breaths. Swam 100 laps. Ate boiled shrimp—but sixteen was too many. To burn off the calories, I speed-walked five miles around the local park by myself, missing Haley. Then I went to the gym to kick-box, pretending I was pummeling Dr. Winters. Pounding too hard, I felt a strain in my back. In a blur of anger and sweat, I didn't realize I was seriously injured until I could barely walk home. Two Aleves didn't stop the ache. I woke up worse.

I'd never had a physical impairment like this before. Aaron offered to come back from L.A. early. I said I'd be fine. I wasn't. My back was throbbing. I could barely sit. I went to the medicine cabinet and took a Tylenol with codeine from Aaron's old back injury. When it didn't work in a half hour, I swallowed another, along with his leftover Xanax. I knew that taking someone else's medication was dangerous, a huge red flag for an addict.

As the medicine numbed my back ache, I scrutinized all of Dr. Winters' case studies more carefully: the male pill popper, the girl who became sleep deprived from too much caffeine, the church-goer so obsessed with charity she neglected her family, and the young man addicted to extreme exercise. I'd been adopting the substance problems of each of his former patients!

It was easy to see why we'd developed addictions when people could be so unreliable and horrible. As the medicine wore off, the pulsating pain returned to my lower spine. Sweating, I had to lie flat on the floor. I picked up my cell phone, about to dial my parents in Michigan. But I was too embarrassed to tell Dad about injuring myself since it was related to therapy, which he always ridiculed. I put the phone down. My father was the last person in the world I wanted to go crawling back to.

CHAPTER 3
THE FORGIVENESS INDUSTRY
SEPTEMBER 2010

"To be wronged is nothing, unless you continue to remember it."

—Confucius

I used to pity friends who stopped speaking to their relatives or colleagues. I didn't want to be an angry person, clinging to an everlasting vendetta. Yet I wasn't a doormat. I adhered to W.H. Auden's poetic advice to "Believe your pain" and Rabbi Hillel's warning, "If I am not for myself, who will be for me?" Still, I'd always forgiven everyone everything. I even forgave my college boyfriend who'd slept with not one, but two of my roommates. I'd also exonerated both of the women *after* they'd explained they'd been under the influence of magic mushrooms and expressed regret. Clearly I was capable of pardoning anyone if they just said "I'm sorry."

Dr. Winters' inability to acknowledge that he'd done anything wrong felt more unforgivable.

I googled "*forgive.*" A billion-dollar Forgiveness Industry popped up: a British charity, a PBS documentary, a Mayo Clinic website. A Lutheran minister in Denver at the House For All Sinners and Saints called her Facebook sermon "Forgive Assholes." A Japanese Apology Agency I saw on YouTube took money to say "I'm sorry" to the clients you offended so

17

you wouldn't have to. I read pages and watched videos on the personal benefits of granting amnesty, deserved or undeserved.

At the Strand Bookstore, I splurged on used paperbacks touting forgiveness from every persuasion. Promoting radical absolution were: an interfaith hypnotherapist, an Amish expert, a reform female rabbi, a Muslim father who forgave his son's killer. A "New Thought" spiritual leader promoted *21 Days to Forgive Everyone for Everything*. A pastor of Christ's Church in Philadelphia offered *Getting Rid of the Gorilla*. I read their words with frenzied hope. But unable to relax, enjoy a meal, rest, or focus, my gorilla grew.

Along with the books, I devoured articles of crimes and cross-fires, where pundits proclaimed that granting clemency—even to someone who wouldn't say I'm sorry—makes you freer, helps you sleep better, ups your sex drive, lowers blood pressure, decreases stress levels, and increases lifespan. These psycho-babbling promises insisted any offense could be overcome even without a sincere apology. My best college friend Judy, a psychotherapist, ran grief therapy groups on turning wounds into wisdom. Alas, with no repentance from Dr. Winters, my angst would not be calmed. Wounded, I was dumber and more miserable.

Still searching for enlightenment, at Holy Apostles soup kitchen—where I taught a writing workshop for thirteen years—I spilled my saga to Reverend Liz, the kindest, most forgiving person I'd worked with. I used to mentally divide the world into "Jew" and "Non-Jew." After doing a charity anthology with Liz to fight homelessness, racism, and homophobia, her congregants deemed me "an honorary Episcopalian."

I knew my tribe had different flavors (Chasidic, Orthodox, Conservative, Reform, Humanistic, Kabbalah, Reconstructionist), which led Dad to say, "If you put two Jews in a corner, you get three opinions." Finding a multitude of Christian branches, I got lost down the internet rabbit hole of deciphering forgiveness differences between Roman Catholicism, Eastern or Oriental Orthodoxy, Assyrians, Restorationism, and Anglicanism. Dr. Winters was born Protestant, but was it their

Lutheran, Adventist, Baptist, Congregationalist, Methodist, Pentecostal, or Presbyterian subset?

"Which are you?" I asked Reverend Liz.

"We are the American branch of the Anglican Communion, with roots in the Church of England," she clarified. "To make it more confusing, Anglicans include both Catholic and Protestant elements."

"What's the difference between your Episcopal outlook and all the other sects?" I asked.

"All Christian denominations believe that Jesus is the Son of God. Our services are similar to Catholics' but our beliefs are more democratic, with no pope, less dogma, and we don't mind saying 'We don't know.'" She added that they had no problem with birth control and their leaders could marry, with female and openly gay priests, deacons and bishops, unlike most Catholic churches. I tried to gather whether that affected their views on forgiving.

Christians repented for sins during Lent, the way Jews did at Yom Kippur, she explained. They were taught to "turn the other cheek" and forgive, as Jesus didn't wait for an apology; he gave forgiveness freely. Confessionals were more common in Catholicism, yet her members still came to her for advice over sins and repentance.

"Why do confessions start 'Forgive me Father, for I have sinned'?" I wondered.

"Admitting your transgressions to God leads to absolution and salvation through receiving Jesus Christ as your Lord and Savior," she said.

"You have to ask and admit your misdeeds before you're forgiven, right?" I was curious why their process appeared to skip the person you wronged.

"Well, sinning against a fellow human is a sin against God," she told me. "And as penitence I might tell someone to make amends with the person they hurt."

"But what about criminals?" I threw out. "On the *Law & Order* show my husband writes for, there's always a priest who won't divulge criminal evidence because confessions to clergy are privileged."

"If someone committed a crime, I'd probably suggest they turn themselves in. And if it involved a molester who was hurting a child, I would feel morally compelled to contact the authorities," she admitted.

I questioned if the line in the Bible where Jesus says, "Father, forgive them, for they know not what they do" meant that her people were taught to *always* show mercy, regardless of guilt, innocence, or contrition.

"That's from Luke, showing the depth of Jesus's love for humanity," Rev. Liz said. "The idea of loving your enemies is in the Old and New Testament."

"After a mass shooting at a Southern church, I heard a victim's family offer unconditional forgiveness to the murderers. Why would they do that," I asked, "even before any remorse was expressed?"

"It's about trying to end a cycle of violence, resentment, revenge, hate, and war," she explained.

That made sense, though I was inclined towards the Jewish view that forgiveness was more conditional and only *following* repentance to your fellow man and the administration of justice. In the 1969 book *The Sunflower*, Holocaust survivor Simon Wiesenthal relates how, as a former concentration camp prisoner, he'd heard a dying Nazi confess all of his war sins, including murder. Wiesenthal listened closely, then left without saying anything.

Over several editions, Wiesenthal asked theologians, scholars, and authors if they would have shown mercy to the German soldier. To paraphrase: Austrian Catholic Cardinal Franz Konig (there's no limit to forgiveness of Christ), South African Anglican cleric Desmond Tutu ("without forgiveness there is no future"), Nazi Albert Speer ("I can never forgive myself"), Islamic historian Smail Balić ("compassion for every sufferer"), Buddhist Dalai Lama (forgive but don't forget), Chinese activist Harry Wu (no, but everyone in your society shares responsibility) and Jewish novelist Cynthia Ozick (hell no).

Rabbi Abraham Joshua Heschel wrote, "No one can forgive crimes committed against other people . . . even God Himself can only forgive sins committed against Himself, not against man." My view aligned with the four-word declaration of Eva Fleischner, Montclair State University religion professor: "Without repentance, no forgiveness."

I was intrigued by an Islamic scholar who felt similarly. Nora Zaki, an astute Muslim chaplain at Vassar College whom I'd met through a student, pointed out that Muslims also saw taking responsibility and action as an essential part of the forgiveness equation. Their God, *Allah* in Arabic, was merciful, but only *after* the offender's apologizing, repenting, and changing. In the Quran, she said, a merciful Prophet Muhammad forgave Wahshi ibn Harb, who'd admitted to killing the Prophet's beloved uncle Hamza in battle. The prophet did not have Wahshi executed but said, "As much as possible do not come before me."

I took that as the ancient equivalent of "get out of my face forever." I really liked the idea that you could forgive someone while still banishing them. Yet what if Wahshi was in denial about his crime? Would Muhammad have exonerated a sinner who didn't think he'd done anything wrong or hadn't sought out any absolution from God or anyone?

Amy, a Chasidic colleague, was more specific about a Jew's method of atonement, called *teshuvah*. "For us, forgiving is a duty and a mitzvah. Jewish law requires a person to ask heartfelt forgiveness three times," Amy said. "If the injured party won't respond, the sinner is forgiven and the non-forgiver has to seek forgiveness for *not* forgiving." But the request had to be inspired by true regret.

I felt vindicated when my lawyer cousin Danny reminded me that admitting guilt and expressing remorse were often the deciding elements of criminal verdicts in the eyes of the law. Yet my issue was more about feelings than legality. A Buddhist yogi friend warned, "If you lost your foundation and feel ungrounded, those emotions could show up in your spine, a body part ruled by the root chakra, the body's first power center." Too late.

Despite being skeptical of interstellar predictions, I phoned the wildly provocative Jungian astrologer (a.k.a. Stargazer) I'd known through Dr. Winters years earlier. When we first met, I thought he was a shrink. "I was," he said. "But I found it too limiting. Astrology is the original psychology. Freud reductively based his work on the Oedipus myth to fit his own pathology. Astrological theories encompass all mythologies."

At a loss for literal direction, I filled him in on the triangle, curious if a planetary take could ease my personal angst.

"Forgiveness is overrated. Holding a grudge can be protective—so you're not a perpetual victim getting hurt," he said. "I blame all the Pluto in both of your seventh houses for shadowing love with abandonment and betrayal."

Stargazer's left-field advice always surprised me. "So I should never speak to him again?"

"Just be grateful you were betrayed by your shrink and not your husband. And you're not done killing Winters off. He needs a proper burial." Stargazer used his typical hyperbolic metaphors. "Then the death can lead to rebirth."

Now *that* sounded Biblical. But it was impossible for me to reconsider trusting Dr. Winters if he didn't offer any explanation or regret. I wasn't in the mood to be a martyr. No wonder I became entranced by the website *SorryWatch*.com. I followed on Facebook and Twitter as two middle-aged female bloggers from both coasts analyzed public and newsworthy faux pas for "signs of defective, weaselly, and poisoned apologies." They broke it down to such categories as "Royal Apologies," "Belated Apologies," "Performative Utterances," "Twitpologies," and "Apologies Not Accepted." I already saw how a passive-aggressive "Sorry *if* I hurt you" could deepen a rift. I heard the echo of Dr. Winters' words: "I hope you'll forgive the imaginary crime you envision I'm committing." That aggressive-aggressive tone made me want to commit an actual crime.

I felt better when my husband came home, but he was immersed in work. He thought I was, too. I was actually just scrawling notes all over the shrewd book *On Apology* by Dr. Aaron Lazare. I read his section "Forgiveness Without Apology," where people forgave to be free from anger, resentment, and grudges. Without remorse, Lazare wrote, reconciliation was unlikely. I underlined the four elements that he felt were needed when somebody apologized fully: 1) acknowledgement and taking responsibility for your mistake, 2) explaining why it happened, 3) showing it won't happen again, and 4) offering reparations for healing. Lazare traced this formula back to Maimonides, the twelfth-century scholar, a Spanish Jew. This philosophy I could wrap my head around.

I called my parents' smart new Conservative rabbi, Joseph Krakoff, to see if he sanctioned this approach. He shared his theory on The Jewish Apology: "I personally don't feel any apologizing has officially taken effect until the offending person is in the same situation again and acts differently, showing they've learned and changed."

"What if someone who wronged you doesn't even feel you're owed any apology?" I asked.

Rabbi Krakoff told me that in his hospice work, when a family gathered around someone very old or ill, he led them in an end-of-life prayer they all shared: "'You are forgiven. I forgive you. Please forgive me. I love you.' Sometimes the best way to get someone to say they're sorry is to say it yourself," he said.

Sounded too kumbaya to me. "Any old coot ever yell 'I have nothing to apologize for?'" I asked.

"Yes, actually," he said. "A difficult father told his oldest child, 'I didn't do anything wrong. I did the best I could.' The daughter gave me a look that said 'See what I've been up against for forty years?'"

"So it was a stalemate?"

"No. I told him that I couldn't make him do something that wasn't in his heart, but it was a good way to end peacefully," Rabbi Krakoff recalled. "The next day he told her, 'I've thought about it. I still don't think I did anything wrong, but I'll say the prayer because the Rabbi says it's a better way to leave the world.' Even saying those words begrudgingly meant a lot to his daughter."

That could have been me, my father, and my grandfather.

As I hung up the phone, my spine was burning, as if my body were radiating red flares.

When I checked the mail, I found the copy of an old therapy bill receipt I already paid. On the bottom Dr. Winters scrawled: "I'm sure you'll write about this."

He sounded like the caustic father he was supposed to be replacing. When my back spasmed, I took more of Aaron's Tylenol. I could only sit up at my desk pain-free for an hour before it ached again. Despite Dr. Winters' sarcastic prediction that I would use our falling out as material, I couldn't type a sentence. For someone normally busy at the computer ten hours a day, it was paralyzing. I wasted hours flat on the floor holding my iPhone above me, anxiously refreshing my inbox, awaiting an apology from the person he used to be.

CHAPTER 4
WHEN YOUR OWN COUNTRY EXILES YOU

"Never forgive, never forget"
>   —lyric by Swedish Death metal band Arch Enemy

"I've been taking some of your old pain killers," I confided to my husband.

Aaron looked worried. "You shouldn't do that. Go see your own doctor."

"I did—I went to Winters," I lamented. "And look what good that did me."

"A medical doctor," he specified. "Or call your father."

"I'm too embarrassed," I admitted.

When the spine twitches didn't go away, I finally relinquished my pride and called my seventy-nine-year-old father, a brilliant, cantankerous diagnostician with a cane. (I was sure the creators of the TV show *House* lifted his identity.) After his emergency heart surgery, he'd spent ten miserable days at the Michigan hospital where he used to practice. I'd assumed the pacemaker that left a savage scar on his chest and his retirement would mellow him out. Instead he became more irascible, berating me every phone call.

"If you want to moon the world, use pseudonyms so you don't embarrass your whole family," he told me after I said "Hello." This was his way of acknowledging my latest personal essay in *Marie Claire*.

I wanted to hang up, feeling trapped inside my aching body and bad mood while worried my piece—mentioning how therapy helped me have hotter sex with my husband—had upset Dad. (Aaron wasn't thrilled either, questioning why I'd publish it. "I was offered $2,000," I admitted. "I'll pay you $4,000 to un-publish it," he'd said.)

While I'd inherited my father's dark coloring, good hearing, and addictive personality, he never approved of anything I did. "You remind me of Shirley," he'd say. His only sister was a sharp-tongued Floridian smoker and drinker who'd had tough marriages and was unable to bear a child. As a childless brunette who'd spent decades smoking, drinking, and arguing like Shirley, I feared Dad and I had recreated their antagonistic relationship. After getting breast cancer, Shirley had died too young, like my grandmother. I guessed that my father had subconsciously chosen his profession to save his mom and only sibling. He and I got along best, I'd noticed, when I had a physical ailment he could cure long-distance.

"I really hurt my back," I admitted.

"What did you do?" He switched into doctor mode.

"Not sure. Can't walk," I said. "Don't know which specialist is on my healthcare network."

Thankfully, he offered to help.

As I entered the subculture of Manhattan spinal specialists that week, my newly retired dad became my partner in navigating the medical terrain. By phone, fax, and email on his new iPad, he gleefully belittled each expert long-distance. He nixed the orthopedic surgeon pushing steroid injections with "If he can't cut 'em up, he'll shoot 'em up." He dismissed the physiatrist prescribing Oxycodone with "Try heroin while you're at it." Of the expensive chiropractor who "realigned" my spine: "Glad that moron didn't kill you." Dad vetoed the neurologist's EMG needle test which he christened "New-age claptrap." Another doc scheduled an MRI at an uptown hospital at 6 a.m., my idea of hell. A squeamish late-nighter, I told Dad I was scared of the claustrophobic, coffin-like machine on TV medical shows, where patients fainted, stroked out, or croaked.

"Don't be Sarah Bernhardt," he said, evoking the overly emotive

Jewish actress whenever he thought I was being melodramatic. "Get a standing MRI. It's open, with no cover."

At Stand Up Open MRI's clinic on Avenue A, a friendly receptionist offered a 7 p.m. slot that night. I was lucky I lived in Greenwich Village, filled with neurotics and night owls like me.

Reading the results on his computer, Dad said, "Good. Let's see what we're up against." I liked the "we," as if my back injury had hurt him, the way his cardiac arrest had somehow weakened my heart too. Other doctors said "pulled muscle," "inflammation," "sprain." Dad insisted I'd torn two ligaments in my lower back. I preferred his extreme verb "to tear." I was honored that he was diagnosing me, as if—with Winters out of the picture—only my actual father could see what was wrong inside.

"Oh boy, my little girl really hurt herself this time," he told me.

At almost half a century, I was still his little girl.

Because I was needle-phobic and the cortisone injections came with side effects and Dad's disapproval, I nixed the shots and oral steroids. Instead the neurologist prescribed physical therapy at a place three blocks from my home.

"My policy covers sixty PT sessions for $40 a pop. Think it'll help?" I asked Dad.

"No," he said. "But it'll give you something to do while it heals itself—and the illusion of control."

He understood control freaks: we were alike that way. Making an appointment with a back specialist did make me feel less helpless. When I walked in that fall Tuesday night, the orthopedic rehab center was populated with perky workers half my age. Two students wearing NYU shirts were doing exercises on the mat—probably sports injuries.

"How we doing today, Susan?" asked the tall spine expert with a Slavic-sounding accent, holding my chart on his clipboard. His patronizing tone got on my nerves. He glanced at me, then at my report. "I'm Kenan."

With dark bangs and a baby face, chinos, button-down blue shirt, and big white sneakers, he looked like a college student. In oversized black sweats and top, flat on my achy back on a table in the corner, I felt ancient. In my purse I had a copy of my favorite magazine profile of me with my glamour shot taken six years before. I was carrying around the younger, happier woman I used to be, as if the picture proved I was still a young, hot, and happening author, not a sour old depressive with a defective spine. Blinking back tears, I avoided his eyes.

"Tell me what is wrong," Kenan said, putting his hand on my arm.

What wasn't? I couldn't tell him that, along with my skeletal dysfunction, I was flipping out about my disappearing doctor and successful career, which seemed over. My unresolved falling out with the advisor whose praise had fueled my ambition was draining my spirit and my mojo. It felt as though, literally and figuratively, losing my main "core pillar" left me unable to stand. I couldn't walk six blocks with my bags to get to classes I'd been teaching for twenty years, down the streets where my twenty-year-old legs once ran. What a wimp I was, crying in front of this kid I'd just met.

"You are in pain?" Kenan asked, hovering over me, worried. "Tell me where." I pointed below my hip. He handed me a Kleenex. "Where is MRI results? You brought?"

I wiped my eyes, shook my head no. I'd misplaced the printout. "Ligament tear. Two, actually."

"Which discs?"

I shrugged, ashamed I couldn't tell the difference between a ligament or disc.

"I do not touch till I know." He put his pen down, annoyed. "Would not guess and make worse."

His mangled tenses and missing connectives made his speech kind of poetic. I didn't know if the doctor who ordered the test was still in his office.

"Show me." Kenan took out a plastic vertebrae, like the physicians and chiropractor had used, lecturing me on the spinal column bones. Dad had one in his den, along with a skeleton that had spooked me as a kid.

"Don't bother, I flunked science." I cut him off. "Wait, my father has a copy of my scan. I'll call him in Michigan." I'd forgotten my cell, but Kenan pulled out his. I was glad Dad picked up on the first ring.

"Hi, Daddy," I regressed. "I don't have my MRI and the physical therapist wants to know which—"

"Lumbar disc," Kenan said.

"Which lumbar discs I tore before he touches me."

"Good, finally someone with a brain," Dad said. I handed Kenan the phone.

They talked for ten minutes. I heard Kenan laugh. None of my other medicine men had spoken to my father. It seemed sweetly old-fashioned. When I was a teenager, Dad scared off my dates by coming to the door in his boxer shorts and T-shirt, smoking a six-inch cigar. I was relieved he'd recovered enough from his heart problems to resume playing the protective dad, as though any new man needed his permission to approach his daughter. I closed my eyes, listening to them talk, feeling cared for.

"Okay, you tore L-4-L-5 and L5-S1 in lower back." Kenan sounded official. "Annular tear. You do not know when you get injured?"

"I'm not sure. I've been working out a lot—swimming, speed walking, kickboxing."

"Kickboxing! Twisting horrible for back," he chided. "Especially at your age."

"What do you mean *my* age?" My face flushed. "Older people do marathons, triathlons."

"Athletes retire early. You not athletic." He read my chart. "Almost fifty. Writer and teacher."

"Why don't I just kill myself now?"

"No, do not!" He sounded alarmed.

Since I'd taken up kickboxing to metaphorically punch the lights out of my former shrink, I now held Dr. Winters responsible for screwing up my head *and* my spine. Kenan must have intuited that I was about to tear up again because in a gentler voice he said, "Don't worry, we figure out."

The last thing I wanted from this guy was pity.

"Okay, first we do stretches." He abruptly pulled my left leg up to my chest.

I felt a sharp pain around my hip area and gasped, pushing him away.

"Sorry. We go slower," he said. "Try leg lift." He lifted my left leg up a few inches, then put it down.

"How old are you?" I interrogated him to distract from my discomfort. "Just out of college?"

He rolled his eyes. "Ten years off."

"Where are you from?"

"Left side worse than right." He scrawled notes. "I'm thirty. Bosnian."

I thought of the literary event, sponsored by Susan Sontag, that I'd covered for *Newsday* in 1993 benefitting families of the victims massacred during the genocide there. "Are you Muslim?"

He nodded.

I did the math. "Were you exiled during the Balkan War?"

"You always so nosy?" he asked.

"Twenty years as a journalist," I admitted. "Have you been back to visit?"

"Went last month with brother and father," he mumbled, lifting my right leg.

"Not your mother?" I asked.

"She always said, 'I'd rather be dead than go back there.' She get wish. Died of breast cancer. I blame war. Mortar shelling every day. Toxic fumes. She found lump the day we escape. Now do bridges, like this." As he raised my left leg, I spied the end of a big green tattoo on his shoulder, under his shirt. Didn't Islam ban body ink, like traditional Jews in my clan? He caught me trying to decipher it.

"Old Bosnian flag," he said.

Burned in his skin, I noted, above his heart.

"Try ten lifts each side." When he turned to assist another patient, I pulled out a stack of papers from my purse to grade.

"Focus on exercise!" he scolded when he returned, putting the stack on the table. "What is this?"

"I have a hundred student essays a week to grade from my class," I explained.

"What I Did on Summer Vacation?" he said sarcastically.

"Actually, my first assignment is: write three pages on your most humiliating secret."

"You Americans." He smirked. "Why anyone reveals that?"

"It's healing," I said. "You can turn your worst experience into the most beautiful."

"I never spill," Kenan said. "I keep to my chest."

"Try three pages about the war," I gave *him* an exercise.

"I do not write. I fix backs," he said. "You very weak. You must listen, trust me. That will be hard for you. There is lot of damage here."

I was thinking the same of him. That night I was moved when Kenan emailed to check on my back and see if I needed medication. To offer him some inspiration to do my assignment, I forwarded him my student Danielle's recently published piece on how she ate bacon cheeseburgers with her mother, a Holocaust survivor, on Yom Kippur, to cope with her father's suicide.

"Touchy," Kenan responded. I gathered he meant "touching."

Next session, as I was lying down in agony on a heating pad, he surprised me with three typed pages. They recounted his return to Bosnia that summer, two decades after the ethnic cleansing campaign he witnessed at twelve. He confronted a neighbor who'd stolen from his mother, and stood on the grave of Pero, his once-beloved karate coach who came to his home with an AK-47, yelling "You have one hour to leave or be killed!" It was Pero—weeks later—who sent Kenan's dad and brother to a concentration camp.

I was stunned out of my self-pity. "This blows my socks off," I told him.

"No good?" He frowned.

"It's great." I marked some notes on it, then suggested he try a three-page flashback scene.

"No, cannot remember."

At my Friday session, he put me on a bigger table, plugged electrodes to my back, then handed me forty-three pages, pointing to the paragraph where he told his neighbor Petra, "No one has forgotten." He stood over me. "What do you think?" I thought: I've turned my mellow Muslim physical therapist into a neurotic Jewish freelance writer like me.

While his grandfather was an Imam, his grandma Nena prayed at the mosque, and his father studied at a Madrasa, Kenan and his brother were raised secular. As a soccer-loving twelve-year-old, he was shocked to witness his country dividing into three teams: the Greek Orthodox Serbs, the Catholic Croats, and the Bosnian Muslims, like him. I read about how his third-grade teacher held a rifle to his head. He'd been grazed by a bullet when he went out to buy bread. Although his whole family survived, he shared detailed revenge fantasies towards the Christian class-mates who'd betrayed him. Invited to put his past trauma into words, he all of a sudden couldn't stop spilling. Could he ever find peace or forgive-ness? As if to answer, his pages ended: *"Nikad zaboravit i Nakad oprostit.* Our motto is 'Never forgive, never forget.'"

The idea of someone living with so much rage seemed scary and self-defeating. "You never wrote any of this down before?" I asked.

"No. Medical reports only thing I write. In Connecticut, my mother tried to type story of how we survive," he told me. "She could not learn English while sick."

He handed me a picture of a pretty redhead who resembled *my* pretty mom Miriam, who'd grown up a poor orphan, and was sent home from school for speaking only Yiddish. Kenan's hard-working dad said, "Whatever your job, do your best," like my father. I was from Midwest Jewish suburbia. He grew up Islamic in Eastern Europe. Though worlds apart, it felt like we both came from the same close-knit, no-nonsense family.

"As kid, I never tell anyone I wished I was eighteen, to be soldier who get revenge with gun," he said.

"That's understandable. Didn't your parents ask about your feelings during the occupation?" I asked.

"No. Too busy telling me to duck," he said, and we both cracked up.

At our next session, he showed me his revision, reiterating how much he hated the Christian Serbs who'd betrayed his family. "It's powerful," I said. "But to publish an essay, you can't start with hate and end with hate. You need what we call a dramatic arc."

"No arc. No meaning. No closure," he insisted. "Never forgiving."

"Try wisdom, a surprise, or an unexpected revelation?" While holding a grudge against my psychotherapist, I was now pushing my physical therapist to let go of his rancor. Kenan mentioned the dinner in Bosnia he'd recently had with his old neighbor Milos, a Serb soldier who'd helped Kenan's family escape.

I asked what he hoped would happen while visiting his homeland. "I wish Pero could say he was sorry," Kenan said. "Just once, I want Serb soldier to admit they started war against my people and apologize."

I was mesmerized by his desire for someone to acknowledge their sins against him, to say they were sorry and ask forgiveness, as if twenty years later, it could make a difference. Without an apology, Kenan's pain had never really abated. I was over-identifying with his anger towards the karate coach, the mentor he'd idolized. I bet the more you looked up to someone, the worse you experienced their slight.

Yet Kenan was a victim of a crime against humanity. He'd lost his homeland, friends, country. Nobody had ever offered reparations or expressed any remorse, so of course he was still enraged. I feared keeping all that fury was limiting his life. I'd been consumed by anger for only six weeks and could barely work, sleep, feel hope, or make love to the husband I adored.

I recalled the book *Radical Forgiveness* by British author Colin Tripping, born during World War II. Had war influenced his theory that you forgive someone not for them, but to liberate yourself? If rage remained unresolved, what did you do with it? What did it do to you? After witnessing true evil, was forgiveness, love, or internal peace even possible for Kenan?

He read me his list of twelve people he wanted to avenge in Bosnia, including his thief neighbor Petra and karate coach Pero, though he was dead. On the next page, he described his mother watching *Schindler's List*, her favorite movie, because she thought their tale of survival was similar. "I'll never forget the people who did us harm. But you have to remember the good people too," she'd told him. I asked Kenan to write a list of the Serbs who'd come to their rescue.

"I could count on one finger," he said with a sneer.

"I already counted more," I argued. "Milos gave you money to escape. And the other day you told me a police captain provided fake documents to get you out and a bus driver waited for your family in the snowstorm to drive you to Vienna. So that's three."

"Why does number matter?" he questioned.

"Sometimes insight comes from reordering facts," I said, repeating a Dr. Winters adage.

At my next session, Kenan handed me a list of twelve Serbs who'd helped his family. When I asked if there was any forgiveness that could provide a cathartic ending or different resolution, he said, "Don't be stupid. Never." But that night he emailed, "I forgive my father for not getting us out of danger sooner, Mom for getting sick when I was a kid. I forgave Milos, who fought against Muslims, but gave us food and money to escape. I remember eleven other Serbs who helped. But I never forgive Serbian president Milosevic or other nationalist monsters who perpetrated crimes against humanity on fellow Bosnian Muslims."

"You have every right not to forgive Milosevic. But he's dead and you're still hurting," I explained. "The war continues inside you. You have the power to finish it."

"Would you expect Jewish Auschwitz survivor to forgive Hitler and Nazis?" he asked.

"My father's seventy-four-year-old close friend survived Bergen-Belsen, the concentration camp," I said. I told him how Manny became a good husband, father of two, and psychologist involved with the Holocaust Museum in D.C. I forwarded Kenan a piece Manny sent me on the film *The Power of Forgiveness* about how, in the year 2000, Elie

Wiesel urged the German government to issue a formal apology to Israel for its involvement in the Holocaust and they did, offering war reparations. Wiesel shared the Jewish view that in order to be forgiven, one must first admit to wrongful action and apologize.

"But Germany lost World War II," Kenan told me. "They officially apologized, made reparations and thrive economically today. Meanwhile my heart—and my country—stay in turmoil."

While my back was slowly improving, so was Kenan's grammar and eloquence as he was gradually articulating his outrage more thoughtfully. Judy, my psychotherapist friend, who'd been widowed young, said that just being there to hear other people's hurt could be healing on both sides. An author friend in Chicago sent me her book on Balkan War trauma, *Wounded I Am More Awake,* the line from a Bosnian poem. I hoped I could channel my physical and psychic injuries to somehow help Kenan. I felt sure this process could ease his emotional agony, the way he was soothing the pain in my spine. "What would you want to hear from the Serbian government?" I asked. "Can you get it down on paper?"

"No," he said. "Nothing."

I wasn't surprised at my next session when he handed me the typed paragraph: "We were responsible for the war and your family's exile. We apologize for genocide and crimes against humanity committed against our Muslim neighbors. We will disclose hidden mass graves and educate younger generations about our violence. We will be part of ethnically mixed country, pay financial reparations to those who had relatives killed or who were wounded or exiled."

"That's really important," I said. "Remember, the pen is mightier than the sword."

"Great line," he said. "I should write that down."

"It's not mine," I admitted, smiling.

After I helped Kenan publish his debut essays in *The New York Times* and *The Wall Street Journal,* my father's favorite newspaper, a nineteen-year-old Serb girl in St. Louis wrote him a letter. She apologized for what her people did to him. "She wasn't born yet. Does not help," he said. Still,

I noticed he kept her letter in his bag. When I gave him framed copies of his pieces, he said, "This is most pride I ever had."

He received interest from a literary agent and from my dad, a history buff, who emailed "Chilling. They didn't hang enough of the monsters who killed for blood lust. This story needs to be heard."

"Wow. We say in Bosnia, 'No hair on his tongue,'" Kenan said. "His words have power, like yours."

I never noticed that I'd mirrored Dad's linguistic intensity, how he'd speak his mind fearlessly, obliterating small talk, unconcerned about whom he'd offend. As we were both on the mend, Dad sent articles comparing the Serb's ethnic cleansing campaign to the Nazis wiping out our Eastern European relatives.

I forwarded my father's emails to Kenan, who asked questions about Dad's medical career. Kenan was in awe that my dad, a Lower East Side street kid, had labored to become a hospital chief of medicine, paid the college tuitions of his four kids, and set up educational trusts for his five grandchildren. Seeing my father through Kenan's eyes, I was awed too. Despite hating what I did for a living, my father had helped pay my rent when I was struggling with two jobs that wouldn't cover it. His worst fear was that I'd be poor in Manhattan, like he'd been. I now saw that the creative dreams he'd disparaged were only possible because of him.

"This Bosnia piece proves how sharp and diligent you are," Dad said. "It makes me proud of you."

I was overjoyed. Then I laughed to myself, realizing it was because I'd helped recreate the story of someone else's family, rather than continuing to overexpose ours. I noted that losing my stand-in paternal figure was leading me back to my father's love. But Dad's renewed attention didn't erase my hurt over Dr. Winters. While my spine was slowly recovering, I was still confounded by the fallout with my head doctor.

The longer Kenan spoke of his global tragedy, however, the more clearly I saw that what happened with Dr. Winters wasn't tragic. Mine was merely "a narcissistic wound," as Freud called a perceived threat to one's self-esteem or self-worth. I'd imbued my addiction specialist with superpowers, but he was just a flawed human being. His sin was far from unpardonable. Unlike Kenan's dead mentor, Pero, Dr. Winters never literally threatened me. He was alive, and there was still time for him to apologize.

Although I wondered what would happen if he couldn't.

CHAPTER 5
WHEN ALL AUTHORITY FIGURES FAIL YOU
OCTOBER 2010

"Forgiveness is not an occasional act, it is a constant attitude."
—Reverend Martin Luther King Jr.

One cold Sunday afternoon before Halloween, my eyes caught the subject heading: "I'm sorry, please forgive me." Praying it was Dr. Winters, I opened the email quickly. But it was from my student Cliff.

"I apologize deeply, professor. I'm having a bad time. I'm homeless. The V.A. screwed up my benefits. Shuffling between shelters, it's impossible to do homework. It would kill me if I failed your class. I have limited internet access, but I'll let you know if I can make it to school tomorrow."

What was this sweet kid apologizing for? I felt sad for the twenty-six-year-old African-American Iraq War veteran. On the G.I. Bill, he'd taken several of my classes. He was in a group of older repeat students I'd befriended and invited to readings and events, the way I'd hung out with my grad school professors. I hadn't noticed anything different with Cliff this term and now feared my preoccupation with Dr. Winters had caused me to miss the more serious problems of the aspiring young journalists I usually kept an eye on.

"You okay?" I asked when I returned his call.

"I'm at this shelter in Brooklyn until my V.A. check comes in. I might have to change the topic of my essay." He chuckled at his quip about my first assignment: "Write three pages on your most humiliating secret."

Good sign that he was laughing, could use his cell phone at a shelter, and had buzzed me back so fast. "Can you write about this? Writing can be a way to turn your worst experience into the most beautiful," I repeated my leitmotif. "Come to class tomorrow night, if you can. I'll pay your transportation," I offered.

I struggled not to ask how much his rent was and cover it, or offer him the extra room we used as Aaron's office. That would upset my husband and break Dr. Winters' rules against being over-involved as a professor. He felt that teaching brought out my maternal instincts, but he'd insisted I not get too emotionally enmeshed. "Not being able to have kids is a biological tragedy you haven't dealt with yet," he'd said. "Your students are like surrogate children. But they have endless needs you can't fulfill."

It came up often over my years at Holy Apostles soup kitchen. Many in the group didn't have homes, families, or money. The time I gave my business card (with home address and phone number) to a fellow teacher, a tattooed member asked, "Hey, ya got a card for me?" So as not to slight him, I handed one over. The next day, this middle-aged man from Staten Island with a Jesus portrait inked across his neck rang my bell, holding an envelope filled with scrawled poetry.

"One of your exes?" Aaron later quipped. He was annoyed when I accepted members' collect calls from prison.

Dr. Winters also fretted when I spontaneously gave any money away, seeing it as another sign of addiction. He questioned why I paid the cab fare for an older guy with AIDS to get home (it was snowing and he used a cane), and covered the dental bill to fix the broken tooth of a Harlem student who had a job interview.

"Who do you think you are, throwing around cash? Oprah?" Dr. Winters had asked. "As of last year, you were in debt yourself. And there are limits to how involved a university faculty member should get with their students."

"I'm not a full-time Harvard law professor. I'm just a part-time adjunct teaching six hours a week in Greenwich Village," I said. "I like helping my students get jobs, internships, and clips, the way my mentors helped me. One protégée makes me touch her papers for good luck before she submits, like Oprah's audience wants to touch her."

"Listen, if *she* thinks you're Oprah, no problem. If *you* think you're Oprah, *huge* problem."

"Isn't it healthy to want to do good in the world?" I'd asked.

"With an addict like you, it can get megalomaniacal," he warned. "You're not a multi-billionaire who can afford to hand out twenties."

"You're saying I shouldn't do charity?" I asked.

"You're such an extremist. After you quit smoking and drinking, you toked too much. Then you chewed an obscene amount of gum. Next you drank a dozen diet sodas a day. You transfer addictions," he said. "It feels fantastic to give away money. Heroin feels great, too. But you have to beware of all excitement, because it takes you out of yourself. And you always have to go back to yourself."

That was helpful, but there had to be a rational way for me to help Cliff. I often told Dr. Winters that writing teachers were like therapists, only paid less. In the throes of my nicotine withdrawal years earlier, he'd warned me, "You shed the armor you used to protect yourself. You're so sensitive and exposed, you're like a burn victim with no skin. Going outside will be difficult. Even the air hurts." That was how I felt now, without him.

Not sure what to do about Cliff, I could hear him telling me, "You're not a doctor. He has a lot of complicated issues. Don't get too involved."

Fuck Winters, I thought. He'd lost the right to protect me. I picked up the phone to call Cliff back.

He'd stood out from the first session of my fall term at the university, when he announced he was writing *Losing My Balls*, a wild chronicle of getting wounded during his military service in 2006, when a Somali pirate attacked his ship and left him without a testicle. As he walked me home from class that night, as students frequently did, he limped, sharing more of his naval disaster. He recounted how, returning gunfire to the pirates, he'd been shot and tumbled down the stairs. He needed four operations and had never fully recovered.

"I have seven screws in my foot and ankle and I'm in pain every day. Without both testicles, I don't feel like a man," he confessed.

His fellow students had lauded Cliff's bravery, honesty, and twisted humor. Then he'd disappeared for two weeks. I worried he'd opened up too much, scaring himself off. But on Monday, after our phone call, I was pleased Cliff came to class early. I slipped him a twenty to cover dinner and the train back to the shelter. The V.A. was untangling his financial mess, so he'd land a new place to live soon, he said. Later that night, a *New York Times* editor visited our class, saying she wanted dramatic personal essays on current events. Everybody crowded around to meet her afterwards. "Tell her what you've been going through," I whispered to Cliff.

"No," he whispered back. "I'm too embarrassed."

"My shrink insists that to be successful you have to 'Lead the least secretive life you can,'" I said. Dr. Winters was gone, but the years of good advice he'd given me hovered.

"I really enjoyed your talk," I heard Cliff tell the editor. "Would you be interested in a piece about how I became a homeless veteran after the V.A. screwed up my benefits?"

"Yes, I would," the editor said, nodding. "I definitely want to read that."

Was it any wonder that I saw the newspaper and magazine editors who helped my students as benevolent gods?

Excited, Cliff sent me three pages the next morning. My own work felt stifled, but Cliff's raw need galvanized me as we edited over the phone. I couldn't heal his homelessness, or my sadness, but I could help improve Cliff's prose for publication. I made it my mission, as if we were on an essential deadline to save the world. I asked him to add lines describing his background for an audience who couldn't see him and didn't know him.

"I was the youngest of eight kids from a black family on Chicago's South Side, raised in poverty," he said. "My parents divorced when I was a baby. My schizophrenic mom left her Baptist church and had no support. She didn't enroll me in school until I was eleven. My dad was in the military. So I enlisted in the Navy at eighteen, to get training and an education like he did."

I taught my students the adage "If you got the story, tell it. If you ain't got it, write it." Cliff had the story; as he dictated, I typed his words verbatim. Every detail was gripping.

After he was wounded in 2008, Cliff had received an honorable discharge. G.I. Benefits paid his rent. He won a New School scholarship and gravitated to my class, interested in writing and stand-up comedy. To afford the city, he took jobs as a server in a pizza joint, a retail salesman, and a maintenance worker at the Bronx Veterans Hospital. But external issues (bad commute, horrible hours, dumb boss) caused him to quit each time. I'd seen him drink too much at school events. As a fellow addict, I surmised that was his bigger obstacle now. When his V.A. payments were delayed by six months, he was broke.

"Describe your days in the shelter system," I suggested.

He told me how mentally unstable vets lay on cots next to soldiers who were just down on their luck, who in turn lay next to ex-cons, so it was hard for him to sleep at night. Every shelter had gang members and stories of violence and theft. Someone was always bragging they'd taken another's life. I held the phone to my ear with my shoulder, weaving in the new sentences on my laptop. He blamed his late mother for having schizophrenia and his dad for abandoning him. He cursed the government that trained him only on sophisticated equipment found in the military, limiting his civilian opportunities, and for failing to put safeguards in place to keep veterans like him off the street.

"The year 2008 was the worst year of my life," he went on. "My sister Yvette died from cancer at forty-one. Then my wife's parents ruined our marriage. They were Salvadorian Catholics who were mad she'd married a black guy."

"I didn't even know you were married," I said.

"It was just for a year, long-distance. We'd eloped before I shipped off," Cliff said. "By the time I was discharged, she'd divorced me."

"You're like a fucking country music song," I told him.

"I know, right? I am!" he agreed, laughing.

I noticed people had confessed more over the last month, as if my vulnerability had made me more empathetic. Full of rage myself, I saw how easy it was to be paranoid and to "catastrophize." Yet I had a great husband, family, and friends who came through for me. *Everyone* important to Cliff had failed him. I was not going to.

My father once told me "If you don't have your mother's love, you have nothing." Despite my dad's rough-and-tumble upbringing on the Lower East Side, his mom adored him. Dr. Winters' wealthy mother had hated and abused him. After his parents' divorce, living with a good father who remarried someone saner might have given him a chance. But maybe that hadn't come early enough.

After Cliff's dad left the family, he'd moved to another state and Cliff's mother had died. Now he had no healthy parent around. While spiritual, Cliff wasn't religious or affiliated with a church. He had little money or support. Still, I didn't think his playing the victim would improve his piece—or his life.

"You have good reasons to be pissed. But do you deserve any of the blame yourself?" I had to ask.

"Yes. It's partly my fault," he conceded.

"Why? What did you do wrong?" I jumped in, the way Dr. Winters used to interrogate me.

He was silent for a few minutes. "My drinking made this all worse," Cliff confessed.

Dr. Winters used to say that verbalizing the specifics was essential for an addict, quoting the AA adage: "You're only as sick as your secrets." I asked Cliff, "How much do you drink?"

"As much as I can," he admitted. "Until I black out."

Did this explain our connection? Different as we were, Cliff's impatience and insatiability mirrored my own. "You have to stop drinking," I said, putting on my doctor voice. "Nothing good happens if you depend on substances instead of people."

"I know," Cliff said. "I haven't had a drink all week."

It was unclear if he'd been sober intentionally or only because he couldn't afford alcohol.

"Keep it that way. Maybe you have PTSD? You have to get a therapist," I pushed.

"I tried seeing a counselor at the V.A. He was condescending. I hated him. It's hard for me to trust anyone now." Then he quietly added, "But I trust you."

"I'm glad," I said, nervous about what that trust entailed. "I've had so much therapy you must have picked up some by osmosis." However, I wasn't a trained doctor with the wisdom or power needed to treat a wounded vet who'd had a mentally ill mom and absent dad. I was only a part-time professor. Still, in two decades of teaching, I'd only seen positive things happen when students were published. It boosted their self-worth. Replacing toxic addictions with writing and encouragement was the plan Dr. Winters had used on me.

"Look, you had it really tough. But your essay can't just be a victimized kvetch, blaming everyone else," I said. "If you want it to see print, I'd go deeper and take some personal responsibility for making the situation worse."

"You really think that'll make my piece publishable?" he asked.

"Yes," I said, also believing it could determine whether or not he'd survive.

He paused, then said, "I'll put in how my drinking too much screwed everything up. That's why I stopped."

I wanted to cry. It felt like a big breakthrough. Alcoholic's Anonymous encouraged members to admit they were powerless over alcohol, surrender to a higher power, turn their will over to the care of God, do a moral inventory, and make amends to the people they hurt.

In Cliff's case, the person his alcohol use had damaged most was himself. Nobody in his family or the military was amending the hurt that Cliff had suffered. I wished he could get a new support system to take the place of his parents and his former job in the navy. He shot down my suggestion of going to AA meetings every day.

"My friend Kate goes to a Greenwich Village church with a black reverend she loves," I threw out.

"My mom was Baptist, I don't have good memories of churches," he told me.

The next day he emailed, "I dreamt about running a Bible group last night."

I took this as another good omen.

Submitting the revision of his essay to the editor for him, I explained that Cliff had only intermittent internet service. The next Monday, he strode in, star of the class, smiling as he said, "*The Times* said yes!" He received loud applause. Within the month his piece ran, he was offered a job as a hospital receptionist by a woman who'd read his essay, was invited to a *New York Times* party, and was contacted by a literary agent. Plus his V.A. money came in. He found a share in Brooklyn with another vet. I was proud of him, feeling immense relief.

A week later, he emailed as I was heading to a former student's book launch. I invited Cliff, hoping it would inspire him to publish a book of his own. He was happy to join me, dazzling the editor and agent there with his losing-his-testicle-to-a-Somali-pirate mayhem. Afterwards I asked him to grab a bite, wanting to make sure he was eating, not drinking. I had the chef salad. He ordered a cheeseburger, fries, and chocolate milkshake. "First clip in *New York Times*. That is really impressive. Screw you! It took me five years of writing to break in there," I told him, smiling, recalling how good it felt when Dr. Winters had profusely praised my last piece. "What's been the best response so far?"

"My father read it and emailed me, 'Good job. I'm proud of you,'" Cliff told me, grinning back.

"That must have felt great. Is he still in the army?" I asked.

"No. He's living in the South, an artist now. He's not very emotional. He never really told me why he left us," Cliff said as the food came.

My father was also stoic and spare with praise. But I was lucky he'd been happily married to my mother for almost sixty years. When I worked at the soup kitchen writing workshop for thirteen years, I noticed that none of the members—who came there for the free lunch—grew up in homes where two parents lived together.

"I read this book by apology expert Aaron Lazare, who claims there are four elements of a good apology," I told Cliff. "Acknowledgment of the offense, explanation, remorse, and reparation."

"I'm down with that." He nodded enthusiastically.

"If your dad could apologize to you, what would you want him to say?" I asked.

"I wished he'd explain why he took off," Cliff said. "Even if my mom was mentally ill, he shouldn't have deserted his kids. He should say 'I'm sorry I've been so tough on you and judgmental and made you feel there was nothing you could do to impress me.'"

"Great one." I wouldn't mind hearing that from my father too. "What about the Navy and the V.A.?"

"I'm still dealing with medical issues. It's unfair the government won't honor someone wounded overseas and apologize for the way I was treated."

"That's despicable," I said, picking at my salad. I hadn't been hungry since my fight with Dr. Winters. Maybe my weight loss was the only upside to his betrayal. Cliff chomped on his burger. I knew I was projecting my desire for an apology onto him, and this resembled therapy, though it was unclear for whom.

Five years after Cliff was wounded, he continued to resent not getting a Purple Heart or recognition, or an explanation why the V.A. screwed up his benefits. He hypothesized that there was a government cover-up, since they didn't want their inability to stop the teenage piracy publicized. That made sense to me, though the only conspiracy theories I'd pondered were in spy novels. However incomparable, I still identified with Cliff's fury at the world; it made me feel normal, as if we all kept a secret list of unsettled scores. But dwelling on the indignities you suffered had poisonous side effects, like drinking to escape.

"What about reparations? Is there anything that would help you feel better?" I asked Cliff.

"Yes. I want an apology from the Navy chief."

"The pirate too?" I threw out, smiling, eating chicken from my salad, then the tomato slices.

"Yes, the pirate who shot me. And the President." He chuckled, on a roll, only half-kidding. "Along with answers for why I was shafted. If it was just administrative, they have to do better."

During therapy to stop my substance abuse, Dr. Winters and I had discussed how, in Step 9 of AA, addicts took action by making amends to restore what they'd broken or damaged, if the person they'd offended was amenable. You weren't supposed to try to reconcile if doing so would cause further hurt, damage, or stress. Though I wasn't in an official program, I did admit my regrets to Aaron, relatives, and old classmates for any harm caused by my past addictive behavior. My friends who were still partying hadn't noticed anything I'd done wrong—that is, until *after* I quit everything. Then I felt like I had to apologize to everyone all over again for changing and becoming what one colleague called "a Type-A workaholic boring stick in the mud."

If you pried, I bet everyone felt emotionally bruised or betrayed by someone close who'd never showed any remorse or an explanation. What if no amends ever came? I asked Cliff the question circling my brain: "If you could hear 'I'm sorry' from the one who hurt you the most, who would it be?"

"My mom," he said quietly, after a pause. "She never took her medication. At my sister's funeral, she said, 'I have regrets about what happened after your father and I divorced.' It helped to hear that."

"But you wished she'd gone further before she passed away?" I asked, sensing he should keep going and might be able to crystallize what he craved but could never receive.

"Yes." Cliff nodded, finishing the last of his milkshake. "I wish she would have said 'I'm sorry I was too sick to be a real mom for you.'"

"It's really smart that you can verbalize that," I said, as the waiter left the check.

From my own therapy, I knew that you only needed one person as a catalyst for transformation, "a change agent," as Dr. Winters had been for me, and naming what you needed but never got was a good beginning. I took out my wallet to pay, pondering how you could get an apology from a dead relative.

"I have money now," Cliff said, sticking his hand out to stop me.

"It's on me," I insisted, ignoring Dr. Winters' advice, wishing I could help more, and feed him the way his mom hadn't.

Standing outside the restaurant, I said, "I'm sorry she was too sick to take care of you. You're a very smart, special guy who got a raw deal you didn't deserve."

Cliff hugged me goodbye. It was the first day in two months that I felt a little better. I'd become what was missing, offering Cliff the kind of remorse I wanted, hoping to mend the rift between him and his late mother, playing the role of a forgiveness surrogate. Would it be possible to heal myself if Dr. Winters and I didn't reconcile? Like Cliff, I could be left unfulfilled, forever wrestling a ghost.

CHAPTER 6
WHEN THE LOVE OF YOUR LIFE BETRAYS YOU

"I could easily forgive his pride, if he had not mortified mine."

—Jane Austen, *Pride and Prejudice*

"Hey, Sleeping Beauty," Aaron said, coming home late that chilly autumn night.

I was on the couch, legs tucked under a blanket in dim light, where I'd been reading poems since he'd left that morning. Eight weeks after my fight with Dr. Winters, I still felt like I was sitting shiva to grieve an irreplaceable loss. That morning I'd called a young female rabbi friend.

"You know, religious Jews who lost someone close have to live through every season, every day, and every holiday without the person they love before they're even required to go outside their house," she told me.

Her words and confessional poems by dead foreigners got me through that cold afternoon.

"How was dinner with Cindy?" I asked Aaron now.

I usually only saw his cousin Cindy at his family's holiday events. Lately I'd been coming up with excuses to avoid all plans, as I'd done during my nicotine withdrawal. Only now I was giving up a person, not a substance.

"You'll never guess who I invited to come to the restaurant," he said, sitting next to me, lifting my feet into his lap. He pretended our role reversal was normal. But he'd been trying to better report gossip when he went out and I stayed home, taking on his role of anti-social misanthrope. "Harold, her ex-husband!"

"What? When? But they split up decades ago," I said, startled. "I thought they hated each other."

"She phoned me today, distraught they're raising her rent. She can't afford New York. She's still blaming her lousy divorce settlement from thirty years ago," he said. "She begged me to get Harold to help her out. I was worried. So I asked him to join us. I couldn't believe he showed up."

Cindy and Harold were married in the 1970s for seven years and had two kids. Their hate had lasted decades longer than their love. After they split, she eked by as a single mom with child support and a little alimony. It worried me that, thirty years later, Cindy still wasn't over Harold's betrayal. When her kids went to college, his payments lessened. She worked full time, but struggled to pay rent and medical bills from breast cancer. Now, alone in her sixties, she could lose her home. Like Kenan and Cliff, her substantive problems dwarfed mine. I wished I could help, unsure how to stop being such a depressed rage-ball.

"I hadn't seen Harold since 1975," Aaron added, massaging my feet.

His hands felt good. I put my book down. "Did you know them back when they were happy?"

"I don't remember." He shrugged. "A mutual friend called Cindy 'a real *hottie*,' saying they were the beautiful couple you hated, making out in the hallway in high school."

"What does he look like now? Fat and bald?"

"No, he's thin, with hair. Average build. I only invited him today to bail out Cindy," he said. "Figures I'm the schmuck who buys dinner for the rich uptown surgeon who dumped my cousin."

"You're such a mensch," I kissed his forehead.

"Her folks are dead. She doesn't have anyone to protect her," he said. I rubbed his arm.

"She asked for you," Aaron added.

I'd thought Cindy disliked me when she'd sent us one single large carving knife for our wedding in 1996. We only bonded after I learned she worked as a sex therapist. Intrigued, I asked her all about it. She sounded smart and knowledgeable, so I took some of her business cards and recommended her to people I knew. She wound up treating Risa, a close twenty-eight-year-old family friend.

"Cindy is so awesome, she taught me to climax by myself!" Risa had emailed, divulging that Cindy treated her on a sliding scale—very generous for someone who was broke. I hadn't known then that Cindy was in financial straits.

"Why didn't her lawyer bring up Harold's future earnings as a surgeon?" I asked now.

"They divorced around 1980," Aaron said. "The lawyer was an older, suburban guy my father found. Probably not a hot shot New York divorce specialist. I've always felt guilty."

Ah, his beloved late father had recommended the lawyer. Now I understood why Aaron felt compelled to be there for Cindy: to assuage inherited guilt. "What happened?"

"Over dinner, Harold said he'd consider helping her. But he wanted something in return."

It bugged me how slowly Aaron told stories. "What did he want?" I asked, impatient.

"He wants Cindy to do something for him."

"What?!" I practically shouted.

"You have to let people tell a story their own way," he scolded. "Cindy's kids liked Harold's second wife, Bonnie. But after she died, they couldn't stand his new girlfriend, Lynn. They won't be in the same room with her. Harold asked Cindy to get the kids to accept Lynn. He wants domestic harmony."

"So she's got leverage." I nodded, sitting upright against the couch arm.

"Well, not much. After Cindy left tonight, Harold tried to slip me money for dinner. When I refused, he said, 'This is the first time I've ever seen her that didn't cost me.'"

"Wow, that is nasty."

"But good line," Aaron said. "Maybe he felt she never really loved him and just wanted to be married to someone successful."

"What is that? A guy's worst fear?" I asked. "You used to say that about me."

"Some women get ring-happy and pick whichever man has the best earning potential," he said, removing my feet from his lap. Was that true of Cindy *and* me? She'd wanted a doctor and I didn't get serious with Aaron until after he had a job, like I did. He was probably just annoyed I'd pushed him to be more social. Or that I felt so wrecked by a man who wasn't him.

That dawn, I was startled awake from another bad dream about Dr. Winters dying. I could tell my miserable state was draining Aaron. Obsessed with my personal Judas, I thought of Cindy's eternal grudge against her husband. Harold's desertion had come close to destroying her. If I never received the apology I wanted, I might grow older and stay bitter too.

"Thanks for loaning me your husband," Cindy emailed the next day.

"Sounds like a crazy dinner," I replied.

"I'll be in your neighborhood tonight. I could stop by at six if you're around?" she asked.

It was sunny, so I suggested we take a walk. She was wearing a black pea coat. She had on jeans and a sweater like I did, but her sneakers were rainbow-colored, while mine were black. She dyed her hair brown, like mine, but hers was shorter, in a bob. We could have been sisters. I led her to Washington Square Park, two blocks east. Since she was well-versed on Freud, I hoped she'd have insight into why images of Dr. Winters and Haley were haunting me.

"So how's everything?" she asked, striding as fast as I did, though she talked slower.

"I'm in a mood. I had a falling out with a mentor I depended on," I admitted. I found it easier to talk and walk since you weren't looking at someone straight on.

"I'm sorry," she said. "The more you admire a person, the greater your expectations."

"I know. I credit this person for helping me off cigarettes, booze, and drugs and getting me married to a great guy." I didn't mention his name, in case she knew him. Nor did I share that being an emotional disaster had become a roadblock in my bedroom. I hadn't wanted sex in two months.

"Aaron is great." She smiled. "He's a Jewish saint for inviting Harold on my behalf."

"How was it having dinner with your ex after so long?"

"I've seen Harold at our kids' graduations," she said. "And last year at my grandson's bris."

"You were high school sweethearts?" I knew from Aaron that her family had gone to a conservative Temple like his, and that she and Harold seemed the perfect Jewish couple. I pictured her as a slim teen beauty in tight jeans, with a V-neck and her mom's pearls. She'd filled out a little since then but still had a cute pug nose and lovely brown oval eyes.

"Junior high. I met him at thirteen. He was my first and only love," Cindy said.

"*Only?*" I asked, marveling at the thought. I'd been in love at least five times before I said "I do."

"Our parents were best friends. We got married when I was twenty-one. Dumb to marry so young."

"I had a pre-med beau too," I admitted. "He got me pregnant at nineteen. He proposed. I said no and had an abortion. After that he slept with my roommate to spite me."

"Wow. That's rough." She patted my arm. "Good you didn't let it ruin you, like I did."

Had it ruined her? After divorcing, Cindy raised two kids on her own and had a great career. She was proud that her daughter was a lawyer and her son an architect. Still, the fissure with Harold did seem to wreck her for romance. I wasn't surprised. I'd read that divorced men remarried at a higher rate than their female counterparts. I knew several divorced single moms whose standard of living went down and never rebounded.

I was eleven years younger than Cindy. If I'd married my high school boyfriend—a Jewish pre-med student—the union wouldn't have lasted. Losing my first amour before we wed or had a baby had actually saved me, as had the advice of Paula, the sharp female therapist I'd recommended to Haley whose words echoed in my head often: "Love won't make you happy. Make yourself happy. Then you'll find love." Maybe Cindy's mistake was being too dependent on a man when she was too young.

"In college, Harold and I were fun and adventurous in bed," Cindy recalled. "He only went cold when I became pregnant. Some men are like that. The mother/whore complex. I had my son at twenty-five. I was five months pregnant with my daughter at twenty-nine. I was due over the summer. It was January 1979." She recited numbers as if grappling with an equation she couldn't solve. As we finished the half-mile lap, I stopped by the park's arch to stretch my calves, holding onto the metal rail.

"You'd moved to the city by then?" I asked.

I'd met Cindy at my wedding when I was thirty-five. She'd come solo, a middle-aged, long-divorced mom, soon to become a young grandma. I had no idea of the lurid specifics of her split. It wasn't something you'd discuss at Thanksgiving dinner. I should have asked her about all this sooner.

"We lived in the hospital complex, next door to Harold's job. I looked out the window of our apartment one day, shocked to see my husband kissing his paramour."

The word seemed aptly old-fashioned for someone stuck in her past.

"She was in a nurse uniform. She was five years younger than I was," Cindy said. "I didn't know what to do." Her voice was raw, as if this scene from thirty-five years ago had occurred that morning. "I called his mother and said, 'Please help me.' She said, 'I'm so sorry he did this.'"

"So his mother knew he was a jerk."

"Not really. I was pregnant and hysterical. My mother-in-law wanted to see her grandkids," Cindy recalled. "But she embraced Bonnie too quickly. When I confronted him, he told me, 'I don't love you anymore.' I gave birth to my daughter Anne six weeks early. From the stress. He remarried right away and had another baby. They lasted three decades. Until she died last year."

Months before, on Cindy's website, I'd read: "I help Women and Men Enhance Their Love and Intimacy." It was ironic that a woman whose mate betrayed her while pregnant and destroyed her ability to love became a sex therapist. Though in retrospect, it made perfect sense. I recalled a Mark Strand poem about how we "become what was missing."

"A month after he buried Bonnie, he brought his new girlfriend Lynn home," Cindy added.

"Aaron said your kids won't meet or accept her," I reported. "Too soon?"

"Too married." She spilled the factoid that Aaron didn't even know.

"He brought a married woman home right after he lost his wife? Is she getting divorced?"

Cindy nodded. "But I heard he was seeing Lynn *before* Bonnie died."

So much for her leverage. I imagined Cindy was too moral to push her kids to accept a married woman he'd cheated with while his second spouse was dying. "Bad karma caught up to Bonnie," I said, wanting there to be consequences for that kind of misbehavior, as if having a morally illicit passion deserved a bitter end.

"I blame him more than her," she said.

"Is it hard for you to see him fall in love for a third time?"

"Actually, it's liberating to see his pattern. He wasn't loyal to his second wife either at the end. He's not close to their daughter. He can't be alone; he already found wife #3. Lots of women want a big surgeon." She shrugged. "It helped me see I wasn't totally to blame for our problems."

"Watch out," I stopped her as a rat scurried by. "Good visual for your story, like a pop-up ad," I joked.

She laughed. "My ex is a rat. He's lawless. He always gets away with everything."

She'd remained mad at the injustice. "Life's not fair," my father often warned me. "If you expect fairness, you'll be very disappointed." Finishing another loop around the park, Cindy told me how her folks had pushed her brother to a career and her towards marriage. Over country club dinners with Harold's clan, they'd decided she and Harold should wed, like an old-world arranged marriage. When they split, nobody wanted to destroy their status quo.

"Your mom and dad took Harold's side in the divorce?" I was stunned that Jewish parents (I'd automatically pictured mine) could be that insensitive.

"We officially divorced in 1982," Cindy said. "My mom died of ovarian cancer the next year. So I can't blame her for not wanting to fight while she was sick."

Since I'd never met her mother, *I* could blame her. "Man, that's hard, losing your mom and husband at the same time." I touched her shoulder.

"Right after that, my father called Harold's dad, determined to stay friends."

"That must have been humiliating for you," I commented.

"It was. But you have to understand the milieu," Cindy responded.

I did. I was from the suburban Michigan version. Her trajectory was familiar, since men made more money and so many marriages ended in divorce. I'd wed a man in a creative field, yet Aaron was more successful than I was. If we split acrimoniously, I'd be in trouble, personally and financially. If I couldn't even cope with my missing shrink, how would I recover from losing a husband?

"The world sided with Harold," Cindy said. We passed a trio of policemen by the park's entrance. "As a kid he'd set a fire in the garage and his mom would say 'It must have been someone else. Not my Harry.' The lawyers, judge, our joint friends and relatives took his side, because he was a male doctor."

Growing up with a father and brothers who were physicians, I'd witnessed the male-doctor-god syndrome firsthand. Outside of a domestic realm, women served as appendages to their spouses. Cindy had probably married young to escape her family. Not the best reason, yet that was also my parents' motive, and they'd been happy for over half a century. "You can do anything as long as it works," as the saying went. The problem was, you had to play it out to know.

"When did you first try therapy?" I asked her.

"During the breakup—but Harold brought his girlfriend Bonnie to our couples' session. It was bizarre. We saw a psychiatrist with Harold, Bonnie, and me, holding my two-month-old."

I was floored that the doctor permitted such a travesty. "Why would the shrink allow it?"

"It's the only way Harold would come. The doctor told him 'What you're doing is wrong. You should leave Bonnie and go back to your family.' Harold obviously didn't listen," Cindy said. "He married her, had another baby, became a big success. I was traumatized. Nobody recognized my loss. I was supposed to move on, like he had. But I couldn't." She looked teary and fragile. I led us towards a bench, buying us bottled waters from a hotdog vendor. We sat down.

"How long was it until you got over the breakup?" I asked, taking a sip.

"In terms of romantic love, I didn't, really," she said. "My kids filled my heart."

I felt sad for her but bet her experience was fairly common. Not exactly an upbeat topic for Ellen or Dr. Phil's show: Women Who Never Recover from Being Dumped by Their Husbands.

"I still don't trust men. I don't know how to meet someone special," Cindy admitted. "Having surgery for breast cancer last year didn't exactly make it easier to date. Neither does the thought of getting thrown out of my apartment because I can't afford the rent increase."

"I'm sorry you had to go through that," I said, starting to understand why a sex therapist might prefer celibacy. Dating took time and money, which she put into improving her health and work, and bringing up her children. Maybe masturbation was easier, as the joke went, because it's sex with someone you love. I bet, after all she'd lost, she was afraid to risk falling for someone new. Surely letting go of the fantasy that her ex might save her financially could help her move on.

"So if you could script the apology that Harold owes you, that might let you forgive him and move on, what exactly would you have him say?"

Cindy looked at me, then said, "I'm sorry I left you pregnant with an infant. And for never explaining why. I'm grateful for how well you brought up our wonderful children." She was speaking clearly, as if she'd rehearsed this in her head for years. "I know you've been sick. I want to buy you a house so you can heal and grow old comfortably. I'm sorry I didn't do this sooner."

It amazed me to think that Harold could buy Cindy's forgiveness simply with a check and apology, and by acknowledging her pain. My student Cliff craved money from the government, but mainly wanted an apology from his mom. To Cindy, the past was gone, but her future was in jeopardy. Thus the idea of financial reparation from her ex-husband—however unrealistic that fantasy was—loomed larger.

"Did anything good come from all the pain you suffered?" I asked her.

"Yes. I have two kids who are happily married, and two beautiful grandkids. That's very important to me." She stood up. "And I was resilient. I did my graduate degree at night, a babysitter watching my two toddlers. If Harold stayed, I might not have found a career I loved." I saw why she was confused. Doing everything right and earning good grades had not led to a fulfilling life.

"Why sex therapy?" I tossed my bottle in the overflowing trash bin.

"I went to a Dr. Ruth Westheimer reading," she said. "I was fascinated to learn that, as an Orthodox Jewish girl in Germany, her parents sent her to Switzerland, then both died in the Holocaust. Yet she's so vibrant, funny, and smart. I introduced myself. I wanted to get rid of the repressed background I came from and be just like her."

Dr. Ruth had worked with Helen Singer Kaplan, as had Cindy. I'd been honored to meet Kaplan in 1981, through my cousin, the author Howard Fast. I was twenty, new in New York, excited to be at a sophisticated Fifth Avenue party. When Kaplan asked me about my childhood, I told her that I'd destroyed most of my Barbie dolls. "That's why you're so happy and healthy. You got all of your aggression out," she said. So sure of my bright future, she even fixed me up with her son (alas, no chemistry).

Thirty years later, I no longer felt like the picture of happiness and health.

"Your mom never brought up sex?" I asked Cindy as we headed back to my place.

"She was insane on the subject, a lot of crossed wires." Cindy had clearly analyzed this. "She was overly focused on looks. She used to tell me to wear my bikini in front of guests."

Yikes! I saw why sex was complicated for her. With that family *mishigas*, it was a miracle Cindy married and had healthy kids. I was thankful for my warm, more appropriate mother. I recalled telling Mom I'd "lost it" to my pre-med boyfriend at fifteen. She'd cried, then said, "Well, the Goodman women were always hot-blooded." That made me feel special, like I was in a secret tribe. My parents hoped I'd marry him. If he hadn't dumped me, I might have wound up with the first guy I'd slept with, like my mom and Cindy. I would have been a wife and mother, with no career, relying solely on my husband. I'd narrowly escaped having Cindy's life.

"Dr. Ruth recommended a class on sexual disorders that I took. That's where I learned to give other people the assistance I couldn't get, to help couples work out the trust and relationship problems I never fixed in *my* marriage. I think most therapists are working out their own issues."

I nodded, reminded that a psychology degree could indicate instability, not the opposite.

"A female patient wrote me and said, 'I wouldn't have been able to have a baby, husband, and happy marriage without you.' That made feel so proud, I cried," Cindy said.

"Risa raves about you," I jumped in. "She said you taught her how to climax with her boyfriend."

She beamed. "I told her, 'Don't expect men to read minds. Take responsibility for your own pleasure.'"

Maybe Cindy thought devoting her life to being a good mother and helping other young women be happier sexually would help heal herself. "That's smart," I said. "You should publish an article on that."

"You think so?" Cindy asked, flattered.

"I'm serious. Few women in college or even grad school know how to orgasm during sex. I sure didn't," I told her. Despite her hardships, she seemed better off without Harold. After all, nurse Bonnie was dead. Cindy could have a third act. "Didn't you have other lovers after your divorce?" I asked.

"I've had desires," she said. "I wish I could meet someone now. Maybe I have to forgive myself for being so blind-sided and naïve about relationships."

I pictured what a letter of apology to herself would sound like. "After a bad breakup with a sociopath, I was beating myself up," I said. "My shrink told me: 'Your only mistake was believing what someone you love told you. And we're all guilty of that.'"

"We are," Cindy said.

Hugging goodbye, I worried about her. I wished Aaron and I had the money to give Cindy. If it were up to me, she'd remarry someone great and publish a bestselling sex book to pay for her apartment.

"You'll help me with the article?" she asked.

"Of course," I promised.

For a second I felt empowered, the way Cindy might have felt helping Risa and others find the pleasure she couldn't get herself. I understood how a head doctor could be your spiritual role model, and therapy could become your religion. They did have a lot of common mandates: Be very honest. Focus on work and love. Nurture meaningful family and friend connections. Don't overindulge in drinking, smoking or drugs. Stop hurting others and yourself. In my case, Dr. Winters told me to "always err on the side of generosity." He'd pushed me towards teaching more. He was right, it became a calling.

My dad—who'd taught medical school—was so gung-ho about my adjunct professorship he'd wanted to come to New York to see me get a teaching award on a Thursday afternoon. But he'd planned to leave before a big book event I was doing that Friday night.

"He loves that I'm a married teacher who's a nice aunt to his grandkids," I'd complained in therapy. "My father is proud of me for all the wrong things."

"Just be glad he's proud of you for something," Dr. Winters had answered. "He likes it when you're like him. Didn't he used to teach?"

"Sharing your wisdom is a gift," my father used to tell me. "A rabbi is a Jewish teacher. For our people, it's a noble profession."

"Too bad writing is my religion," I'd told Dr. Winters.

"The function of the Jewish people is to be a light unto nations," Rabbi Pindrus once told me. "We exist to serve as inspiration, as mentors, guides and educators. God desires that every person maximize their unique potential to reach excellence. But you can't self-actualize unless your goal is to enable others to."

That sounded surprisingly modern and shrinkadelic for an Orthodox grandfather. I recalled that Freud had called religion "a collective neurosis" about "longing for a father" in *The Future of an Illusion*. Yet in his eighties, in his last book *Moses and Monotheism,* Freud relented. He decided that Judaism's internalizing of God and the prohibition against recreating His image helped Jews gain intellectual strength. Their powers of introspection, Freud argued, led to remarkable achievements in literary art, math, and science. My father's education is what led my family to a better life.

Walking back into my building's lobby, I realized I had to resolve my conflict soon. I missed my speed-of-light energy, ardor, the joy I used to feel and be able to share. I saw why my father and Dr. Winters had pushed me towards teaching. It took me out of myself and gave back to the world. If I didn't get over my resentment, I could lose decades.

CHAPTER 7
WHEN YOUR WHOLE CONTINENT BETRAYS YOU
NOVEMBER 2010

"Those who cannot learn from history are doomed to repeat it."
—philosopher George Santayana

"Susie, good to see you," Manny said, using my old nickname. "Tell me about your Bosnia project."

I'd been nervous to meet with Emanuel Mandel (a.k.a. Manny) that November day in Washington, D.C. He'd been a buddy of my father's for half a century. I hadn't seen him since my wedding eighteen years before. As a Hungarian Jew, Manny had been the victim of ethnic cleansing. His mother was from the former Yugoslavia, which riveted me since I began researching the Bosnian War for the book Kenan asked me to coauthor.

Now I felt surprisingly comfortable greeting Manny at the Sea Catch restaurant. "Kenan's like the Muslim Anne Frank who lived to tell the story," I said, sitting down, eager to share my newfound interest in history. "It's shocking there was another holocaust in Europe in 1993 that most Americans don't know about."

"Well, we only use *Holocaust* for what happened to the Jews in Eastern

Europe in World War II," he corrected. "You know, I survived Bergen-Belsen, where Anne Frank died."

Damn. In seconds I'd already insulted a seventy-four-year-old survivor, retired psychologist, and close family friend. Growing up I'd found my dad's buddy Manny intimidating, with his strong baritone voice. He was more erudite than other Midwest dads. He was the only person I knew personally, aside from Kenan, who'd escaped a war and knew the Balkans.

"I'm sorry," I said.

"I use *genocide*, not *holocaust*," Manny made clear. "Look, it's despicable that Serbs murdered their Balkan countrymen. But in our case in World War II, the Germans went into twenty other nations to kill Jews. Because of the number and magnitude of Hitler's Final Solution, we feel proprietary about the word."

I kept apologizing as the waiter brought menus, though Manny said it wasn't necessary. After losing Dr. Winters and being immersed in Kenan's family history, I was consumed with questions of mortal sins and forgiveness. Here was a male psychologist who could tell me how he forgave, or lived without forgiving the evil forces who'd tried to annihilate our whole tribe.

Kenan's people actually fought to call what happened to Bosnians a *genocide*. The Serb government claimed the dead were "war casualties," as if the deliberate murder of more than 100,000 Muslim civilians killed didn't qualify as genocidal. When I later emailed that Manny objected to the use of *holocaust* for the Bosnian massacres, Kenan found an Oxford English Dictionary entry showing the word was derived from the Greek *holokauston* (a burnt sacrificial offering) and had been used to describe massacres since 1142.

"But you never call what happened in the Balkans a *Holocaust*," I'd argued.

"I know, but I want the option to," Kenan admitted, then chuckled at his stubbornness.

It was probably human nature to compare atrocities, wanting your tragedy to be the worst ever, not downplayed or ranked less severe. Of course, by comparison, my fight with Dr. Winters was getting exponentially smaller. It made me want to ask more people I knew who'd endured horrible traumas how they'd coped and forgiven their offenders. I knew my misfortune was a minor estrangement that might be fixable. That perspective should have made reconciliation easier, but I didn't know how. If anyone could teach me, it was a successful shrink who'd survived war atrocities, like Manny.

I felt lucky to interview one of only 500,000 survivors still alive. He looked younger than his age, slim with salt and pepper hair, bushy brows, brown eyes. At six feet, he was an inch taller than my dad. As a kid it freaked me out when my father said Manny was "a Holocaust survivor." I'd pictured the piles of emaciated corpses from documentaries shown at Hebrew School, as if he'd been hiding in there. As an adult, I'd sidestepped Manny's invitations to the U.S. Holocaust Museum, where he volunteered. A friend who went to a special program there said what happened to Hitler's victims was reenacted for visitors, who were pinned with yellow "Juden" stars, asked to remove their shoes, and given fake arm tattoos.

"Oh good, a vacation that'll give me nightmares," I'd told Aaron. I blamed my alienation on how my childhood temple had shoved the Holocaust down my throat, then felt guilty for my reaction. Visiting Dachau on a high-school trip made me mistrust Germans and I carried ongoing suspicions of European anti-Semitism. Yet suddenly everything I'd found scary about my father's friend Manny enthralled me.

"Did my parents know your whole past?" I asked, bubbling with questions.

"I didn't discuss it much, until the World Gathering of Holocaust Survivors in 1981," Manny said. "At Central High in Philly, I played soccer with Charles Roger, a survivor from Brussels. It was never mentioned until we remet at a commemoration five decades later. There was an irrational fear that once you started remembering, you couldn't stop." I nodded, thinking of all the pages pouring out of Kenan.

We'd lived near Manny, his wife Adrienne, and their kids in middle-class Oak Park, Michigan, in the 60s. As a classmate of their daughter Lisa, I'd fixed her up with the guy she dated for four years. Before I'd taken the train to D.C. that morning, I'd called to ask my folks about their memories.

"Adrienne was funny, short, very pretty. She was the vivacious one," said my mother, who was very pretty and charismatic herself. "Manny was drier, intellectual. He seemed European," she added.

"How did you first learn he was a Holocaust survivor?"

"He had an accent, so I asked where he was from," Dad recalled. "My family was from the Ukraine, but came to America sooner. We found out we both had our bar mitzvahs at the Orthodox Roumanian Synagogue on Rivington Street, on New York's Lower East Side. Manny's dad was a cantor there."

"An Orthodox temple? Why? You were never religious," I said.

"I played hooky and gambled, running a numbers game," Dad said. "I got thrown out everywhere else. My grandfather made a deal with the Rabbi of *Roumanishe Shul* that I'd learn my *Haftorah* there."

I relished hearing about Dad's early days as a troublemaker, before he'd become a staid Republican. "So that was a bond between you and Manny?"

"Yeah. He was a better student," Dad said, laughing. "We always talked history. His dad was a cantor. So I was impressed that he knew all the different cantorial schools in Europe."

My parents, who'd hated anything personal I'd ever published about myself or our family, sounded gleeful that Jewish history was my new subject, as if I'd finally seen their light.

"Dad and Manny fought politics," Mom piped in from the other line. "Manny was more liberal."

"Now he's less liberal, and I'm less conservative," Dad told me. He'd called my candidates Hillary and Bill "Bonnie and Clyde" and nicknamed Obama "Oprah." *This* was his idea of being less conservative?

"We shared an obsessive loathing for Nazis who got off too easy," my father went on. "The second A-bomb should have hit Germany, not Japan."

Dad's characteristic hyberbole underscored Manny's typical understatement. But I didn't want a history lesson from Dad. I wanted him to like me more, respect my work, and treat me the way he did my brothers.

"Manny used to confuse me as a kid," I admitted. "You were blunt, but he'd talk in a roundabout way that I didn't get."

"Yes, he had a more dry, ironic sensibility," Dad said. "He was Talmudic. The commentators always answer questions with other questions."

"He had a sibling who died," Mom said. "Ask him about that."

Although Manny kept the laws of Kashrut at home, we both ordered shrimp cocktails and lobster, which felt thrillingly illicit. I'd rarely had a meal alone with my dad. Reaching out to his friend made me feel closer to my father. I fired away queries, taking notes. "You're from an Orthodox Hungarian family?"

"I was born on May 8 in 1936 in Riga, Latvia. I would call us Observant Jews."

"You're Taurus the bull, like my mom," I said, then felt like an airbrain for bringing up astrology.

"Yes, I am a Taurus in many ways," he admitted, "horoscopes notwithstanding."

Kenan, too, was fiercely stubborn. Was it a survival technique they'd learned as kids who lived through wars? Manny's mother's father was a rabbi in Novi-Sad, Serbia. He was an only child who resembled her side. He pulled out pictures. "My dad was five foot seven, stocky, with black hair, brown eyes."

The elder Mandel looked friendly but, oddly, he resembled Hitler with his short, stubby mustache.

"He had a magnificent voice. He left Hungary for an important job as cantor in Riga from 1933. My mom went with him. Since you have to be born where your mother is, my birthplace was Riga. Then he took a higher position as one of four chief cantors in Budapest at the

Romabach Street Synagogue there, where we lived until 1944, when we were deported."

"Were you aware of rising anti-Semitism?" I finished my water, eager to get to the forgiving part.

"As a kid, I was in a bubble. Initially I saw the yellow star I wore as a mark of heroism, since the adults wore it. I thought it was terrific. I was proud. I didn't know it was demeaning," he said. "At seven, I asked Dad for a new two-wheel bicycle. He said no. Our fifty-year-old building had old elevators. The machinists in factories were busy making guns and bombs, my father said. If the elevator broke, I'd have to carry my bike up five flights. Riding in the park with a yellow star was dangerous; we didn't want more attention. No bike. That hit me. That was my first clue."

In a photo from age three, he was driving a fancy toy car in a park in Budapest. The image conveyed how beloved he was, as well as his wealth and privilege. My parents had grown up poor.

"After anti-Jewish laws in Hungary in 1938, Jews were harassed. A kid with a yellow star would be hit on the head, dumped in a gutter, left alone to die," Manny added. "Dad was afraid someone might push me into traffic. He let me go to school four blocks away, but somebody walked me there and back. I was never alone. I still went ice skating, wearing my yellow star. But my father was there too, that made it secure."

"How old was your mother when she had you?" I asked.

"She was twenty-eight." When our dinner came, I ate quickly, taking notes, not wanting to miss anything.

I flashed to my mother's words. "Wasn't that late for a rabbi's daughter to have a first kid?" I asked.

"Oh, she'd married at twenty-two and had her first son, Rubin, when she was twenty-five," Manny admitted. "He had enteritis. He couldn't absorb food. He died at ten weeks. Now they'd probably give you a shot and pills and send you home to play baseball. Adrienne and I recently visited his grave, in Yugoslavia."

No wonder he'd been so cherished by his parents.

Manny was seven when Germany occupied Budapest. He was sent to

Bergen-Belsen in July 1944, on a Kasztner train transport. He was told it would be a rest stop before boarding a ship as part of the Nazi plan to make Europe *Judenrein*, Jew-free. His father was sent to a different work camp. For six months, Manny lived in a "family" barrack, sleeping on a bunk bed above his mother. He was afraid of the armed soldiers and barbed wire. For the first time he was hungry.

"We had two meals a day," he said. "The first was black bread and a brown coffee-like liquid. In the afternoon, vats filled with soup, stew with vegetables or horse meat. My mother, a great cook, brought three things with her to the camp—a jar of honey, chicken fat, and a slab of bacon. Weird for someone kosher. People told her these condiments might help make the food edible. For us, Bergen-Belsen wasn't as bad as Auschwitz. We didn't have numbers tattooed on our arms. In 1944, the war was ending. To save their skin, the Nazis kept us healthy as barter."

"My grandfather used to say 'Nothing's so bad it can't be vorse,'" I said in a Yiddish accent.

"I was extremely blessed to always be with my mother," he restated like a mantra.

Like Manny, my dad was an only son adored by his mother. (His father was a different story.) I thought of how Dr. Winters' mother had hated him, realizing how much harder that made his life. I had my mother's love (albeit shared with three brothers born too close in age). Still, if Dad's belief was true, I didn't know why I was an emotional mess. Because my connection with my Dad had been fraught and difficult? That male parental gap might be why I'd glommed onto Dr. Winters so tightly.

"Many had it worse," Manny said. "For gold and loot, Adolf Eichman was coerced to transfer 1,670 Jews to Bergen-Belsen. Unlike Auschwitz, it was an intern camp, not designed for extermination."

Thus Manny and his mom were sent to Switzerland, where the Red Cross brought potatoes to their hotel. "We weren't scarecrows, like others in the pictures you've seen." They took a British troop ship to Palestine, where he reunited with his father after two years apart. "My mother's parents and two of her brothers died in Auschwitz. To Nazis, the old and young were useless; they killed my little cousin Judy. Mom's two sisters, strong and in their thirties, survived. My father lost his mother. He didn't know what day she died, so he lit a Yahrzeit candle for her every Yom Kippur."

I thought that was poetic, picking the most sorrowful day to remember.

"My worst shock was in 1949, when my thirty-four-year-old uncle, Dad's youngest brother, died in Israel. It was a stroke or heart attack, but clearly related to his concentration-camp stay. He left a wife and two babies. I was thirteen. I was living with my parents in New York, an apartment on Barrow Street."

"Right by me," I said, amused to think of Manny living in the now hipster West Village.

"I was home alone when the telegram came: 'Daniel died yesterday. He'll be buried tomorrow.' I didn't know how to tell my parents," Manny said. "I told my father to come get the mail with me where I gave him the bad news. We didn't tell my mother until the next day, knowing she'd be grief-stricken."

When I asked his worst loss from the war, he said, "My whole family was shrunk forever. My mom was one of six kids but they only had five offspring altogether. Nobody would bring another child into the world after the war. We didn't madly procreate to repopulate our people, the way some survivors did."

I couldn't wait to get his reaction to the official apology in 1990. Pulling out a printout, I read, "East Germany's first freely elected Parliament admits joint responsibility on behalf of the people for the humiliation, expulsion and murder of Jewish women, men and children. We feel sad and ashamed . . . Jews in all the world and the people of Israel are asked to forgive us for the wrongs they experienced."

"It didn't make the Germans who did this less guilty," Manny said. "The murderers are dead. If I could get an apology from the criminals who did it, that might mean something. For survivors, it's hard not to have a long-term committed hatred of Nazi Germany."

Interesting he still wanted the late perpetrators to apologize, as did Kenan. "So you found ways to live with your rage?" I asked.

"I wouldn't call it rage," he said. "Well, it was 10 percent rage and 90 percent thank God we're still alive. Being here and successful said to Hitler: *Up Yours! We refuse to let you control our life.*"

I thought of George Herbert's line, "Living well is the best revenge," feeling a little taken aback by the lesson Manny had to teach: Don't forgive, but find a way to thrive without granting mercy. Out of spite.

"How?" I asked, wanting to do that myself. "You compartmentalize?"

"Ask yourself, 'What's enraging you?' and 'What do you want your life to be about?' he threw out. "Then you find tiny ways to lessen the pain or remove it, pebble by pebble."

"Is that how you counseled your patients who'd been through similar atrocities?"

"Hundreds of survivors came to my private practice," he said. "Their problems seemed the same as anyone from Montana. The Holmes-Rahe's studies show the worst stresses are death of a spouse, divorce, marital separation, detention in jail or another institution, major personal injury or illness, loss of job."

Finishing my seafood, I was stunned that Manny didn't see his experience as singular. "So your treatment was the same for anybody who survived any war, illness, or a traumatic change?" I asked.

"Yes," he said. "My feeling is: the more we blame the past, the harder it is to move on. There's a way to remember and understand trauma without dwelling on it. Feeling stuck without a choice is demeaning and devastating. In my career, I've spent forty years helping people learn they had choices."

"But how do you get unstuck?" Completely mired, that was my million-dollar question.

"Start by talking it out with someone you trust—a clergy, sponsor, therapist, or mentor," he said.

Well, I'd lost the one I went to for enlightenment. "I fell out with a parental figure I looked up to for a long time," I ventured. "I'm having trouble getting over it. Any advice?" I hope he didn't mind that I'd just turned our forgiveness interview into a free therapy session.

"You can get over anything," he said. "Make art from your pain. Try a group, new interest, or mentor. Education helps. Do the Bosnia book. Anything to remove the barriers and offer fresh insight."

"So you're behavioral, not Freudian?" I asked.

"If a patient came to my office bleeding, my job is to stop the blood," he said. "Later I'll ask 'Where did the wound come from?' Some Freudians spend so much time on the origins of the wound, the patient bleeds out. But I was lucky. I didn't lose my parents. We started over and were monetarily compensated."

I'd forgotten about the reparations that were paid. "How did they decide who got money?"

"It was a complicated process. My dad lost his pension and employment, though being a cantor was a portable profession. He got jobs in Israel and America."

I asked him how much difference the financial restitution made. I guessed not very much.

"I was given a one-time sum of $500. It paid for my honeymoon to the Concord Hotel in upstate New York," Manny said. "That money didn't restore anything. My murdered grandparents, cousins, uncles, and aunts had perished. But my father received $1,000 a month from the German government between 1950 and 1994, until he died. It meant a great deal to him. It allowed us to live better and move on."

Oh. Since people who did well had less resentment about the past, I wondered if reparations could actually be the most important part of forgiving. If the Serbian government had paid for Kenan's higher education, he might have been a doctor. Cliff would have thrived with a Purple Heart, better veterans benefits, and medical attention.

"The last payment came after my father died. I returned it," Manny said. "It didn't belong to me."

"Didn't you want to keep the money?" I asked. "Even after witnessing the worst atrocities of the century against you and your people, you maintained a clear sense of right and wrong?"

"Not really. It would have been a hassle to cash. Not worth the trouble for $1,000," he said.

When the waiter brought the check, Manny tried to pay. I insisted, feeling very adult.

"My dad used to say, 'If you have your mother's love, you have everything.' Freud agreed," I said. "Is that why you healed and had a great life? Because you were the apple of your mom's eye?"

"Well, she had very few apples." He smiled and told me how his work in the Peace Corps and running teen programs for B'nai B'rith gave him a sense of purpose. "When we met, Adrienne was her B'nai B'rith district president," he said. "You were in a B'nai B'rith group in high school," he remembered.

"I was president of my chapter," I said proudly. But actually, at thirteen I was a chain-smoking troublemaker, like my dad. I'd get stoned and make out with my boyfriend on the camp retreats. "Did the war mean you couldn't rebel?" I asked. I told Manny how upset Kenan had been when a dorm mate teased him, saying "You're calling your mommy again? The whole point of college is to escape your family."

"'He had no idea the real enemies I escaped,' Kenan said. 'I thanked God every day my parents were not murdered in war. I couldn't relate to the superficial rebellions of my classmates.'"

"I understand. After what we went through, rebellion was not an option," Manny agreed.

"Did you work in Jewish groups and help teens as a shrink to avenge the Holocaust?"

"Not that I'm conscious of," he said. "Remember, I had it easier than most."

Indeed, his mother adored him until her death, when he was thirty-one. Manny had his dad and stepmom until he was sixty.

"Your connection to your parents seems like the essential part of the forgiving equation," I told Manny. "I love how you learned to have a great life without really forgiving anyone."

"I went back to Germany for the sixty-fifth anniversary of Bergen-Belsen's liberation five years ago," he said. "After, I visited Berlin as a tourist. A young guide, a nice history professor, said his grandmother was a proud card-carrying Nazi. I felt no animosity for him, though his grandmother was eligible for hatred."

I showed Manny a controversial study from a research team at New York's Mount Sinai hospital on "epigenetic inheritance" that found Holocaust survivors' trauma was passed on in their children's genes, affecting subsequent generations. "I didn't realize you could inherit a memory of trauma."

"Perfectly legitimate researchers often prove whatever they wish to prove," he said.

A week later, Manny's granddaughter Gabriele emailed. She was studying forensic science at John Jay College of Criminal Justice near us. Teenagers her age usually asked me about how to publish an article or a book. Gabriele became entrenched in a conversation with my husband, who'd worked on *Law & Order*, about his interviews with forensic experts on serial killers.

"Strange obsession for a young girl," I'd told Aaron later.

"Not if your grandfather was a Holocaust survivor," he said.

Insignificant as my problem was now starting to feel, I wrote a list of what would help me truly forgive Dr. Winters: acknowledgment that he hurt me, an explanation and an apology. I contemplated what I would do if he couldn't cough it up. Manny's take was that you didn't need anyone to say "I'm sorry" to have a good life, and that reparation was actually the more essential ingredient in moving on. Yet I had no control over the only act of restitution that would really do the trick: that Dr. Winters would come clean. Or did I?

CHAPTER 8
CRAVING AN IMPOSSIBLE APOLOGY

"To err is human; to forgive, divine."—Alexander Pope

"It's not easy being the boss's daughter, especially when you're really his son," cracked Chris Edwards, to loud applause. His darkly funny speech at a Boston advertising conference revealed how he'd had twenty-eight surgeries to become a man. "Changing from female to male takes balls," he added.

Beneath his witty banter about "rebranding himself," I questioned how the cute, short, bearded forty-two-year-old creative director really felt. We'd become friendly after he'd hired me to help edit his memoir-in-progress *Balls: It Takes Some to Get Some* over the last two years, and he'd invited me to hear his talk. I hoped getting out of town for a twenty-four-hour work jaunt would chill me out. But in the midst of contemplating the stories of ethnic cleansing against Muslims and Jews, I thought: a transgender adman with an Armenian background had to be filled with pent-up rage. In the process of discussing his book outline, I wanted to know who'd hurt him most and owed him an apology.

Having drinks at the hotel bar after his speech, I said "My student Liza Derymerjian joked that Jews got better PR for their Holocaust. As an Armenian, did you feel that way?"

"I'll say! Fucking Turks," he said. "They act like it never happened. It's a sore spot with all Armenians."

"So you have a life-long hatred of Turkey?" I poured myself green tea as Chris squeezed lime juice over his Stoli and soda, then took a sip.

"Not really. I grew up assimilated. My mom was a Boston Protestant, Dad a Pennsylvania Catholic. I felt like a good Christian, going to church and Sunday School. I didn't even learn our history until I was sixteen. At my grandparents' Armenian Apostolic service, the minister brought in a guest speaker who spoke about the million and a half Armenians who were killed by the Turks in 1915. I couldn't believe it. I'd learned about the Jewish Holocaust in school, but nothing about the slaughter of my own people. I rushed out to get a book on it. It was very disturbing."

"Are you Armenian Orthodox?"

"No. My sisters and I were brought up Protestant like my mom."

"Your parents never talked about the genocide with you?" I asked.

"Not much. Sometimes I'd hear my older relatives make negative comments about Turkish people, but I didn't understand. When I learned that Turkey wouldn't officially acknowledge what happened, I was outraged. Did I hate what the Turks did to Armenia 100 years ago? Absolutely. Do I hate Turkish people? No."

"Do you think the Turks should apologize?"

"Now I think the country of Turkey owes Armenians as a people an acknowledgment and apology," he said. "But growing up, I hardly knew anyone like us. There were only two other Armenian families in our town. I was the only transgender."

"In your talk, I loved how your parents supported your transformation," I said.

"My parents were amazing." He smiled.

As a straight, married, cis-het female from a reserved Midwest family, I'd learned a lot teaching in downtown New York City, where students across the sexual spectrum exposed intimate secrets. I told Chris about the trans-female doctor in my class who'd been upset to learn her mother's OBGYN prescribed Diethylstilbestrol (DES), a synthetic estrogen to help morning sickness during pregnancy, a common practice starting in the 1940s. It had caused many of the babies to suffer from genital abnormalities and gender dysphoria, the feeling they were born the opposite of the sex they were supposed to be. The drug wasn't banned until 1971.

"I always wished I had a biological defect to explain my problem," Chris said. "So people wouldn't think I was crazy. So I wouldn't think it was my fault."

He asked about the book proposal I'd written with twenty-three-year-old Andreja Pejic, the first trans model featured in *Vogue*. She'd described growing up with a Serb mother and macho Croatian father during the Bosnian War. Her Catholic dad claimed her half-Serbian side and effeminacy brought "a double curse to the family." She hated the homophobia in the Balkans and gave herself "how to be a man" lessons as a teen: speaking in a flat monotone, walking straight with no arm swings. Even with fame, an agent warned: "It's better to be androgynous than a tranny."

I expected Chris to share his own transphobia stories. But all he said was "Andreja's ravishing, but way too tall for me," and winked.

"You seem really together and well-adjusted," I said. "I read that a high percentage of the 1.5 million transgender people in the U.S. are depressed and suicidal."

"Yes, I speak out because 50 percent of trans kids try to kill themselves after family rejection," he said. "They get bullied at school and kicked out of their homes. I feel that more success stories will breed more supportive parents. They'll be able to look at me and people like me and say, 'That person transitioned and turned out okay, so my kid will be fine too.' Thankfully my relatives were great. My father even paid for my surgeries."

I grew up the black sheep in picket-fence suburbia. I didn't believe everyone in his bloodline was accepting. Maybe he was putting on a happy face for me. Was Chris a reliable narrator?

"When I started my transition in 1996, insurance didn't cover anything," he added.

Maybe he hated insurance companies, at least? "That sounds so unfair. Did the injustice upset you?"

"Kind of. I mean I wasn't surprised it wasn't covered. At the time it was classified as a mental disorder. I was just lucky my parents were generous, could afford it, and were willing to help me. If that wasn't the case I would have been way more upset."

Either his family was superhuman or he was in denial. Comedy often masked misery. Or was he just an upbeat, rich Massachusetts businessman, not a cynical Manhattan shrinkaholic, like me?

"When did you realize you weren't female?" I asked.

"I always knew I was a boy," he said. "I was the middle child, between my older sister Wendy and the youngest, Jill. One day when I was five, I was on vacation at my grandmother's cottage on Cape Cod. Wendy and I were in the family room coloring and Gram yelled from the kitchen, 'Come on girls, dinner is ready.' Wendy immediately sprung up, but I didn't flinch. I honestly didn't think Gram was talking to me. A minute later she came back into the room to reprimand me. 'Didn't you hear me say "Come on girls"?' she asked.

'I'm not a girl,' I told her.

'Yes you are.'

'No, I'm not. I'm a boy.'

'No, you're not, sweetheart,' she said.

'Well, I'm gonna be,' I insisted.

'You can't, darling.'

"I remember thinking, *Whatever, Gram*," he said. "I wondered how she could possibly make such a dumb mistake. Then I thought, *Oh, I know what happened. Girls have long hair; boys have short hair*. So I told Mom I wanted my hair cut, like Daddy's. In my five-year-old brain, I was sure that would solve the problem. My parents let me cut it. They just figured I was a tomboy. Wendy was, too, so they probably thought I'd grow out of it like she did. Obviously I didn't. I've had short hair ever since."

"But then it got worse?"

"Yes. The next summer on Cape Cod, I was on Gram's back deck eating popsicles with Wendy, when my cousin Adam, who was a year younger than me, said 'Watch this' as he peed in a perfect arc over the deck rail. Stunned, I asked, 'How did you do that?' I thought he had a squirt gun in his pants.

'Duh,' Wendy said. 'With his penis.'

"I didn't know what that was and wanted to know why I didn't have one. I assumed mine just hadn't grown in yet. Every night I asked God for one, to turn me into a boy and prove to everyone they were silly for thinking I was a girl. Puberty hit and my body betrayed me in the worst ways. I went into a deep depression. I knew then I was stuck in this body for the rest of my life, like I was born wrong. My personality darkened." His voice was quieter. "One day I noticed my sister Wendy sitting in a dress and eating a cupcake, looking very happy. I punched her. I wound up asking God for forgiveness. I never wanted to hurt her. I was just so unhappy."

"Were you isolated and ostracized by other kids?" I felt indignant for him, picturing a football-playing bully ruining Chris's school days.

"No. I was popular. I was smart, on the honor roll every term."

"I thought you were flipping out because you were in the wrong body?" I asked.

"I was—on the inside. Getting my period every month was devastating. Wearing a bra was a constant reminder I wasn't who I was supposed to be. I couldn't control what body I was stuck with so I tried to bury my anxiety and discomfort and focus on what I could control: my friends, grades, and clothes. My anxiety would creep up when I had to wear a bathing suit, or a dress to a classmate's bar mitzvah. I was uncomfortable—like I was in drag. I didn't want anyone to know I was attracted to girls. To avoid going out on dates with guys, I would steer clear of make-out and spin-the-bottle games. I faked answers when asked who I had a crush on. In the locker room I'd change privately in a stall with a curtain. My classmates liked me. But I never dated," Chris said. "In that way, I was isolated."

"So nobody was cruel, but you *felt* alone?" I wanted him to clarify.

"Yes. First I thought I was gay. But I didn't want to be a woman with a woman. I wanted to be with a woman as a man. I didn't know anybody like me. I thought I was a freak. I'll never forget in college when I went with a friend to see *The Silence of the Lambs*. There was a scene where Lecter describes this psycho-killer, Buffalo Bill, as a 'frustrated transsexual who was rejected from all three gender clinics in the country.' I was amazed to hear there were gender clinics. But it made me sick to think that's how people might see me. I couldn't envision a happy future for myself. So I decided to spend my four years of college partying it up, then I'd kill myself."

"That's horrible." Now I felt badly about pushing him to recall these memories.

"After I heard the trans-model Tula on Maury Povich's TV show saying a chromosome test proved she had a defect, I took a chromosome test too. But my results came back normal. I explained my problem to my doctor. She sent me to a therapist with the diagnosis *hirsutism*, too much hair."

Chris hadn't been taking hormones yet, but I gathered that being dark and Armenian caused the doctor to label him a hairy lesbian. "Didn't that doctor distress you?" I asked. I couldn't imagine how unsettling it would feel if my physician didn't know what sex I was meant to be. "Do you want an apology for being misdiagnosed?"

"No. She was just ignorant on the subject, like most people—including the therapist she sent me to. I saw that woman for almost a year and she didn't really get it either. To her credit, she emphasized that I needed support and encouraged me to tell my parents and sisters. She said to reveal who I was in stages, so they could digest it, not to drop the surgery bomb on them right away."

It struck me that Chris focused on what his shrink got right rather than her mistakes.

"One Sunday dinner after college, when I was twenty-four, I finally told my family. They were all joking around and I didn't say anything. 'Shtiny, what's your problem?' Jill asked, using my nickname. I broke down sobbing. Finally I said I was depressed, seeing a therapist because I'd always felt like a boy. I reminded them how I'd hated dresses and loved action figures and superheroes as a kid, so they could link past memories to slowly put it all together. I explained I'd always been attracted to girls.'

Chris continued: "'So you're gay?' Wendy asked, trying to complete the picture.

'No, it's more than that. I'm in the wrong body,' I confessed.

'We'll join a gym. You'll feel better if you lose a few pounds,' Mom said. 'I'll go too. We'll do it together.'"

"Were you overweight?" I interrupted.

"Not really, for a boy. But I had put on the freshman fifteen. So at five foot three and a half, I was 135 pounds. 'You're not getting it,' I told them. 'When I go to sleep, in my dreams I'm male.'

"Dad said, 'Gender is a spectrum. There are females who are very feminine and others who are more masculine. You're on the masculine end.' I thought that was progressive of my father, but was a bit pained by his implication that I was a butch dyke."

When Chris confessed how suicidal he'd been, his relatives cried and hugged him, trying to understand. Two weeks later, he told his father, "I don't see a way out of this—except surgery."

His dad said, "That's a lot to go through," asking Chris if he could just "live with it."

Chris said he couldn't. "Were you angry that he didn't really grasp that you were in agony?"

"No. He tried," he said quickly. "I was hurt, but I put myself in his shoes. I'd been living with this for decades. He was hearing it for the first time. He was trying to protect me, scared I'd end up worse off than I already was. I was proud of my dad. He was this Armenian-American kid from Telford who went to Harvard Business School and became a CEO. I wanted to be like him."

Chris had done research and gave his dad a few articles on the subject. He called one of the clinics mentioned in *The Silence of the Lambs*; the scene in the movie that creeped him out led him to a Cambridge shrink experienced in transgender patients. He saw her twice weekly for nine months before talking about hormone treatments. The wait was a precaution to make sure he wasn't "just gay" or "going through a stage." He legally changed his legal name from Kristin to Christopher and took his dad's first name as his last, as a way of starting over.

"Did you intentionally pick an Anglo-Saxon name?" I couldn't help but ask.

"My sisters asked me to keep our surname, since they took their husbands' names and wanted it to live on. But Eskandarian in Boston is unique. It could have led to trouble in the future. Somebody might say, 'I went to school with a Wendy Eskandarian, but she had sisters, one Chris's age,' and figure it out. Also, since I was working as a copywriter at my dad's company, every new client didn't need to know I'd been his daughter."

At twenty-four, Chris had to wait a month and file a newspaper announcement to ensure he wasn't changing his name to defraud anyone to get out of debt. "It doesn't have to be *The Boston Globe*," whispered a woman at the courthouse. He sent notice to a tiny obscure local paper who ran it. Next: a new birth certificate, Social Security card, and driver's license. The people he encountered in the process sounded supportive. Perhaps not everyone felt they needed an apology? I was about to give up probing when Chris said, "There was one horrible passport agent."

"What did he do?" I leaned forward.

"He looked fifty, like a middle-American high school math teacher. At first, he was friendly. Using my deepest voice I said I'd changed my name and needed a new picture. I handed him my old passport and documents. He looked at me, then at the photo of me as a seventeen-year-old girl. He was confused. Then his face changed to disgust. He turned his back on me. I felt degraded. He went to show a female supervisor, shaking his head, sneering. I heard her say, 'It's legal.' He told her he refused to wait on me and walked away from her. She approached the counter, embarrassed and apologetic, and said, 'I'll take care of this for you.' She took the forms and told me my new passport would arrive in four to six weeks. But I couldn't get over the way that man acted towards me."

"Why was an ignorant reaction from a bigot you didn't know so shattering?" I asked.

"My family said, 'I'll love you no matter what.' The Social Security and DMV people were nice," Chris said. "After years of confusion and doubt, I felt accepted, normal, hopeful, expecting it would go smoothly. So I didn't see it coming—especially with him being nice to me at first. It was the first time I was treated badly. I feared more ugly prejudice would come."

"So in some ways you'd been very sheltered and he represented society's disapproval and shame?"

"Yes, he embodied my biggest fear. His behavior is what made me live with this secret for twenty-four years. He stood for the chance of bad treatment from the public," Chris said. "He definitely owes me an apology."

When I asked what words Chris wanted to hear, he recited: "I'm sorry. I had no idea how degrading my actions were. I now understand I sounded like a nasty, ignorant, closed-minded bully. I beg for your forgiveness." His tone showed he was still pissed.

"Is there any reparation you want that might make you feel better?" I asked.

"Yes. He should be accepting of all transgendered people from now on and never act that way to anybody else again," Chris told me.

"And then you'd be able to forgive him?" I asked. He nodded.

I suspected something more personal was haunting him. "No one else owes you an apology?" I didn't mean to be pushy, but surface answers didn't satisfy my forgiveness quest. Plus I had a train to catch and hoped he'd go deeper before I left. "What about Gram?"

"One day my mom told me she'd sent those articles to my grandmother. I was stunned."

He recalled Gram's letter from Florida. "My darling Chris," it said. "I'm so sad that you've been unhappy all these years. I remembered what you told me when you were five. Everything makes sense now. My concern is that after surgery, you might not look like a man and you won't be able to pass and you'll be worse off." She feared Chris would look like her hairdresser, "a mannish woman."

"Don't worry," Chris wrote back. "I was walking outside the other day and a carful of girls honked and waved at me, seeing only a cute guy in a baseball cap. I waved back."

In January 1996 Chris had his first operation, a mastectomy. His father paid upward of $150,000 for more than two dozen subsequent surgeries. Both his parents accompanied him to meet a specialist who gave a PowerPoint presentation on which kind of penis he could get.

"I decided on the deluxe model. My mom liked the surgeon, who was from Greece. It seemed Armenians and Greeks both hated the Turks."

Aha! I had a feeling some ethnic hatred lingered. "Did they talk about the Armenian genocide?"

"No. Mom wanted to bake puklava for him—the American version of baklava. It was surreal."

As Chris won top advertising awards and acclaim at his father's company, his therapist suggested he make a list of people to tell that he'd transitioned. It added up to eighty-four. "I used a rating system for how safe or difficult the risk would be and knocked off the safest ones first to build my confidence," he said. "My mother told our family friends. My dad and I announced it to the executive board at work. At first they were shocked, then they dealt with it well. Some guy colleagues took me to a strip club to celebrate. I was a bit worried that the strippers didn't turn me on—like maybe I needed to up my dose of testosterone. But they were old and kind of haggard. I was glad when two of the guys whispered they weren't turned on either."

It seemed sexist and ageist to judge strippers so harshly. Yet at this point there'd been a deeper meaning for Chris to be part of typical male rituals. "Who was your first girlfriend?" I asked.

"I developed a crush on Jess, an Irish blonde college friend," Chris said. "After we graduated, even though she was straight, I told her how I felt. We dated long-distance for six months. We fooled around, but I wasn't ready to go further while my body was changing," he admitted.

"When I was twenty-nine, Lorraine, a great looking intern at work, had a crush on me—until she found out I was transitioning. Then she backed off. Months later we wound up in Australia, doing a commercial shoot together. It was romantic and she fell victim to my charms. But the sex was very one-sided. I didn't have a penis yet and didn't feel comfortable with her touching me down there. It just didn't seem right to me and it was a bit weird for her to have me insist on an 'off limits' rule. We wound up seeing each other for nine months. I wanted to keep it casual—I'd just started dating and figured she would too because she was only twenty-three. But she wanted a commitment. We're still friendly now."

"When were you finally able to have sex?" I asked.

Chris explained that at thiry-five he was in Nashville for what he called "bottom surgery," when the Greek doctor asked what he thought of Karen, the sexy aesthetician who worked in his office.

"She's really hot," Chris said. "Way out of my league."

"She thinks you're cute. I gave her your number," the doctor told him.

They dated long-distance until they finally were intimate.

"But then the equipment didn't work," Chris said. "There was a glitch with the implant. Picture a windsock on a breezeless day."

From his pained expression, I gathered it was humiliating. But he seemed nostalgic talking about his exes. "When did it work?"

"Not until I was forty and involved with Laura, another beautiful, petite Irish woman who worked at my office. She was eight years older, an art director. It was 2009. She wanted to see all the Oscar-nominated movies before the award show. We went out to dinner and then back to my place to watch *Hurt Locker*," Chris recalled. "Over dinner and a bottle of wine, in a flirty voice, she said, "I can't believe I'm on a date with you."

"So this is a date?" I asked, hoping it was.

When she said yes, I made sure she was aware of my background.

She nodded and said, "As far as I'm concerned, you're a very attractive guy."

A few weeks later, they went to bed and he was thrilled that his new penis worked. He'd lost his virginity at forty. This could be optioned as an LGBTQ update of *The 40-Year-Old Virgin*, I thought. "Could you have an orgasm?" I asked.

"Yes," Chris said. "I'd had a nerve transplanted down there from my arm, so I had sensation. It probably wasn't as powerful as what biological men had but good enough for me. Of course, there was no semen, which—for women who don't want kids—is kind of a plus. But Laura said it was great for her and that it didn't feel any different than with any other guy. Remember I had the deluxe model." He laughed.

Over the next three years they fell in love. But the relationship didn't last. "Horrible breakup?" I asked, guessing she owed him an apology for not being open-minded enough to marry someone who was transgender.

He explained he was the one who'd ended it, because she was easy-going and outdoorsy while he was a type-A urban workaholic. "I tried to figure out why I was hesitant to go forward," Chris said. "I didn't want to marry the first woman I felt comfortable sleeping with. That wasn't a strong enough reason. It just came down to compatibility. We didn't have enough in common and I felt like I was keeping her from doing the things she enjoyed. I felt terrible about it, like I owe her an apology. We're still friends though. She's engaged to someone else. Funny, my sisters married Irish guys and I'm attracted to fair-skinned Irish girls with freckles, like Laura. Maybe you fall for your opposite?"

"My husband always says you marry your dark side," I told him.

Along with his advertising job, Chris became a transgender lecturer and spokesperson. In the speeches I watched on video, he was a charming mix of an inspirational TED orator and stand-up comic. He spoke of being an advisor for Camp Aranu'tiq in New Hampshire. The non-profit, founded in 2009, was a safe haven for transgender kids from eight to eighteen and their families, with the hope of lowering the alarming rate of suicide attempts for kids who didn't have the amazing support Chris did. His parents made a substantial donation with one request: that "Edwards Hall," the main lodge/dining area named after their son, serve chicken and pilaf every Sunday for dinner, the traditional family meal they were having when Chris had finally shared his truth.

He was so rational and resolved, I assumed our conversation was ending and asked for the check.

"You know, there is someone else I want an apology from," he threw out. He paused, then looked at me and said, "I think God owes me an apology."

You couldn't go any deeper than that. I was floored. It reminded me of the "doorknob syndrome," where a patient mumbled a late-breaking revelation at the end of their session, just as their shrink was showing them out. I felt guilty I hadn't grasped the enormity of Chris's longing and sadness. I touched his hand.

"What should God apologize to you for?" I asked, wanting the exact words.

"For putting me in the wrong body," he said. "I wouldn't wish this on anyone."

"What do you want God to say to you?"

"I'm sorry I did this to you and made you so suffer for so long," Chris said.

I'd always vaguely believed a divine spirit watched over me. Dr. Winters had been a more concrete figure of the Almighty father figure whom I'd seen as my higher power. While getting him to express any remorse felt futile, I was actually lucky I had someone specific to blame, a face to focus my fury on. It jarred me to think someone could feel wronged their whole life with nobody human at fault, craving an apology from their *real* deity.

My former shrink had debated why the righteous suffered. "Born sick, with a mother who hated me, I saw myself like Job," Dr. Winters once revealed. "I questioned what I'd done wrong. But I was an innocent baby. She'd turned on me because I was weak. Suffering can't be seen as a consequence of bad choices or actions. Life isn't ever fair," he warned. "If you expect fairness, you'll suffer more. Focus on what you have, what's good, and what you can change," was his advice. Could this help Chris?

"You've described your life as good in many ways," I told him.

"Externally as a kid, I was fine, I felt loved," he said. "Puberty was a disaster. I was edgy, uncomfortable, anxious, in turmoil. I wasn't carefree. In high school I was voted 'most likely to get an ulcer.'"

"But you felt better once you were on the mission to change?" I asked.

"Emotionally. But twenty-eight surgeries were grueling," Chris said. "I'm still having urology issues."

"I'm sorry to hear," I told him. "Though your speech was terrific and hilarious. And what a happy ending." What a hypocrite I was being now, holding a grudge against Dr. Winters while aping the so-called forgiveness experts shouting "don't worry, be happy," and "forgive everyone everything."

"I was happier three years ago," Chris said. "When work and love were going better."

If there was a certain type of secure personality more prone to forgive, Chris had it. "A Holocaust survivor told me that if you had your parents' love, you could heal from anything," I threw out.

"My parents' devotion and support is the backbone of my strength," he conceded.

Manny believed therapy could get people unstuck, as if living well really was the ultimate revenge. Despite my cynicism and personal angst, I hoped that would be true for Chris. Meanwhile he was already well off, and money couldn't shield him from sexual dilemmas. "What reparation would you want from God?"

"I want his help finding a wife," he said. "I fear I missed the window for having my own family."

"And you blame God for taking that away from you?"

"Well, I wonder how different everything would be if I'd been born genetically male," he said.

"Is there any way to forgive God?" I wanted to know.

"I'm trying," Chris said. "I might not be traditionally religious, but I'm an optimist and spiritual and believe in a divine plan, that things happen for a reason. So I'm thinking he must have chosen to do this to me on purpose. Maybe he figured I'd have the most chance of success."

"What do you mean?"

"Well, what if he thought I could be the best person to change society's perception of what it means to be transgender?" he asked. "I mean, if anyone was going to get through this and come out on top, I had the best chance. I had a loving family and great friends who fully accepted me. Because I worked for my dad, I had job protection. I was in a field where I learned the art of rebranding that I could apply to myself in my new gender. Not to mention having the financial means to get the medical treatments and surgeries I'd need. I also have the stubborn personality of a Taurus so I never give up when things get tough. And I've always been funny and articulate. I tell myself God did this to me because he knew I could make a difference as a spokesperson. That's why I'm writing *Balls* and doing speaking engagements."

I was inspired that he felt his suffering could help others. I wanted to channel my problems into a bigger purpose too. As a teacher and recovering addict, maybe my job was to champion young aspiring writers and addicts who wanted to get clean. My mind flashed again to the line of the Bosnian poem: "Wounded I am more awake."

"But still," Chris added, "I really wish he would have chosen somebody else."

CHAPTER 9
DEPENDING ON SOMEONE WHO WON'T APOLOGIZE

"The weak can never forgive. Forgiveness is the attribute of the strong."—Mahatma Gandhi

I was giving up hope for his apology. Three months after my fight with Dr. Winters, I was eating, sleeping better, and making love to my husband again. Yet my anger remained, like the mole on my chest I'd had for years. I tried to ignore it, pretending it wasn't a problem. Then I feared it was malignant and would grow and kill me. Finally I had it excised, which left a pale scar. Although I'd cut off my former confidant, he was still there too, like the mark on my skin, shadowing my heart. No wonder I was so taken by stories from people struggling with dilemmas more extreme than mine.

That was the case with Sharisse. The tall, pretty forty-one-year-old Army wife first entered my graduate seminar carrying a thick purse, a book bag, and wheeling a suitcase. Sharisse literally came with baggage. And style. She was dolled up in red lipstick, eye shadow, and a pantsuit with leather boots, a standout from the grungy grad school crowd. (And their teacher: in my usual black jeans, Gap sweater, and sneakers.) I would have guessed a fashionista from Parsons School of Design had stumbled into the wrong classroom.

Yet I knew better, from Sharisse's first email a week before: "I'm determined to take your two-week workshop," she wrote. "But my husband is deployed in Afghanistan. I have four children—one with special needs—a disabled mother, and a three-hour commute from West Point. So I have to miss the first session. I greatly believe you can help me publish my memoir on surviving incest. I know missing half your course is not something you'd normally allow, but I urge you to consider my circumstance. What do you think?"

I thought: big headache. Before we'd even met, this middle-aged MFA candidate was defying all my rules that students had to attend both sessions, over-sharing, prematurely anointing me her literary fairy godmother, and adding an intense hard-luck pitch to guilt me into accepting her terms and schedule. Of course, I said yes. I liked complicated women. I was one myself.

After the second part of the seminar, Sharisse begged me to be her thesis advisor, the equivalent of proposing marriage on a first date. When I said I was too busy, she decided to take my fifteen-week class. That semester, moved by her troubles and her obsessive drive, I helped her focus, pen provocative titles and timely leads, steering her fascinating pages towards publication. *The New York Times, Ebony, Essence, Washington Post, Salon* and *Dame Magazine* soon ran her essays about returning to the university as an African-American high school dropout. Raising an autistic son. Confessing that her late father raped her when she was thirteen. Allowing her mother, who'd betrayed Sharisse by staying with him, to move in with her. Sharisse's complicated life was publishing gold. I was impressed how she compulsively revised each piece until it found a home.

"You're my good luck charm," she told me. I was afraid all my luck and charm couldn't calm her chaos. She wanted to be an author too. But she was broke, with no job or childcare for her four kids from three husbands—another topic I encouraged her to explore.

"While Donald Trump, Kate Winslet, Melanie Griffith, and Christie Brinkley have a trio of kids with three different spouses, it's called a trend. When I do it, it's ghetto," she pitched.

"Excellent angle," I said, hoping that didn't commit me to edit seven drafts over the next seven days.

Yet I heard my shrink saying "You can't just take from the world, you have to give back." On some weird cosmic level, maybe I hoped that taking his advice and helping Sharisse might return the good Winters to me. I imagined it was excruciating for her to live in the same house with her aging mom, who'd let her be violated but showed no remorse.

I wasn't sure in her case if forgiveness would ease anything in her life. After getting her graduate degree, her spouse was reassigned. Moving to a regimented Northwest army base, she felt trapped as a military wife and special needs mom, unable to afford to come East often. Susan, a playwright living in my building, was taken with the work of Sharisse's I'd posted on Facebook and asked for her number. Susan ended up using Sharisse's account of the incest for an Off-Broadway play about women who were sexually assaulted. No money exchanged hands, but Sharisse felt honored, especially when her mentor Susan #2 flew her to New York for an advance reading of the show and put her up in her extra bedroom, six flights above my place. I sensed I wasn't helping Sharisse's career fast enough, so she'd somehow cloned me.

"Can I come by? You're geographically desirable," Sharisse joked.

I invited her over for an hour that Saturday, mentioning an afternoon appointment.

"It's hard living in Seattle now, working without you," Sharisse said, unzipping her lilac parka, sitting down on the leather couch in my living room. "I really miss coming to your New York class every week."

"Congratulations on the show." I veered from her latest obstacles to her new triumph. "Tell me about it."

"A hot TV actress plays my role. We're using my real name. It's surreal to hear my words from her lips, like I'm helping the younger me verbalize what I went through at thirteen. I hope it'll make other women feel less alone," she said. "You should cancel your class and come with me."

"I wish I could." Her desire that I'd blow off my current forty students to see a play about her brought back the subtext of her first email: drop everything to take care of me.

"You're my Jewish mom," Sharisse added. "And now we're neighbors!"

Oy. I couldn't keep up with the multiple roles she'd assigned me. No longer officially her teacher or advisor, I'd felt overwhelmed with her endless online requests and replied, "One question at a time." But that Saturday, after reading her rough new essay on trying to forgive her seventy-year-old mother for staying married to her dad after the rape, I was transfixed. It reminded me why Sharisse needed to be taken care of and had trouble with boundaries.

When Dr. Winters' old emails popped up in my computer searches for addiction pieces I'd published, I was reminded of his support. "Very smart," "beautiful clip," "this shows amazing progress" he'd responded thousands of times. After I showed him early pages, he'd say, "dig deeper, don't be afraid of your darkness." He had no literary background, but commented astutely, and even foresaw the public response I'd get. Each project he loved found an editor. Whatever he didn't like wouldn't sell, until I revised it his way. He found my last potential memoir "excruciating to read." No editor bid on it. "Try fictionalizing and being funny," he advised. Once I did, he found it "delightful" and the comic novel sold. I knew other therapists who'd read their patients' work, but none with superpowers to predict success. I nicknamed him "The Book Swami," casting him in as many roles as Sharisse gave me: editor, critic, shrink, career guru, parental surrogate, lucky charm.

When I quit cigarettes, Dr. Winters felt I'd emotionally regressed to thirteen, the year I started smoking. Sharisse's father's betrayal happened when she was that age. Despite her tough, sassy façade, I wondered if emotionally she was stuck there too. As she sat across from me on my leather couch, asking career advice, it seemed she wanted me to be her Dr. Winters.

"Can you believe I'm living with the person I can't forgive?" she told me.

"Jeez. What's it like having your mom as your roommate?" I asked, getting her a soda.

"It's a trip," Sharisse said. "She's older now, with severe asthma and diabetes."

"So *you* have to take care of *her*?" I sat back down. "How can you do that if you're still angry?"

"No choice," she said. "I'm an only child. She's widowed with nobody else. We do love each other."

I sympathized. I was close to my mother and called her every night since I'd left for college at sixteen. I was annoyed she didn't take my side when I argued with my dad and brothers about politics or sexism. But she'd never denied me her protection or put me in harm's way, as Sharisse's mother had.

"Have you told her you want an apology?" I asked.

"Yes. She reminded me that she always believed me and confronted my father immediately after it happened," Sharisse said. "She went to the pastor at our California church."

"What denomination?"

"My mother was born again. But she joined this black Baptist church in Pasadena because they had a Sunday school I could go to."

"Did you like it?"

"I was an only child, so at first I loved all the Sunday school activities where I met new friends," she told me. "But when I wasn't even in junior high, a preacher came onto me. So did a deacon. They seemed like hypocrites. I felt betrayed by all these high-ranking church men. So did my mother."

"Because her pastor didn't help when she told them your father had abused you?" I asked.

"He didn't do anything. He bought into the front my father had put up. He pushed the three of us into counseling. But the psychiatrist we saw was my father's pal. This so-called doctor insisted that my dad was sorry, he wouldn't hurt me again, and that keeping our household *stable* was the way for us to heal."

Uh oh, bad shrink alert. It reminded me how perilous and re-traumatizing an inept doctor could be.

"So we stayed living together, a rare intact black family in our neighborhood, a pretty picture, like the Huxtables," she said sarcastically. She'd told her truth many times, but still sounded outraged.

It was a prophetic comparison, though this was years before Bill Cosby's sexual assaults became headlines. Rape and incest seemed too horrific to forgive. Yet was her mom's denial equally unpardonable? When Kenan spoke of the genocide he'd witnessed at twelve, it wasn't the soldiers or Serbian president who haunted him, but the betrayal by his karate coach. However, his mother and father were his protectors, as were Manny's mom and dad. In the case of Sharisse, her parents themselves were the monsters. How do you recover from that?

"My father did apologize," she said, her eyes scrunched. Reliving this was harrowing, twenty-seven years later. "He took our family to Disneyland, of all ironic remedies for rape. My mom forgave him, offering another chance. I said I did. But at thirteen, I was too young to understand what that meant. My mother, the reverend, and doctor expected me to, so I tried. But I never forgot. Then he came on to me again."

It was hard for me not to wish her father dead, although he already was.

"I was sixteen, about to take a shower. My mom was at work," Sharisse said. "He caught me in a towel going into the bathroom. 'Leave the door open. I want to watch you lather up. Then I'll let you practice driving in my pickup truck,' he tried to bargain. I charged at him, with intent to kill. But my towel fell down. I didn't want him to see me, so I ran in my room hysterically crying, afraid he'd rape me again. This time I screamed, locked my door, and called my best male friend to come rescue me."

"I don't know how the hell you could even consider forgiving your father," I said.

"After the second time, I was done with him forever," she told me. "I was sure my mother would take my side. Throw him out. Get divorced. But she didn't. He had sickle cell anemia so she stayed and took care of him." Sharisse's eyes were bloodshot. "She went back to that same sexist minister and incompetent shrink who gave her ignorant advice. AGAIN! 'Keep it in the family.'"

Outraged, I was about to repeat Dr. Winters' saying "Secrets are poison." But his adages now seemed tainted. Sharisse's father's second offense proved there were horrific risks in accepting someone's repentance. You couldn't know if they'd replicate their past crime or do something worse, until they did.

"Then I moved away," she said.

"Why do you think your mom took your father's side? Some kind of pathological co-dependency?"

Sharisse nodded. "It was her second marriage. She was afraid to be alone," Sharisse guessed. "As he got sicker, his legs and back would be in pain for days. He could only drive a taxi and own a food cart business since he'd be in bed or the hospital for weeks at a time. Her position at the phone company came with medical insurance. She didn't need his money. She supported him, for twenty-seven years. Without her, he would have died broke and alone. But his illness was no excuse. What he did was evil. I was angry that she was weak and wrong to choose him over me."

She finished the soda and I gave her another. "I had to get away from my church, my father, and that house. It wasn't safe. That's why I married at nineteen. My first husband was twenty-four. But it didn't help me escape."

"Why not?"

"My father was so ill his last year, begging for forgiveness. The minister, counselor, and my mom pushed me to forgive him," she said. "Want to hear something ridiculous? At the Vegas chapel, I asked him to give me away. My mom and fiancé looked at each other. My fiancé knew my father raped me; for a second I hoped he'd knock my dad to the ground. But he shook his hand. I was hurt, but not surprised."

"You wanted your fiancé to punch your father—who walked you down the aisle?"

"My dad was an amateur photographer. Pictures were important to me," she said. "I worried my wedding album would be incomplete with no father. I had no brother or uncle to stand in. It had to be my dad, as if I could erase being the daughter of a rapist. Instead I'd be the pretty bride. Picture Perfect."

I nodded, understanding how her desperation to be part of a normal family clouded her judgment. Stockholm Syndrome? Staying in denial was safer? Another student wrote about how, in shock, she'd begged her rapist to sleep over after he'd attacked her, as if she had the power to turn his violation into love.

"I picked the chapel with the best picture deal," Sharisse recalled. "Five hundred dollars for thirty-six portraits, a special frame, small cake, and bridal bouquet. On the drive there, we crammed into my groom's car, my parents crushed in the back seat. Janet Jackson's *Black Cat* was playing. *Heartbeat, real strong but not for long/Better watch your step, or you're gonna die,*" she recited. "The lyrics were an omen. My dad looked worse. I thought he'd have a sickle cell flare-up, collapse, and croak on the day of my wedding. Then who would walk me down the aisle? The photographer said, 'Father and daughter look so much alike.'"

"You resemble him?" I was struck by that eerie, cruel detail.

"I have his slender build, brown eyes, and cheek bones. The photographer joked, 'Daddy's little girl.'"

"It must have been torturous at your wedding, to both need and hate him so much," I said.

"It was. My mother wanted me to grant him some kind of true pardon before he passed away, six months later. It was hard to watch him suffer. She said he was holding on until I would see him. I was only nineteen and felt guilty. I wanted him to die, so I could live in peace. I pretended to forgive him. But really I still can't," she admitted. "Even though he's gone."

The forgiveness industry claimed it was never too late to exonerate someone dead. Yet Sharisse and her dad had shared phony apologies. I wondered if an inauthentic pardon could actually do more harm.

"He messed me up," she said. "On the honeymoon my husband and I took months later in Hawaii, I arranged the photos in a wedding album I hid away. We had a son. Then I cheated with an abusive guy. We divorced. By twenty-one, I wound up with two sons by two different fathers."

"Without a healthy paternal figure, it's hard to have a good compass with men," I said. It took me years of therapy to find a husband who was sweet and sensitive, like my mom. But then I gravitated to Winters, an arrogant doctor who was a Leo, like my father. "Anyone else owe you an apology?" I asked.

She tapped her foot. "Yes, the idiots at my mother's church who told our family to stay together and the psychiatrist pal of my dad's. The pastor eventually did apologize to my mother for not helping us."

"Did that help you at all?"

"No," she said. "Too little, too late."

"Did you ever go back to church?"

"The last time I was in a Baptist church was for my father's funeral," she said.

"I read about how in 1995, the Southern Baptist Convention apologized to black Americans for owning slaves in the past and denouncing their racism," I told her. "Did that make any difference to you?"

"Not really. I was just a kid going there in the 80s. It was mostly black, with black leaders. I think they stepped away from the traditional doctrine. Truthfully, I couldn't wait to get away. For a decade, I was a single mom, raising my boys alone. I didn't remarry until I was thirty-three. It's still hard for me to trust anyone," she said.

"So you don't consider yourself religious?" I asked.

"I can't walk into a church without crying. I still feel betrayed by my father, the pastor, and those supposedly religious men who came onto me," she said. "I did find a non-denominational church in California I liked. Though I'd rather watch the services streamed online."

That made sense. Given her experiences, it was safer. "What about your kids?"

"Their father, Aaron, is Catholic. So sometimes he takes them to his church. But since our youngest son is autistic, with ADHD, it's complicated. We don't have enough help."

Talking about all my addictions and relationship issues at an early therapy session, I was hurt when Dr. Winters had said, "You have so many problems." He'd meant it sympathetically, but it felt condescending. So I avoided saying this to Sharisse. "Is that why it's good having your mom there?" I tried.

"It's mixed. Last year she wouldn't get rid of my first wedding pictures. 'They're beautiful photos,' she said." Sharisse's voice was trembling as she added, "Beautiful and meaningless. You know, I trusted her more than anyone in the world. It was like I lost my father and mother at the same time. It screwed me up that she never apologized or got it."

"She never *once* said 'I'm sorry?'" I couldn't believe it.

"In her mind, she did. She told me 'I can't ever make up for what happened. But I can try.' She moved in with me in Seattle to be my childcare when my husband was away. Even while she's sick, she fries me bacon, eggs, homemade potatoes in the morning, the way I like." Sharisse smiled, as if this proved her mother loved her. It was scary to think her mom did, and at the same time could make such a deplorable mistake. Twice.

"She gets up at 4:30 in the morning to feed my son breakfast. She's not young and her health is getting worse. It's hard for her," Sharisse added. "That's her way of apologizing to me."

Oh, so these were the terms of their reconnection: her mother babysat and cooked, instead of coughing up the apology she couldn't muster. "She overcompensates because she can't say the words?"

"She spoils me, spending her Social Security check on a flat screen TV, fancy pens and purses for my birthday and Mother's Day, and for my kids," Sharisse recalled. "I know it's partly from guilt."

Was it bribery? I flashed to Manny, who was glad the German government gave his father a monthly $1,000 for decades after the war. The monetary assistance allowed his family to start over. All reparations were a form of blood money, but sometimes an external Band-Aid could be healing.

"What's weird is that her gifts feel sincere," Sharisse added. "But I'd rather hear her say she was sorry."

For Manny, the payments were more important than the pardon. Financial restitution also would have helped Cliff, Kenan, and Cindy forgive, by making their lives easier. Yet when the betrayer was a parent, maybe the pain was so personal, the admission of guilt would be the ultimate validation.

"What did you want your mother to say to you?" I asked Sharisse.

She rearranged the chenille pillows on my couch. "I'm so sorry this happened," she recited like an actress in a play. "I should have been there for you. When I found out, I should have thrown him out. The religion clouded my head with hogwash about how black families need to stay together, no matter what. I wished I'd left him, to protect you."

"Have you told her this is what you need to hear?" I asked.

"Not in those words," she said. "But I show her everything I publish, even stories that upset her."

"First piece you write that your family hates means you've found your voice," I repeated my rule.

"When I was a teenager, I never told her all the details of the rape," Sharisse said. "My mom just learned it recently, reading what I wrote. She said, 'This is very hurtful to me. But I'm glad if it helps you heal.'"

It sounded like her mom still didn't quite get it and was confused that following what her doctor and clergy told her turned out to be so wrong. Google forgiveness images, you get sunsets, kittens, a palm freeing a butterfly heart. The road to real reconciliation was sometimes ugly, jagged, paved with passive aggression.

"I think it's good you keep demanding your mother know what happened and discuss it," I said. "There's a saying: *Writing is like talking without being interrupted.*"

"Yes! We relive the rape every day, since I show her my essays and the book I'm working on," Sharisse told me. "I'm calling it 'In Spite Of.'"

"What a fantastic title for a memoir," I commented.

"My mom reads and edits every line I write. I need her to fix my spelling, grammar, and punctuation. She was a poet. That's where I get my talent," she said proudly.

That was Sharisse's mother's punishment and repentance: to keep reading and editing the sin of the husband she should have left. It made me think of *Gray Gardens*, the film about the old mother and middle-aged daughter who grow old and demented together.

I didn't know why I connected so much with Sharisse's story. My dad had committed no sin against me. I couldn't blame him for favoring his sons, who'd shared his vocation, city, and politics. He'd merely hated reading personal details about me and himself in my work. Hearing Dr. Winters call my pages "moving" and "exquisite" felt like I'd designed the ideal substitute to compensate for what my father didn't give me. Maybe my strong link to Sharisse was my obsessive need for validation through publishing. I wasn't sure if an editor's acceptance could ever replace parental love. But Sharisse and I were both lucky our emptiness and anger created an endless need that fueled us artistically. "What does your mother think of your work?"

"Sometimes she'll say it's very good. Other times she'll tell me, 'This is too painful. I need a few days to prepare myself,'" Sharisse said. "Once in a while she'll beg off, saying, 'Let's agree to disagree.'"

"Agree to disagree you were attacked by her husband in your home?" I said. "What an anti-apology."

"I know! Isn't it? I tell my mom 'I appreciate your support.' But I'm still in shock that she didn't leave him. In the meantime, we keep doing this word dance around the rape. It never ends."

"But you're making art out of your pain. It's impressive," I said, thinking of the Adrienne Rich poem that ended: "her wounds came from the same source as her power." "What else can heal you?"

"Therapy. Writing about it using my real name. Not being scared anymore," Sharisse listed. "Talking openly. Reaching others through the play and seeing my work in print."

Dr. Winters was right about "leading the least secretive life." What happened with Sharisse's parents was a paradox. She'd become successful by repeatedly asking for the apology she deserved, pushing the bounds of what her mother could give and accepting childcare, food, gifts and editing as the reparation she needed to move on.

Yet the repeat offense by her late father also unnerved me. It offered a strong argument never to give the person who hurt you the benefit of the doubt; you could be doubly punished for your generosity of spirit. You should protect yourself instead. Sharisse's pain felt like an ancient parable on the dark side of forgiveness. Her greatest triumphs: un-forgiving her father as an adult and becoming the mother she wished she'd had.

Indeed, two weeks later Sharisse surprised me by stopping by with her daughter Sophia, a tall, pretty nine-year-old in a purple parka, with matching purple ribbons in her hair, Sharisse's little clone. "We were at Susan's upstairs," Sharisse said. "I wanted Sophia to meet my favorite professor."

"What a big place," Sophia said, looking around. "So many books. You read them all?"

"Not yet. When your mom publishes her memoir, maybe I'll throw her the launch party," I said.

"I'm coming to the party. When is it? What should I wear? What kind of food will you have? I write too," Sophia said, sensing I'd just become her Jewish grandmother. I pointed to my Barbie collection. She went to inspect.

"She's just like you," I told Sharisse as Sophia pulled the mini turquoise doll convertible from the shelf.

"But when I make a mistake with my kids, I say 'I'm sorry, I screwed up. I was wrong. I should have done better,'" Sharisse said, glancing at Sophia. "And if my husband ever tried to touch my daughter, he'd be out in half a second."

CHAPTER 10
WHEN ADDICTION RUINS YOUR FAMILY

"Forgive the inexcusable because God has forgiven the inexcusable in you."—C.S. Lewis

"David just stopped by with the kids. They're all watching *Shrek* in the basement. Jane's a disaster—don't mention her," my mother whispered, though we were alone in the airy, pastel Midwest kitchen where I grew up, loading the dishwasher after Thanksgiving dinner.

David was my brother Ben's best friend in high school. Whenever his name came up, I winced at the thought of his ex-wife Jane, an alcoholic who gave up custody of their kids. How do you forgive a mother who deserts her children? My mom and I felt complicit, since we'd originally conspired to fix him up with Jane in the 90s.

"Where is he living now?" I asked.

"Texas. I'm going to go watch the movie too," Mom said, turning towards the steps.

I was leaning on the granite island, checking my cell to see if Aaron had emailed, when David walked upstairs. "Hey, Susie! How's my favorite New Yorker doing?" He hugged me.

Hearing my old nickname again made me smile. He was a big, sweet papa bear with silver-rimmed glasses. In his late forties, he was still cute, but heavier and balding, with a goatee. The pain of his acrimonious divorce showed in his weary eyes.

"Dave, so good to see you. It's been a few years. How's everything?"

"Been better," he said. "But I got a new job in Ft. Worth. The kids like it there."

"Nina got so tall and pretty. I'm her Facebook friend. Can't wait to see her."

"My little girl's in ninth grade already," he told me. "Can you believe it?"

I'd first met David here, in my childhood house, at a party of Ben's, after their football team had won the championship in the mid-70s. David was always so polite, saying "Hello Dr. Shapiro, Hello Mrs. Shapiro, it's very generous of you to host us." I'd nicknamed him Eddie Haskell, the suck-up from *Leave It to Beaver*. I saw Ben's teammates as beer-chugging jocks and assumed David—their starting center—was also a typical Budweiser-guzzling, well-off galoot from Bloomfield, our Detroit suburb. But I learned his background was much more intriguing: he and his twin brother had been adopted at birth by a local Presbyterian minister, who was now eighty-three. While the family didn't have much money, their dad was a traveler and published author who spoke several languages. David's brother had a happy marriage and an international career. I felt bad that David was now a divorced, struggling, single dad.

"Come sit down," I told him. "Want a drink?" He took a liter of Coke from the fridge and poured himself a glass. I grabbed a bottle of water I opened as we sat down at my mother's long kitchen table.

"You quit alcohol?" David asked.

"No drinking, smoking, or toking in almost a decade," I smiled, taking a sip of my water.

"I remember you telling me about your addiction specialist," he said. "Jane could have used him."

I'd wanted to go twenty-four hours without thinking of Dr. Winters. I didn't know whether to divulge the truth about our rift to David or pretend he was still my exalted guru.

"But you were never an alcoholic, like Jane," David went on. Or was it a question?

"Cigarettes and pot were toughest for me to quit since I did them every day," I said. My wedding photo flashed by on the video picture frame my brothers had set up on the counter, an anniversary gift for my folks. It was unnerving to see old pictures of myself I didn't remember, as if someone else owned my past. I didn't mention stealing Aaron's pain medication when I'd hurt my back. "So tell me what's been happening with you?"

"Oh man, where do I start?" David asked.

"I feel bad that I fixed you up with Jane," I admitted. I recalled Dr. Winters telling me "Once you introduce people, you can't control anything that happens."

In my amateur matchmaker stage when I'd set him up with Jane, I'd thought she was pretty, smart, bubbly. Like David, she was Christian who wanted a big family. Dr. Winters labeled my matchmaking preoccupation "a counter-phobic erotic obsession," since it began when I was single and hadn't found someone for myself.

"That's bullshit! I'm putting good love karma out there," I'd argued.

"What about *bad* love karma?" Winters countered. A divorcé, he knew the underside of marriage. He felt my fix-up mania was "playing with fire," motivated by a superficial urge to be powerful. Since a friend had set me up with Aaron, I took it is as proof that I'd accumulated karmic points for passion. After we wed, my list of unions grew to thirty which produced twenty-five children. I felt proud and useful, until five of my matches split up. Then I saw why Winters was cynical. With David and Jane, at least my mother and I shared the glory. And the blame.

Whenever Mom used to shop at Saks, she'd talk to Jane, the cute blonde salesgirl, who knew Ben and David from their football days. A decade after college, Jane had continued to moon over David. In 1994, hearing that he was still single, my mother took her number. Conspiring with me on a visit home, we both pushed David to call her. That led to their marriage of thirteen years and three adorable children.

I'd claimed David and Jane as one of my success stories, along with my brother and his wife, a New York friend I'd introduced to Ben around the same time. Though Aaron and I weren't able to have children, between the two couples I'd matched, there were seven kids. "You've repopulated the Wolverine State," David had kidded. Now I felt sad that three of those kids were growing up without their mother.

"It's not your fault," David said. "Jane was hot for me since high school."

"But you didn't like her then?" I asked.

"I had a girlfriend, so I barely noticed her," he said. "After college, when you gave me her number, I called to say hi, mentioning I worked at a Troy car dealership. Next day she shows up there, all dolled up, asking me to lunch. She was impressed I took her for sushi. Guess a Bloomfield girl didn't expect Japanese from a football player." He laughed.

"Did she drink at lunch?" I asked. Dr. Winters had a theory that people told you who they were right away—if you listened. My first dinner with Aaron, I ordered the least expensive chicken on the menu and brought my own diet soda. "You're a cheap date," he'd commented. "Not emotionally," I joked. He later said it was the most honest I'd ever been and he should have paid more attention.

"Jane had some saké," David said. "I had two beers. We all used to binge-drink in high school, and we'd always have a few when we went out. I didn't notice anything excessive."

Aaron knew I smoked cigarettes and pot while we dated. He never complained and even lit my More Menthol Lights and joints for me.

"When did you see she had a problem?" I asked.

"I knew she was depressed after having three miscarriages. Who wouldn't be? But she went on anti-depressants. We had our twins in 1996, and our youngest son two years later. I thought she was better," he said. "Then, after Nina and Peter's first birthday party, Jane passed out and wouldn't get up. I called an ambulance. Turned out she took leftover Paxil and Zoloft with alcohol. While she was in the hospital, I found discarded booze containers all over the house. In her walk-in closet were thirty-seven empty champagne bottles and wine jugs, flasks tucked in suitcases. I was stunned. I didn't know what a serious disease she had. I later found out that her father was an alcoholic and her mother was in denial about it. I made Jane see a psychiatrist."

I'd kept the darkest side of my addictions from Aaron: going through the garbage, desperately undoing roaches to roll a joint on the floor at 4 a.m. while he slept, meeting shady dealers in horrible neighborhoods in the middle of the night. In grad school, I'd taken my visiting kid brother in a cab to JFK airport and barely had enough cash to take the bus home. I was the only passenger. After I shared the driver's cocaine-laced joint, he dropped me off right at the door of my apartment. It seemed like cool karmic payback for being kind to my sibling. Until my roommate said, "You were basically smoking crack and he could have raped or killed you. And what if you'd both been arrested for endangering lives on the highway?"

When I asked Dr. Winters why I'd seen partying with that bus driver as manna from heaven, he said "You were thinking like an addict," and he also warned that "Feelings misinform." Like Jane, my husband pushed me into therapy. The day after we wed, Aaron insisted I quit smoking and partying.

"Not fair," I said. "If you bugged me about my habits before, I wouldn't have married or dated you."

"I know. That's why I waited," Aaron told me.

"A spouse can't demand you stop being self-destructive," I'd complained in therapy.

"Of course they can," Dr. Winters said. "And should. That's why married couples live longer."

"Or why half of them divorce?" I threw out.

After five years of trying to quit myself, I finally acquiesced. Not to get healthier or please my family, but because Dr. Winters convinced me my bad habits were keeping me from career success. He said I'd been working like an addict, impatiently cutting corners, being a control freak, not delegating or accepting help. Within a year of getting smoke-and-drug-free and sober, I sold three books and finished another. In some ways, since Dr. Winters was a father figure whose approval I craved, I'd partly quit to please him.

"Jane went to rehab five times," David said. When he finished his Coke, I poured him more.

"But it never worked?" I asked, tossing out my empty water bottle, taking a new one from the fridge.

"She'd be fine for a while, then she'd relapse. She used to accuse me of cheating." He shook his head. "Turned out Jane had lots of affairs. One day I followed her to a bowling alley where this sleazy guy was waiting for her. It killed me to think I spent thirteen years with a person I didn't know. Maybe I travelled for business too much."

"Addicts are good at hiding their secrets," I said. I'd been stunned when an attractive forty-year-old blonde in my building died of alcoholism. I'd see her at the pool, jealous of her slim figure. I didn't understand why she stopped swimming, or that she'd been drinking, instead of eating, for years.

"It freaks me out that I didn't know about my neighbor. Why do you think?" I'd asked Dr. Winters.

"Sometimes you're self-involved and myopic," he'd told me. "You get so inside your own head, you're not really in the world." I'd nodded, appreciating his candor. I depended on his brutal honesty. I was comfortable arguing with him; his voice echoed the critical bluntness of my father. Dr. Winters ultimately admitted it could even be hard for loved ones to learn the secrets of an addict who didn't want to be caught.

"When I found out Jane was screwing around, I never cried so much," David went on. "Learning that she was bipolar and tormented, I felt sorry for her. I stayed for the kids. To be home with them, I couldn't travel anymore. It made me lose my job. But the last straw was the night she came home drunk with Chinese takeout, asking for money. I knew it was to buy booze. I said no. She freaked out, tossing the food on the floor. Nina came in to see why her mom was screaming. Jane threw her against the wall. Nina hit her head. I punched Jane in the nose, an automatic reaction. There was blood on my hand. Susie, I never hit a woman before." He looked down at the kitchen tiles, eyes squinting, barely able to stand the memory.

I reached over, touched his hand across the table. "You instinctively protected your daughter."

"Jane could be abusive to me, but I couldn't let her hurt my kids," he said. "Nina was crying. She had a lump on her head." He spoke faster, as if to exorcise the decade-long disaster. "I told Jane I wanted her out. She threatened to call the cops. I said 'fine' and handed her the phone. The police came, three cop cars. A female officer interviewed her in one room. A male cop talked to me and the kids. Jane was wasted and belligerent. They saw what was going on. They took her out in handcuffs. Our kids were watching."

How could we not have realized that anything was wrong? I'd seen Jane as fun, great looking and friendly. There must have been clues. Four years after they broke up, David still looked shocked it happened, the way cousin Cindy did talking about her husband's betrayal decades before. Cindy had married at twenty, too young. But David tied the knot at thirty-five, like I did. I'd thought waiting until you were older made a marriage stronger. And that a good precautionary measure was therapy, which I termed "getting a PhD in yourself." What if I dropped out now because my therapist had flunked the trust part? I wasn't sure I could be smart, clean, and have a solid union if my core pillar deserted me.

"After Jane left the state, she stopped calling and texting the kids," David said. "That's what gets me the most. She's hardly had any contact with her own children for three years. That's unforgivable! It kills Nina. My mother-in-law hired a fancy divorce lawyer who fought for Jane to get alimony. My damn legal fees were $200,000, money I could have spent on the kids. She's supposed to be in rehab and AA, but she never made amends. I hear she's still drinking, living with a guy in Ohio."

For kids that age, three years without their mom was real abandonment—of course I recognized the difference between the symbolic desertion I'd felt after my fallout with Dr. Winters. Aaron tried to help me stop smoking, toking and drinking the first five years of our marriage, but his nagging just made everything worse. Without a substance abuse expert to guide us, I would have been like Jane, destroying myself.

"Growing up with a minister Dad, did you learn about Christian forgiveness?" I asked.

"We did. But it mostly seemed to be about doing good work and charity for the less fortunate," David said.

"If Jane apologized, would you forgive her?"

"If she straightened up, maybe," he said.

I asked David my big question: "What exact words would you want to hear?"

He thought for a moment. "She'd have to tell the truth and say, 'I falsely accused you of cheating. I was the one who had affairs. I fucked up our beautiful family. It was my disease that ruined everything.'"

"In this book I read about forgiveness, the author lists four aspects to an effective apology," I told David. "Acknowledgment of the offense, explanation, and remorse. The last one is reparation. Do you think there's anything that would help you forgive Jane?"

He thought for a moment. "Actually yes," he said. "She should write a letter, apologizing to me and each of our kids. And then use her family money to pay for their college tuitions, which I can't afford. That would make a difference. It would be a huge burden off of my back."

For David, the *reparation* seemed most essential to help him move on.

"That's what I care about," he said. "That my kids will be okay."

"My addiction specialist's mother was a raging alcoholic. She beat him up, told him she hated him, and wished him dead," I said, vividly recalling the poem Dr. Winters showed me about his sick mom. "He grew up to be a sober, acclaimed psychologist with a great wife and three kids, even though his mother never apologized, or even acknowledged her problem. In her nursing home after a stroke, they still allowed her a glass of wine a day. She didn't remember her son, but the booze she never forgot." Even while I was not speaking to Dr. Winters, it still felt fair to use his tenets to be of service to someone I cared about.

"He's really successful?" David asked.

"Yes. He says you can recover from a horrible childhood, especially if you have one good parent. Like your kids with you." As I said it, I believed it. Yet clearly having an abusive mother wasn't a solvable problem. That kind of loss could keep ruining future connections and sabotaging closeness later on. I felt for David and his children—and for Dr. Winters, who I suddenly understood better. He'd been an innocent victim of a violent alcoholic mom, not unlike Nina. Again, I felt blessed I had a good mom and the good Dr. Winters as core pillar for fifteen years, along with such a supportive life partner.

"Your husband didn't join you this trip?" David asked.

"He had to work." I'd actually decided that Aaron needed a break from me and my Winters obsession, which was dragging us both down.

"Ben said you're dating someone new?" I asked David.

"I met a great lady the kids love," he said as we heard squeals and footsteps coming up the stairs.

"That's what friends do, they forgive each other," his son said in singsong voice.

"You're right, Donkey. I forgive you," his daughter yelled in the ogre's Scottish accent, adding with spot-on comic timing, "FOR STABBING ME IN THE BACK!" They cracked up as we walked into the foyer. Funny kismet that was the film scene they'd chosen to quote just now.

"Still awesome the fourth time you've seen it?" David chuckled and Nina gave him the thumbs up.

He seemed like such a good dad. I was happy to hear he'd found someone new, though I stopped myself before I mentioned the word "marriage." The one I needed to fix now was me.

"My father's the one you should ask about religious aspects of forgiveness," David told me, and gave me his number.

Later that night, I called his dad to try out my theory. "So does Christianity offer more unconditional forgiveness than other religions?"

"Well, it depends," the Reverend said. "In fundamentalist and other extreme factions of Christianity, hell is a place of eternal torment with no second chances."

I thought of the passages in *Portrait of an Artist as a Young Man* where the Catholic-born James Joyce described hell as "a strait and dark and foul-smelling prison, an abode of demons and lost souls, filled with fire and smoke . . . the torment of this infernal prison is increased by the company of the damned themselves."

"What do you preach about forgiving at your Presbyterian congregation?" I asked.

"That Jesus teaches us to love our enemies," he told me. "But in the major Abrahamic religions—Judaism, Christianity and Islam—forgiveness is absolute and essential."

"So have you forgiven your daughter-in-law?" I wanted to know.

"Yes. I feel badly for Jane. She's sick. We tried to push her into rehab but it didn't take," the Reverend told me. "She didn't come from a loving background. She had a lot of baggage. You know, her father drank himself to death. Imagine growing up watching the person you love most succumb to their addictions. Poor girl. Never recovered from that."

It was striking that David left out that horrible final detail about Jane's father that David's own beloved dad now filled in. The thought of it threw me back again to Dr. Winters, who'd recovered from an abusive alcoholic parent by centering his life on helping others conquer addiction. It must have been hard for him to always remain stable for me, even after his home was destroyed during 9/11. I felt gratitude for how he'd led me out of the maze of illness that wrecked Jane and her father. I'd been able to quickly stop taking pain medication for my back, replacing it with physical therapy exercises—proof that his behavioral rules were still in place, the wisdom he'd shared etched in my brain. Without him, I needed another higher power.

Rabbi Moshe Pindrus and I discussed how, on the high holy days, Jews were taught that God records all your good deeds and sins. The names of the righteous were inscribed in the Book of Life, the evil were put in the Book of Death, and everyone in between had judgment suspended until Yom Kippur. During past high holy days, I'd worried how my behavior would be judged. Now I wanted to weigh everything that happened with Dr. Winters. While enraged at his actions in the present, I still felt indebted for his help in the past. Maybe that was already enough to get him into The Book of My Life, warranting forgiveness?

Years later, I reconnected with David's daughter Nina, who was in college in Austen. She heard I'd interviewed her father and grandfather for a book on forgiveness and wanted to add a coda to the story from her viewpoint.

"When I was thirteen, my mom sent me a friend request on Facebook," Nina told me over the phone. "I thought it was cool. So I said yes. After a few instant messages, she said she'd like to speak with me and gave me her number in Ohio. The only contact we'd had in years was when she'd call to talk to me and my brothers together. My dad would put her on speaker phone. But when she was drunk, he'd hang up."

"So what happened when you spoke to her one-on-one?" I asked.

"She told me 'I never got a chance to say I'm sorry,'" Nina remembered. "I told her 'It's okay, Mom.' But she said 'No it's not okay. My drinking got out of hand. I wish things could have been different. I love you and I'll always love you. And you can always call me, you know.'"

"Wow," I said, tearing up hearing Nina repeat her mother Jane's apology. "Did you keep in touch after that?"

"Yeah," Nina said. "I haven't seen her in ten years. But we talk on the phone, maybe every week. If I call her and she slurs her words, sounding drunk, I just say, 'I can't talk to you when you're drinking. I'll call you back tomorrow, Mom.' And I do. I understand alcoholism is a disease she suffers from. But when she's sober, she listens and gives me really good advice."

"So even though she still drinks, her apology made a big difference to you?"

"Yes. It was a big deal for her to openly admit what she did wrong," Nina said. "She was taking responsibility, trying to step up and be a mom."

"How did it make you feel?" I asked.

"Like it was my healing my heart," Nina said. "Like I wasn't crazy and hadn't made any of it up in my head. I went from feeling abandoned to knowing I could have a nice talk on the phone to share things with my mother, who still loved me. Her apology opened a window to allow the forgiveness to come in. I totally forgave her. It's kind of crazy how much one apology can do."

CHAPTER 11
FORGIVING THE UNFORGIVABLE

"No sin is so light that it might be overlooked. No sin is so heavy that it may not be repented."—Moses Ibn Ezra

"I got a call from the hospital saying, 'We have Sam.' He was my youngest," Gary told me. "I jumped into my car to rush to my boy without asking why. I called my wife's cell phone, but it went to voicemail. I dialed my older son's phone. Voicemail too. Helicopters were flying above. I wondered how Sam got to the hospital. My mind couldn't process what was happening."

Gary and I were sitting in the lobby of my hometown's Maple Theatre in Birmingham, Michigan. My best college friend Judy Burdick's poignant documentary *Transforming Loss* had just screened. Watching six families cope with sudden death, I was riveted by what Gary Weinstein had been through. The screen displayed newspaper clippings of the car accident, eight years before, that had killed his nine-year-old son Sam, twelve-year-old son Alex, and his wife Judith, a pretty redheaded forty-nine-year-old business coach who wore glasses, like him. During one close-up shot, the widowed jeweler revealed that he'd made national news by publicly forgiving the drunk driver who'd killed his family. After the Q & A, I'd introduced myself, anxious to speak with him in person and learn how he could forgive something so completely unpardonable.

At forty-seven, five foot five, slim and balding, Gary was warm and friendly, like the brainy self-effacing suburban Jewish guys I grew up with (and the one I married.) As we sat on a bench while the audience and film crew mingled, he answered my questions, retracing the Tuesday afternoon he'd never forget. On May 3, 2005, his wife picked up their sons from school to take Sam to the orthodontist and Alex, the eldest, to Birmingham Temple for his bar mitzvah practice. Alex was in front, Sam in back. They were on 12 Mile Road, east of Orchard Lake.

I knew the busy intersection, which was near my childhood home. I'd had an accident myself on that road when I was sixteen, emerging unscathed but destroying my car. I didn't drink or toke on the night of my crash but I was ashamed to admit I'd operated a vehicle high a few times as a teenager. Hearing more about Gary's enormous loss, I felt complicit, myopically mortified to think: that driver could have been me. I was an addict, "still recovering, never recovered," as Dr. Winters used to tell me. Everything was coming back to addiction on this trip, like an inverted bizarro world version of *It's a Wonderful Life* where Dr. Winters was haunting me with the damage I could have caused, had he not intervened.

"When I reached Beaumont, they escorted me to a waiting room for relatives," Gary spoke slowly.

I pictured Beaumont's vast high-story concrete medical complex in Royal Oak, where my father worked for decades.

"The doctor said my wife and sons had been in a car crash. They did everything for Sam but he didn't make it," Gary said. "'Do you mean no one made it?' I asked. He confirmed: 'No one made it.' My kids and wife Judith were gone in an instant. For twenty years, she was my best friend, co-parent, business advisor, golf partner, fellow traveler. I lost everything. I was alone. My life was over." He sounded clear yet distraught. I wondered if he'd learned how to tell the tragic story in an impactful way, to help others.

Gary traced the details of his family's final hour: Judith was waiting in the center lane to turn into the parking lot when a GMC Yukon Denali rear ended her and drove over her Honda Accord. It pushed her into oncoming traffic, flattening her and Alex in their seats. The Denali crashed into a Jaguar in the next lane, then rolled over and struck a Ford Escort. The other drivers escaped physically intact, but pictures of the site showed four vehicles totaled beyond recognition. Judith and Alex were pronounced dead at the scene. Upon impact, Sam was ejected from the car to a parking lot driveway twenty-five feet away. Two witnesses rushed to his aid to find him breathing, but unconscious. They stayed with him until paramedics sped him to the hospital.

At a news conference that day, the police chief said the driver's blood alcohol level was five times the legal limit, the highest ever recorded by the precinct. The chief was amazed that Thomas Wellinger, a sales director, could still drive; someone with numbers that high usually ended up in a coma or dead from alcohol poisoning. He was charged with three counts of second-degree murder. Along with his broken neck, Wellinger was suffering tremors from severe withdrawal. His car's "black box" showed he'd been going 70 miles an hour and hadn't tried to hit the brakes before ramming into Gary's wife. Wellinger was arraigned in his bed at Beaumont, the same hospital where Gary's youngest son was declared dead.

"It was right before our twentieth anniversary. I was planning a secret romantic getaway weekend," Gary revealed.

"I'm so sorry," I said. "I can't even imagine…"

"I called my parents and siblings, who dropped everything to run to me," he continued.

"You're from around here? Can you tell me about your background?"

"Yes, I'm the youngest of six kids from Detroit. I grew up in a house full of love," he said, explaining how his family had moved to Southfield when he was in fourth grade. He'd had trouble academically, with reading, so they put him back a year. He was a theatre nerd at Southfield Lathrup High School, where he found his passion was entertaining people on stage.

Before first grade, my family moved to Southfield, where I would have gone to "SL," had I not switched to a smaller school for artsy misfits. I bet my parents knew many of the fifteen hundred people who attended the funeral, including classmates of Gary's sons, who'd brought stuffed animals and candy. Gary had his wife and children cremated, their remains buried in a memorial garden at their temple. That struck me as unusual. According to the laws of our people, dead bodies were to be returned to the earth as undamaged as possible. Cremated remains were usually not interred at a cemetery for Jews. When Gary said he belonged to Birmingham Temple, I understood better. I knew their founder, Rabbi Sherwin Wine.

"Oh I always adored Sherwin," I jumped in. "He was our closest friend's Rabbi." I was surprised someone who seemed as mainstream as Gary was a follower of the Midwest's most infamous intellectual gay atheist leader, who didn't believe in God and ran a Humanist congregation. I was about to ask if he knew the Greenwalds but caught myself before playing Jewish geography during a discussion of Gary's wife's death.

He spoke of the slow days following the tragedy. "It was a dark time, devastating, surreal." He called upon what he'd been taught at The Landmark Forum's "personal development" workshops he'd taken years before the crash. The "transformative learning" center's creed was to take complete responsibility for your life, be true to your word, and inspire others. Asked to design a possibility of who he could be, Gary described his potential self as full of "aliveness, fun and joy," traits he wanted to achieve through creativity, participation in the world, and contributing *Tzedakah*, the Hebrew word for "justice" or "righteousness." It was used to signify giving to those less fortunate, which was seen as a moral obligation in our religion. Most helpful to him during the crisis were the prophetic instructions on how to avoid letting pain from your past define you.

While skeptical of "mind-expansion" programs, I recalled a high school classmate had sworn by the EST program of Landmark's leader Werner Erhard (born John Rosenberg). Another school chum called it a cult, while *The New York Times* saw it as "Zen Buddhism meets Dale Carnegie." I'd found my own therapy with Dr. Winters to be mind-blowingly helpful, while colleagues had criticized it as unorthodox. I felt bonded with Gary over our liberal views, psychological searching, and love of the Midwest's most controversial clergyman. In short, Gary wasn't a typical Southfield, Michigan, guy. I saw why my classmate Judy, a psychotherapist who'd also been widowed young, had featured Gary in her movie. I asked him if Landmark's radical self-confrontation, which focused on taking control of what happened to you and not blaming others, meshed or clashed with Birmingham Temple's view that we had power to shape our own destiny, without ancient traditions or supernatural authority.

"They actually mapped very well together," Gary explained. "They both helped me separate my horrible loss from who I was—and still am. Though I loved my family, I was not my family. I was still me. To not have them did not make myself go away."

*   *   *

I wanted to know more about the Jewish Humanistic outlook on forgiveness, so Gary put me in touch with Tamara Kolton, the rabbi who'd presided over the funeral of his wife and his two sons.

"I was close with the whole family. I was at our summer camp with Alex and Sam," said Kolton, a vivacious blonde from Michigan a little younger than Gary, who spoke with me over the phone. "Here's what I remember most. Right after they died, Judith and Alex's spirits came to me in the middle of the night."

"In a dream?" I asked.

"It felt real," she said. "Alex told me he still wanted to have his bar mitzvah in the fall. And Judith—who was always trying to push me to go to Landmark—told me I had to try it. The next day I called my mom to tell her, asking why Sam hadn't come too."

"What did your mother say?"

"She said that Sam didn't have any unfinished business with me. I didn't want to try Landmark but Mom told me I didn't have to. 'You mean you don't have to obey spirits?' I asked her, amazed. It was the first time I'd ever been visited by the dead, so I wasn't sure of the rules."

I was a shrinkaholic ex-poet whose mother often reminded me that the women in our family were witches. So who was I to question Tamara's apparitions?

"Did you tell Gary?" I asked.

"Yes! And we had a posthumous bar mitzvah for Alex at the Temple. It was beautiful and joyous, not the least bit maudlin. Gary spoke stirringly about how much fun he'd had acting with Alex in *The Wizard of Oz*. He played the music Alex used to play when he'd started a little business selling ice cream. Gary was a great father."

"Did you tell Rabbi Wine about your spiritual encounter?"

"No way," she said. "My supernatural powers were too far out—even for him." She laughed, adding that her clairvoyance and radical feminism led her to leave the temple and strike out on her own.

"From a religious view, were you pushing Gary towards forgiving the drunk driver?"

"No. It was all Gary. If I woke up one morning and my spouse and two kids were gone, I might want to check out, to go be with them. How could you live, or forgive the person who did this? Gary is a fucking miracle. I call him 'a light worker on the planet earth.' I follow his lead. He's like *my* Rabbi."

"Did you ever go to Landmark?"

"I tried one introductory session," she said. "But it wasn't for me."

*   *   *

Not long after the crash in 2005, Gary's jewelry store was destroyed in an electrical fire. With a million-dollar settlement from Wellinger's insurance, he slowly rebuilt his business. Yet calamity kept striking. In 2007, Gary lost his mother, followed by his aunt. Then his older brother died at fifty-two of a heart attack, and Rabbi Wine died in a car crash in Morocco. Mourning his wife, sons, mother, brother, and Rabbi left Gary too traumatized to return to work for four and a half years. To me, he seemed like Job, a righteous man who had suffered excessive loss. Yet Gary wasn't self-pitying. He described his grief as "a brick in my pocket. It didn't go away, though I learned I could handle it. I realized I was strong enough to carry the weight and move on. I had the brick, it didn't have me."

I kept firing away questions, wanting to pinpoint whether it was Gary's spirituality, logicality, illogicality, or the psychological tenets he held to that allowed him to be so forgiving.

"When I heard a drunk driver caused the crash and was five times over the legal limit from vodka at 3:00 in the afternoon, I knew he was very sick," Gary said. "I didn't hate Thomas Wellinger; I hated what he did. That's a distinction I was able to make. And maybe I wasn't totally free of culpability. Who didn't *I* stop from drunk driving in the past?"

He sounded so rational, it was almost otherworldly. I looked for signs of sorrow creeping through. In the film, he cried while reliving what happened. For the criminal case against Wellinger, his "victim impact statement" was a letter Gary wrote to his wife. He told her how heartbroken he'd been to cancel their twentieth anniversary party and how distraught he felt to lose his children, who were his legacy. Even harder was losing the important contributions his sons might have made to the world. The letter was read at the sentencing trial. Wellinger pleaded no contest. From the Oakland County Jail, a sober Wellinger sent Gary a handwritten letter filled with remorse and regret.

"So I decided to meet him a year after the crash," Gary said.

"Why? What did you want?" I asked.

He shrugged. "I had no agenda. As a father, the first thing I asked was how his children were. He said he hadn't seen his son since the crash because the jail didn't allow minors inside."

"I haven't seen mine either," Gary told him.

"Can you ever forgive me?" Wellinger asked.

"Can you ever forgive yourself?" Gary responded.

He learned that Wellinger was sober for seventeen years before relapsing. He'd been on his way to see his psychiatrist, having taken an antihistamine and an anxiety drug to ease his alcohol withdrawal. Drinking again on medication made it much worse. I found myself identifying with Wellinger. I silently thanked Winters one more time for getting me clean and sober.

Gary was already struck by his own similarities to Wellinger, who was fifty, only three years older. "He lived less than a mile away. Since our last names started with *WE*, we were on the same phone book page. His two kids were in the same school district as mine." Wellinger had no recollection of the accident or that he'd swerved over the lanes. A newspaper report said the reason he didn't use his brakes was that he had been blacked out for miles.

Judith, like her husband, was a humanist who didn't believe in God or an afterlife. She was kind, fair, and open-minded, he said, sure she'd want him to forgive the man who killed her. He thought alcoholism was a disease, and that disease caused the crash. So in Gary's mind, blaming Wellinger would be like blaming someone for having cancer.

Dr. Winters opposed that line of thought, saying most people with cancer could only dream that willpower, AA, or talk therapy might cure their sickness. Addicts, in his view, had the power to be cured that cancer patients were not afforded. The judge may have felt that way too, since Wellinger was convicted of three counts of second-degree murder, sentenced to thirty years, no chance of parole for nineteen. He had to pay reparations to Gary. "He wasn't in good health," Gary said. "He wasn't likely to get out of jail. If he did, I requested that he never be allowed a driver's license again. So a year after the tragedy, I publicly forgave him."

It seemed a beautiful gesture. Yet there was messy fallout from his generosity of spirit: Judith's relatives refused to pardon Wellinger—or Gary. "My forgiveness caused contention," he told me. "I was basically ex-communicated from her family. The discord started after the funeral."

So forgiving a stranger divided his family. Had they objected to the burial decisions he'd made? Both Judith's sisters requested some of her remains. "Why aren't there more ashes?" one had asked Gary.

"How many ashes do you need?" he'd replied.

"We had to go back to the Temple to dig up ashes so they could get more," he recalled.

I thought maybe Gary's reconnection with his ex-girlfriend Eileen was the hidden source of his sisters-in-law's ire. Gary had originally met Eileen and her father on a senior class trip to Miami when he was eighteen. Eileen's dad was the stage manager of the Ann Margaret show at the Fontainebleau Hotel. Eileen and Gary hit it off, dating long-distance for two years. She was his first love. She flew in for Southfield Lathrup's senior prom, a memorable night. But at twenty, Gary wasn't ready to marry. They lost touch when he went to school at the Gemological Institute.

Gary met Judith in 1984, when he was twenty-six. She was twenty-eight, out at a local club with friends. "It was the day Marvin Gaye died," he said. "I started this odd conversation with her about the Dover sole I'd had for dinner. We danced to *Sexual Healing*. I was too shy to ask her out. Before I left, Judith's girlfriend said, 'She wants you to have her number.' I didn't have paper. I wrote it on a dollar bill I kept for years," he recalled with a shy smile.

They wed the next year, when he was twenty-seven. After two happy decades, looking forward to their eldest son's bar mitzvah and Gary's Farmington theatre group's *The Wonderful World of Oz*, Gary had planned to go to a jewelry show in Las Vegas, where Eileen's father was living. Gary called him to reconnect. On the phone he mentioned that his daughter Eileen, now divorced, lived there too, and suggested they all get together. But that never happened. After the car crash, Gary cancelled his trip. Eileen phoned her condolences and asked if it would be appropriate for her to attend the funeral.

"I can use all the friends I can get now," Gary said, still in shock.

Eileen came, blown away by the support Gary had. He realized she saw him as "the one who got away." Twenty-nine years after their prom date, they rekindled their romance. I'd read that male widowers and divorcees generally remarried much faster than females. Dr. Winters once told me: "Women mourn, men replace." Gary did nothing wrong, but clearly Judith's sisters were hurt by Gary and Eileen's quick reunion.

"Did having Eileen there help you cope?" I asked.

"Yes, leaning on someone made it easier," he said. "I believed that love could heal all. And that Judith would want me to keep living. Forgiving Wellinger seemed critical. If I held onto regrets and rage, it would have been diverting, keeping me miserable in the past, away from my future."

Eileen moved to Michigan to be with Gary. With her by his side, he didn't feel isolated or bitter, stewing in loneliness like Cindy or David had. Manny felt that having adoring parents empowered you later in life. If there was such an equation, I decided the proof was Gary, whose happy childhood and easygoing personality made him the posterchild for forgiveness. While my mantra from years of therapy was "Love doesn't make you happy, make yourself happy," I could also see that it was easier to let go of resentment if you were cherished and taken care of. I was fortunate to have loving parents and a great husband. I should have been able to grant pardon easily, too. So what was my fucking problem?

"Eileen's over there." Gary pointed to a woman with salt-and-pepper hair talking with the film crew near the popcorn counter. "Eileen's birthday is June 22, the same as Judith's." He was awed by the coincidence. He saw it as fate.

By rekindling their relationship so fast, was he denying his grief? Judy, the insightful therapist who made the film, often spoke of the importance of letting yourself mourn. After her husband died, it took her a long time to remarry. But considering the catastrophe Gary had lived through, he had a right to find comfort however he could, in whatever time frame he needed. Didn't he? Although Gary wasn't ready to remarry, he called Eileen his "life partner." She was proud to accompany him to the documentary screenings and forgiveness panels, as if she'd made room for his lost wife and sons in her life. You couldn't blame her for wanting to help her first love, the one who got away, recover from tragedy. But it couldn't be that simple, or happy relationships would eradicate all rage.

"Did your psychological beliefs push you towards forgiving too?" I asked.

"Yes, I had a strong sense of who I was, even while mourning," Gary said. "I refused to hate Tom. I hoped to contribute to conversations about how forgiveness and healing could come from traumatic losses. Without my wife and sons, I needed a new way to contribute to the world. I am not what happened to me."

"I am what I choose to become," I finished what I thought was his use of the famous Carl Jung quote.

"No, I would say, 'I choose what I have,'" Gary said, which I took to mean that self-acceptance was his main ambition at this stage of his life.

Although you couldn't erase your suffering, I liked the idea that you could decide what you did with it. I thought of Chris being a trans spokesperson, and Sharisse publicizing incest to help ease others' pain. Gary had launched a charity, giving theatre scholarships so other children could enjoy the stage like his sons did. He gave talks to schools on the perils of drinking and driving. As in the definition of karma: "If we do good, good will come to us," Gary's outreach was empowering. Talking about the film and his speeches on forgiveness, this soft-spoken Southfield man gained stature. He joined Project Forgive, a nonprofit founded by Shawne Duperon, an Emmy Award–winning Michigan filmmaker. I found the website a little sentimental (toddlers said "Forgiveness is a bunch of sorries," and "It means you don't hate anyone"). Yet Gary's capacity for forgiving still felt impossible to me. I couldn't exonerate Dr. Winters for a mistake that hurt my feelings, while Gary exonerated a man for the triple murder of his family.

Was it simpler to forgive a stranger than someone close who came with baggage? Did getting a complete apology encourage Gary's magnanimity? Indeed, Wellinger explained his alcoholism, begged for forgiveness and was jailed, paying a million dollars in reparation. The public took Gary's side, punishing the criminal behavior. He found another partner, a good career, had no financial issues. Was that the criteria for compassion? There must be more to it. Leaving the screening, I bumped into my old buddy Andy, who went to elementary school with Gary.

"What was he like as a kid?" I probed.

"Gary was the oldest in our grade, the first with a mustache and jean jacket," Andy said. "We called him *Head*, maybe for *ahead*. He was like The Fonz. He's been acting since sixth grade. He played the rich butcher in *Fiddler on the Roof*. He was really good." Andy forwarded me Gary's senior photo (cute with shaggy bangs and big ears) and recent Facebook shots of him in costume for his theatre ensemble's *The Diary of Anne Frank*, *Full Monty*, *Boeing, Boeing*, and *How to Succeed in Business* (*Without Really Trying*). Gary did seem alive, joyous, and popular, but it felt like a piece was missing.

Researching Gary's case later on, I stumbled on a messier coda. The news reported that Wellinger had shown up to work drunk that fatal morning and was sent home. That meant, instead of calling him a cab or having someone drive him, his boss at the Texas-based manufacturer knew Wellinger was getting behind the wheel. Employees confirmed that this boss had scheduled an intervention the week before, to confront Wellinger about his alcoholism. Wellinger never showed up. Gary brought a wrongful death civil lawsuit against UGS Corp. His lawyers argued gross negligence, since the company knew he was driving drunk and had willfully looked the other way for six months prior to the crash. Reconstructing the day, lawyers proved that Wellinger drank six ounces of vodka before 10 a.m. Or could he have been still drunk from the night before? A co-worker said that after Wellinger returned from lunch, "he came behind me and playfully hit me in the back. I turned around. He was grinning, in a boxer's stance with his fists up. He looked scary, with a wild look in his eyes." At 2:45 he left for his fateful doctor's appointment.

Gary was upset that a federal jury ruled in favor of UGS in 2010. Bizarre angry blog posts and newspaper comments called Gary and his lawyers greedy, since a million dollars from Wellinger's insurance had already been paid. Gary responded: "I want to thank everyone who supported my effort to seek justice for my family. I used part of the insurance settlement for charitable foundations to enrich lives of children in this great country that my wife and children will never see again. This lawsuit isn't about money. It's a call to action to make a corporate giant step up. They should be punished for allowing a drunk employee to be a menace on the road and kill people."

It was satisfying to hear Gary sound so irate, even at a corporation. It made him more human.

"My wife used to say 'You need something to look forward to,'" Gary said. "For me that was raising our sons. Suddenly they were gone. She once joked I was happiest on the golf course. Thinking of that, I set up a golf road trip, where I'd play two championship courses in all fifty states. Talking about my loss is also therapy. When you repeat the painful details almost daily, they lose their charge."

I thought of Freud's repetition compulsion theory, where you subconsciously repeat a traumatic event, as a way to master it, to control the torment so it's not controlling you.

Leaving the movie theatre that day, I'd gone back to my parents' house, where I was staying for the week. My folks were having coffee at the kitchen table, reading newspapers. I felt lucky they were there for me.

"How was Judy's documentary?" Mom asked, putting down *The Detroit News*.

"Amazing. Blew me away," I answered, sitting across from her.

"Hungry?" she asked, getting up to put out grapes and chopped melon.

"No, I'm fine," I said. "Dad, what were you doing at Beaumont Hospital in 2005?"

"I was the medical director overseeing patient care," he told me. "Why?"

"I spoke with Gary Weinstein, who was interviewed in Judy's film. He rushed there when they tried to save his son after a car crash."

"That would have been the trauma unit," Dad said.

"I remember hearing that horrible news," Mom jumped in. "His wife and little boys were killed by that drunk driving idiot in Farmington."

I nodded. "Isn't it odd that a Jew would pick cremation over burial? I read that, after the crematoriums at concentration camps, it was taboo for us to burn ourselves, even after death."

"Many Jews don't feel that way anymore. My cousin Big Jack chose cremation. He had his son cremated too," said my dad, who was also named Jack. (I'd loved his story about how their rich relative Jack on Dad's side generations ago led his family to name their kids Big Jack, Little Jack, Jacob, Yaakov in Hebrew, Yonkel in Yiddish, and Jacqueline.)

"It's cheaper," Mom said. "Cremation is only about $1,500. A burial could be $15,000 and the maintenance can be expensive. Not that many mourners still visit gravesites. It's a pain in the neck."

She was right. I felt guilty we'd hardly visited Aaron's dad at the cemetery in the years since he'd died.

"Money's not the only reason why," Dad interrupted. "It's because it gives the mourners more choices and control. Remember our neighbor Jim who loved trains? So after he passed away, his wife spread his ashes at the Pontiac railroad tracks. And when Big Jack died, his wife wanted him closer. You can take the cremains home with you in an urn, to keep your loved one nearby."

Since when was my father the romantic?

I assumed only reform or humanistic rabbis like Gary's would accept cremation. Dad surprised me by saying that our conservative rabbi, Joseph Krakoff, had been known to compromise. While he tried to be discouraging when a member of their Shaarey Zedek synagogue insisted on being cremated, Krakoff made sure their cemetery had a separate section for it. Burying at least the remnants of the body was better than scattering them in the wind, adhering closer to the biblical mandates to *bury* the dead, and the Genesis line, "From dust we came, to dust we will return."

"The only caveat is that you can't reserve cremation space in advance," my father added.

"Why not?"

"You know rabbis, they keep trying to talk you into doing it their way until the last second," he said, laughing.

"Dad, one more question," I said. "The driver who crashed into Gary's family had a blood alcohol level five times the legal limit, the equivalent of twenty-two vodka shots. His black box showed he was driving way over the speed limit and never even hit his brakes. The paper said he'd been blacked out for miles while still driving. Is that possible?"

"Yeah, he could have been so drunk, he was in and out of consciousness. What happened to him?" he asked.

"Broken neck, but he survived," I reported. "He got nineteen to thirty years in jail."

"Good," said my father—unforgiving.

CHAPTER 12

WHEN LOVE MEANS ALWAYS HAVING TO SAY YOU'RE SORRY

DECEMBER 2010

"Hurt people hurt people."—author Will Bowen

I was sitting outside at Blue Moon Fish Company, in Florida, where I met my parents over the holidays. I had a lunch date with Leah, one of my mother's best friends. She was an effervescent blonde I'd grown up with. Her sons, Jordan and Zack, used to come over to play so often, it felt like I had five little brothers. In my family of arguers, screaming and swearing were more common than the silent treatment. So I was stunned when my mom told me that Jordan and his mother became estranged. I had to find out why. Leah struck me as incredibly warm and kind. Jordan was a handsome, shy mensch I'd had a "crunch" on in fourth grade. She was especially proud at his law school graduation. Many people had issues forgiving their mothers and fathers. I was curious to hear a parent's view of falling out with their child.

"Jordan was the sweetest guy. I remember you two were so close. What happened?" I asked, picking at my seafood salad.

"His wife happened," Leah said. "When my oldest son Jordan got married and cut me off, I kept writing and calling him—for eight years." She choked up. "From the minute he was born, I'd adored him. I couldn't believe he wouldn't speak to me. But I wanted him to know my door—and my heart—were always open."

She'd always adored her oldest son, she explained. At thirty-two, newly divorced, she and Jordan would go to movies, sports games, and shop together. Even at sixteen, he was never embarrassed to hang out with her. He was very protective. In college and graduate school, he'd call her every day, sometimes just to say hi. When Leah first met Kara, she found her son's pretty, petite girlfriend to be polished and polite. Leah was glad her son had fallen for a nice Jewish girl. Kara seemed wild about Leah too.

The first red flag came when Kara, at twenty-six, admitted to her future mother-in-law that she was divorced from a local doctor who'd paid her a big settlement just to move on. The second red flag was Kara sharing how much she hated her ex in-laws. Another bad sign: Kara trashed her own mother, whom Leah knew as a sweet woman.

"I had a rash once and had to go to the hospital but my mom first put on makeup," she complained to Leah.

"Well, some ladies are like that. It doesn't mean she didn't love you," Leah told her.

"I remember crying in the crib at six months old and my mother left me there," Kara added.

Leah doubted the memories of a six-month-old. But since Kara had obviously felt neglected, Leah tried to be especially kind to her. Unfortunately, Leah's intuition was accurate. Her problems with Kara and her son surfaced right after their wedding in 1990.

"I drove them to the airport for their honeymoon. They came back never wanting to speak to me again," Leah said, a stunned look in her eyes, as if she still couldn't believe it. She took a sip of wine.

Concerned to not hear from him, she called her son. He wouldn't pick up the phone. For weeks. Finally Jordan left her a message saying only, "We're back." She drove to their house and knocked on the door. They both welcomed her in, said "Hello, how are you?"

"Is everything okay?" she asked, nervously.

"Everything's fine," Jordan told her.

"Why don't you answer my calls or messages? What's wrong? I've been worried," Leah said.

"Nothing's wrong." Then: a void.

Leah was forty-four at the time, single and broke. It wasn't the life she'd envisioned back when she was a suburban housewife. She'd grown up sheltered in Detroit, the second of two naïve Jewish girls. Her parents worked in the furniture business and belonged to the reform Temple Israel. She met her husband Pete at Mumford High School, when she was a freshman and he was a senior. "He was tall, handsome, and he drove a yellow Ford convertible, which was very impressive to a fourteen-year-old," Leah said. "He was chivalrous, a total gentlemen. We dated four years, but I was a virgin at my wedding, a month after I turned eighteen. I had Jordan ten months later," she smiled, finishing her shrimp cocktail.

My mother married young too, at nineteen. Leah and Pete befriended my parents in the 60s when they'd moved into our apartment complex in Oak Park, Michigan, the one where Manny Mandel's family also lived. Pete was a tall, skinny, chain-smoking salesman who'd seemed funnier and faster-talking than the other dads. He'd watch Tigers and Lions games on TV with his boys and my brothers. "He knew so much about football," my brother Eric told me. "I thought it was cool that a dad was around during the day. I didn't know it was because he was in between jobs and had bet money on the game."

Pete sold my father a fancy-looking IBM Selectric typewriter for his new medical office for $100, which was a steal, Dad said. They usually went for $500. But months later, when it broke, he told Dad, "Don't call IBM. Call this special number."

"I gather it fell off the back of a truck," I heard Dad tell Mom, shaking his head. At five, this made me laugh. I pictured a typewriter tumbling out of a truck and bouncing down the road.

Pete's sales jobs sounded sketchy. By 1970, after he and Leah had two sons, Pete descended into a troubled underworld of cocaine, alcohol, hookers, gambling, and scams that landed him in legal trouble—a spectacular scandal for our boring Midwest community. I was mesmerized that we had a nice Jewish grifter in our midst.

My father once told me that Pete was involved with a scam involving the mafia and a truckload of TVs stolen off the interstate highway, a federal offense. The FBI caught Pete at a warehouse at dawn with $20,000 in cash on him. He stopped by our place one September day, when he was out on bail awaiting arraignment. One Yom Kippur, my mom didn't feel well and couldn't go to temple with my father. Pete took her ticket. "It turned out the judge in his case was seated a few rows behind us and stared at Pete. He wound up with a light sentence, only twenty years' probation. Nobody had ever heard of that sentence before," my dad said. He recalled that Pete's father was also a "son-of-a-bitch." Pete never filed a tax return, so his father had to sign the lease for his apartment. When Pete and Leah divorced, Pete's father evicted her and her sons—his own grandchildren.

"Pete told me if he wasn't a success by thirty-five, he didn't want to live anymore," Leah said. "I thought that sounded really off-base. But at thirty-five, when he wasn't doing well professionally, he started drinking Scotch every night. His personality changed. If I wasn't in the mood, he'd rape me."

"What? He was violent to you?" I put down my fork.

"Well, he never hit me," she said. "He'd only force me when he was drunk."

She'd pushed him into a thirty-day rehab. The doctor told her "There's 3 percent of addicts we can't help. He's one. He doesn't like himself or his life and doesn't want to stop." She told the doctor his line about not wanting to live after thirty-five.

"He's not really living now," the doctor replied. "He'd rather be dead."

I recalled Dr. Winters's adage, "Underlying every substance problem is a deep depression that feels unbearable," astounded that so many forgiveness sagas involved substance abuse. Or maybe, as an addict, I was always looking for, finding, and focusing on it?

After leaving her sixteen-year marriage, Leah moved to a tiny apartment where Jordan and Zack shared a room. She struggled to support them with a job in electronics sales. When Jordan became a lawyer and found Kara, Leah was thankful he'd escaped his father's vices. But soon she feared that his new wife was controlling him. Kara seemed threatened by Leah's closeness with her son and became unable to share Jordan. Leah couldn't figure out if her daughter-in-law was just insecure, selfish, or sociopathic.

For two years, Leah left messages, wrote and mailed many letters to her older son, apologizing for anything she might have done wrong. She cried all the time. She analyzed what had happened, guessing that her acrimonious divorce had something to do with why Jordan wouldn't see her. "I was not an intrusive single mom," Leah said. "I had a life. I worked. I had two Maltese rescue dogs I loved. Having two boys, I was very excited to have a daughter-in-law. I knew I'd never done anything bad to Jordan or his wife. I didn't know why my son was being so distant. He was from a broken home, with an alcoholic father. Was that why?"

When she asked him, Jordan wouldn't reveal anything. She felt guilty for marrying the wrong man when she was too young to choose a responsible husband. But she hadn't known that alcohol and drug use would ruin Pete's personality. Leah felt she was the one owed an apology for the horrid way Jordan treated her. Yet, embracing a maternal role, she sucked it up, reiterated her undying love, and kept her eye on the goal: reconnecting with her son.

"I just kept saying, 'I'm sorry if I hurt or offended you. You know I love you,'" Leah told me, still mortified at the thought that her son didn't want her around anymore. Post-divorce, she'd dated several men who Jordan didn't like. Was that why he was being so cold to her?

Running into Kara's aunt, she learned Kara was pregnant. Leah kept in touch with Kara's relatives to find out when the baby was born. She called again to ask, "Can I see the baby?"

To her pleasant surprise, Jordan invited her to the bris at their new home. Leah came, dismayed to see no other relatives she recognized. She wasn't the only one who'd been cut off. She wasn't allowed any time with her first grandchild and she left crying, feeling dejected and ashamed. A year and a half later, she learned—through friends—that she had a granddaughter, too.

Leah phoned her son and daughter-in-law, reiterating she was sorry if she'd done anything wrong. Though she didn't understand what was going on behind the scenes of his home, her disarming strategy eventually worked. One day in 1995, four years later, she received a letter from her son that said, "Yes, you can see your grandkids. You just can't ever ask why we cut you off." The kids were now three and four. Leah had remarried a kind, charming man in the scrap metal business. They were both confused as to how she should handle the reunion. She saw a therapist, who told her, "Look, your daughter-in-law is obviously nuts. It sounds like she has borderline personality disorder. You'll get close, then get cut off again. It could be damaging—for you and your grandkids."

Leah didn't agree with her therapist's perspective. "It can't be good for his kids to not know they have a grandmother who loves them," she argued. I want to see them, no matter what." She went to her son's house at the designated time.

"Hello, Grandma Leah," the kids said, sounding like puppets who'd been programmed. Still, Leah was overjoyed. For the next year, she was allowed to babysit Andrew and Sarah on weekends. She picked them up from nursery school and met their teacher. She brought them presents. They slept over at her house every Friday, where they'd watch cartoons with her, cuddling in bed. She paid for the whole family to come visit her in Florida for a fun week-long trip. Leah took three albums worth of pictures, trying to make up for lost time. She showed me one on her phone from 1997, with her arms around the angelic little Sarah and Andrew, who had the same shaggy blonde haircut with bangs. They looked just like her.

Then, as her therapist had predicted, she was shut out again—this time for eight years. She received a typed letter from Jordan on his legal stationary saying, "We don't want you in our kids' lives." There was no trigger Leah could think of. She'd never said a negative word to Kara or her son. Leah was devastated, confused, and more depressed than ever.

"Imagine living in the same town as your son and grandchildren, but not being able to see them," Leah said. She shook her head, explaining how grandparents had few legal rights and she didn't have money for lawyers anyway. She tried to focus on work, fixing up a condo she and her new husband bought in Florida, her husband's kids, and her younger son. Zack had a son she saw all the time, but the two brothers barely spoke, and the cousins hardly saw each other.

"I walked my dogs a lot. Then I told Howard I need to be alone. I went into my room, shut the door, and let myself mourn. I felt like I was losing the religious feelings I'd grown up with," Leah admitted. "When I emerged, Howard asked if I wanted to spend half of the year in Fort Lauderdale from now on. I said yes, to escape the pain of being in close proximity to my son and grandchildren who I couldn't see," Leah told me. "When people asked if I had kids and grandkids, I told the truth and said, 'I'm not allowed to speak to two of my grandchildren.' I was amazed how many responded, 'Oh that happened to me too.' Or, 'That's the same as my sister.' It always seemed because of a disgruntled spouse." Kara's own mother used to call Leah crying.

When Leah kept trying to keep the lines of communication open, sending birthday and holiday cards to her son and grandkids, her therapist warned her, "You'll get hurt again."

Undeterred, Leah found a new therapist. She only saw Jordan twice in eight years, at the funerals for Kara's grandmother, and then at the one for Kara's mother, who'd died before reconciling with her daughter. At the services, Leah caught glimpses of her grandkids at eight and nine, but they didn't speak. Jordan came up, kissed her and said "Thanks for coming, Mom."

"It was mind-blowing, because then he wouldn't return my messages," Leah said. I'd lay in bed with my dogs, weeping for days. I had a hole in my heart."

When her eldest grandson Andrew was turning thirteen, she phoned a cousin to find out the date of his bar mitzvah. She wrote another letter to Jordan. "I'm coming. I'm not going to make a scene. But I want to see my grandson get bar mitzvahed. It's a public temple."

"You're welcome to come be part of it," Jordan responded calmly, inviting her to see the kids before the events. When she came over to their house, the kids hugged and kissed her, as if no time had passed. Leah went to the service and the party, at Peking House. Her son greeted her, saying, "Hi Mom. We're so glad you could come," putting his arm around her publicly, as if nothing was wrong. She had no idea why and assumed he didn't want anyone to know their issues.

"I remember how we watched cartoons and ate breakfast in bed," Andrew told her at the party. She was so happy they knew who she was and remembered her love.

"We hated Grandparents Day at school, thinking we didn't have any grandmas or grandpas anymore," said Sarah, now twelve. They'd only been told they weren't allowed to see her or their other grandparents. They never knew why. Leah wanted to quiz them but didn't. Trying not to say anything negative about their parents, Leah made it very clear how hard she'd tried to stay in touch.

Through the Jewish grapevine, Leah found out that Kara's mother and grandmother didn't leave her anything in their wills, though they left each grandkid $10,000 for college.

"Kara was the only girl in that family," Leah said. "What a nightmare it was, if they didn't even leave Kara a bauble or family heirloom."

Knowing that Kara was estranged from her own relatives made Leah feel exonerated, as if wasn't her fault. Since Kara had cut off her own mother, grandmother, brother, and brother-in-law, Leah felt like she was a victim of Kara's pathological pattern. She knew she'd never receive an apology from Kara. Yet she craved an explanation from Jordan about how and why he'd erased his mother from his life. At sixty, Leah went through breast cancer treatments. As Jordan tried to be there for her, he confessed he was having serious marital problems. Kara also opened up to Leah—too much. One day Kara called her to say, "Jordan has been cheating on me for years. When he took the kids on vacation, they told me he hugged a woman they bumped into."

"It was probably an old friend," Leah said. "Jordan is the last man who would ever cheat."

"You don't even know him," Kara countered. "Do you know that he was sexually abused by your husband as a teenager?"

Leah was sickened to learn that when Jordan was sixteen, visiting his father in Florida, a cocaine-riddled Pete had told him, "Suck my dick, you motherfucker," taking it out of his pants. Her son Zack confirmed that Pete had behaved that way. Leah didn't think it went much further than stoned, dirty talk. Still, her therapist explained that Jordan could have been traumatized. Leah felt horrible that she hadn't known how out of control her ex had been and that she didn't keep her kids away from their addict father. She realized she'd been too immersed in her own difficult dating relationships at the time to protect her sons. Now she questioned if Kara—however misguided—had been protecting Jordan from both of his parents out of fear this abuse and neglect could be repeated.

It was harder to understand Kara in 2004, when she accused Jordan of cheating in front of the kids. They divorced. Sarah moved in with her father while Andrew stayed with Kara.

A year later, Jordan was dating a new, healthy woman. He told her what had occurred with his family. "You owe your mother a huge apology," she insisted. Finally Jordan called Leah, begging her forgiveness. He explained how impossible he'd found it to juggle a struggling law practice, a difficult wife, and two kids he was supporting. It was easier for him to give into Kara's demands than fight her. Jordan was afraid Kara would leave and take the kids. He said, "I'm sorry, I don't know how that happened to me, you've always been the best mom."

"Explain it to me better," Leah begged.

"Kara only wanted to be around me and the kids. Nobody else," Jordan said, offering a completely unsatisfying explanation, over the phone.

Leah gave up on the idea of her fantasy explanation and reunion. "I had to live with never really knowing or understanding why my son didn't stand up for me," she said. "I let that go."

She and Jordan forgave each other and have been extremely close since then. Scheduling another operation in the aftermath of breast cancer surgery, Jordan flew to Florida to help take care of her. He and his kid brother Zack also reunited. Leah remained involved with her grandchildren. In college, she pushed them to see different therapists, insisting she would pay for it. "You don't have to tell me—or your parents—anything. Just send me the bill." They both went separately, to many sessions. It seemed to help in every way.

Upset that her parents weren't speaking, Sarah asked, "But what am I going to do when I get married?"

"I'm throwing you any wedding that you want," Leah promised.

When I looked up her grandkids on Facebook, I saw their cover photos both used the 1997 picture Leah had showed me, with her arms around them when they were three and four, with matching bangs. Neither kid had any photos of their parents in their cyber-albums. Leah insisted they all remain nice to their mother.

"When Jordan would see Kara, he wouldn't acknowledge her. I told him, 'You married her, she's the mother of your children. Show her some respect.'" Oddly, when Kara remarried, she invited Leah to come to her third wedding (though Leah begged off).

"My grandkids tell me I'm their anchor." Leah smiled. "I'm so glad I kept sending letters and apologized during those years we were apart. Now they know how much I fought to see them."

"So sweet they both use that picture of yours for their Facebook cover," I told her.

"They do? I didn't know that!" Leah said, tearing up. "That makes my life."

I took her hand, grappling with the wisdom she was sharing. Forgiveness wasn't a one-shot apology and answer. It could be a long, confusing, drawn-out process. If someone you love didn't respond to a few calls, emails, or letters, that didn't mean they couldn't change their mind, or their situation, later on.

Leah's journey made me reconsider what was going on with Dr. Winters. Given how long it took her to break through, I debated if I should keep trying. Sometimes getting the apology and elucidation you longed for required patience.

Yet the rest of Leah's account underscored the need for boundaries. Even a forgiving momma had her limits.

"What about Zack?" I'd casually asked after Leah's younger son, who I'd heard was now a successful businessman.

"Oh, Zack and I don't speak much anymore," she said.

"What? Why?" I asked. "I thought everybody reconciled?"

"For a few years we were fine. Then, in 2006, Pete's girlfriend threw him out and he moved into Zach's Florida home. Zack's wife didn't want him there. But Pete told him, 'You can get a new wife, but you'll never get a new father.' Pete ruined Zack's marriage. Then they started drinking and doing cocaine together. Pete died of a heart attack in 2010."

"How old was he?" I asked.

"He made it to sixty-eight," Leah said. "I joke that it was because he had no stress. Whenever he was stressed out, he'd drink or do drugs."

Unfortunately, Zack got addicted too.

"I begged him to stop, to get into rehab and get clean," Leah said. "But he refused."

Hearing Zach's nasty tirades was a trigger for Leah. "I have to watch my health. Seeing my son become everything he hated in his father makes me sick. He sounds exactly like him," she said. "Genetics is scary. It's like having to deal with an abusive husband all over again."

Putting up with Zach's verbal abuse made her relive the worst years with Pete, reminding her how his substance use led to the demise of her family. While she tried to remain close to her third grandchild, who she texted with weekly, Leah made the decision that—as long as Zack wasn't clean and sober—she was cutting ties with him.

"When he became abusive to me like his father used to be—nasty, swearing—that was where I drew the line. People say addiction is like a disease. But it's really not," Leah said. "If you have cancer, no amount of willpower can get rid of it. But with drug and alcohol abuse, most people can get into a program and at least try to learn how to control it. If you really want to."

Her feelings echoed Dr. Winters' belief. So did mine.

Leah picked up the check, insisting on treating, eternally inhabiting the maternal role, in charge of feeding.

"What if Zack did get clean and sober?" I asked.

"Then I'd be the happiest mother in the world," Leah said without hesitation. "I'd forgive him everything."

CHAPTER 13
CRAVING AN APOLOGY FOR SOMEONE ELSE
JANUARY 2011

"An eye for an eye, and the whole world would be blind."

—Kahlil Gibran

"My father should have apologized to my mother for the insulting way he took a second wife," Raheem said.

While others craved remorse from children, parents, in-laws, and exes who'd wrecked *their* marriages, Raheem still couldn't forgive or forget his father's role in the fissure of his folks' union. Yet his late dad hadn't left his mom for another woman: he'd lived with both wives in the same house for twenty-five years. What would Dr. Winters make of this double Oedipal drama?

"Shouldn't your dad have apologized to *you* for screwing up your life with his polygamous *mishegoss*?" I asked. Back in New York, I was sitting with Raheem in a booth at Cozy's Diner, around the corner from my apartment.

"That means cuckoo in Yiddish?" Raheem checked.

I nodded yes.

"No. Two wives sharing a husband is weird to Western culture, unless you live in Utah," Raheem joked. "It's not unusual where I'm from in South Asia, even in a liberal Muslim family like mine."

"Something common in the culture can be destructive," I said, spooning vinaigrette on my chef salad. Raheem sipped green tea and forked lox slices on his salt bagel, joking, "I must have been a Jew in another lifetime."

"If you were in my tribe, you'd order cream cheese and Dr. Brown's cream soda," I countered.

Divorced, bespectacled and a few years older than me, Raheem was from Kashmir, where men in *his* tribe could legally have four wives simultaneously. A high-end textile importer by day and poet by night, he'd been in my writing workshop for a decade and a half. He blew us away with dark poems in his schizophrenic mother's voice, detailing her depressive madness and anguish over his father's remarriage. In *Hallucinations* he wrote, "My husband says I don't need a doctor/But that doesn't keep his new wife/From going to Combined Hospital/I am still the head of this household/O Wind tell my son/The dollars he sends/The new wife misspends . . ."

"My mother Maryam was an orphan," he said. "Her mom died when she was six and her dad at eleven."

"My mom, Miriam, was an orphan who lost her parents around the same age," I said. "We both have inherited sadness." I'd stolen the phrase from Dr. Winters, who'd felt I was still wrestling with my parents' ghosts.

"To fellow poets mining intergenerational pain," Raheem toasted, clinking his glass against mine. I'd actually given up poetry years before, when a mentor declared my work had "too many words, not enough music." Conversely, Raheem was gifted with a musical ear, especially when chronicling his unstable early years.

"She was the sole heir to her father's vast fortune, which was in the care of her uncle," he recounted. "My grandfather learned of this fourteen-year-old girl of means and arranged her marriage to his son."

"My mother was poor," I said. For the first time I considered whether

her lack of funds and family saved her, since she'd married my father when she was nineteen, for love.

Raheem's dad Ameen was twenty-five, eleven years his mom's senior, in law school, when they'd wed. Raheem saw no love or passion between them, but they respected each other and functioned well as a family, proud of their six offspring. "As the fifth child and third son, I didn't get much attention," he admitted. "My younger brother Saleem, the baby, was Mom's pet."

I identified, since I'd feared my folks favored my younger brother Ben. But then Raheem added, "I still can't tell her that Saleem died. She just knows he hasn't been to visit in a while." I'd learned from a poem Raheem sent me that his brother had drowned in a riptide in Goa at age sixty-three.

"I was so sorry to hear," I said. I'd met Saleem, a tall, handsome charmer in the imported furniture/fabric business. "I still have the bed frame your brother gave me a discount on." I recalled Saleem's turbulent affair with Lisa, a world traveler from our workshop whom he met at one of my parties. "He was your closest sibling, right?"

Raheem nodded. "I remember my mother giving Saleem and me a bath in an oval tin tub under an oak tree above our house, on a hilltop," he said.

"As a kid, did your mom seem healthy to you?" I asked, glad the restaurant was quiet tonight, nobody sitting in the next booth to overhear our intimate conversation.

"My memory of her is moonfaced, five feet five, hearty and strong when I was little," he said. "She was a good storyteller who shared tales from the Old Testament and the Quran." It was a talent Raheem inherited.

Funny, I thought my father's Jewish storytelling also had a biblical component.

Unfortunately, like Manny and Kenan, Raheem's childhood was ruined by war. He explained how, as the eldest son of a prosperous father, his dad had befriended Pakistani statesmen he visited in 1947, at the worst possible time. After three hundred years in India, the British finally left and the continent was divided by The Partition, making India and Pakistan separate states. Military conflict ensued, with a million people killed in genocides between religions. Fourteen million Hindus, Sikhs, and Muslims were displaced in the largest mass migration in history. When Raheem was born in Kashmir in 1948, his father wasn't allowed to leave Pakistan. Maryam and her younger kids were able to join him, but Raheem's grandfather decreed the two eldest children stay in India. Separating the siblings was a disaster that hurt Maryam and estranged their whole family. She wound up moving back to Kashmir, with all her kids, but without her husband, for another decade.

"What the Brits did in India, they'd already done in Ireland. Kashmir is the world's most militarized zone. India controls Kashmiris the way the Zionists control Palestinians," Raheem said.

I was confused, as if following territorial wars over Kashmir wasn't complex enough. I understood why he hated British colonialism and supported a Muslim-run Kashmir. Yet as someone with close Israeli relatives who wanted a two-state solution, I'd long argued with Raheem about his anti-Zionist stance. I connected his sympathies to his feelings of exile from those "occupying" his childhood. "I find the personal roots to your rage more heartfelt," I said calmly, the way I'd critiqued his poems.

"Touché," he told me, sticking out his tongue. I signaled the waiter to bring us more water, hot and cold.

"When did you figure out something was wrong with your mom?" I asked.

"When I was five, I knew she heard voices," Raheem said. "Trying to get her the best medical treatment in Pakistan, my father took her to military doctors, who did electro-convulsive therapy. My grandfather had the procedure continued when they returned to Kashmir. I saw it happen when I was eleven."

"How did you see it?" I asked, trying to take notes, chew my lettuce, and ask questions at the same time.

"One night I hid in the oak armoire in her bedroom and watched what the doctor and his male nurse did to my mother," Raheem told me. "She was lying on her back saying, 'Is this necessary? Please be gentle.' The nurse unlatched his bag, pulled out a small machine that looked like a radio, and plugged it in. From a compartment he took out a syringe and gave my mother a shot. Then he put a sponge in her mouth. She squirmed, her eyes wide open. The nurse took out a long leather belt the doctor used to tie her hands and feet. Dr. Kaul put earphones on her temples and flicked a switch of the box. A red light came on. He gave the knobs a twirl. Mother shut her eyes. Doctor Kaul turned the knob. There was beeping and a low buzzing. The lamp on the nightstand flickered. Her body arched and slumped back. The doctor unplugged the machine and left the room. The nurse untied her, pulling the sponge from her mouth. After I heard Dr. Kaul say goodbye to my grandfather downstairs, I opened the armoire door and tiptoed to her bed. She calmly asked, 'What's your name?'"

"That must have been so traumatizing," I said, putting down my fork and pen.

He nodded, then walked me through how a college classmate of his father's finally arranged his dad's visa back to Kashmir, in 1966. But by the time Ameen could return for good, Raheem was finishing college. In 1971, he moved to America to get a master's degree in political science at The New School, where I taught, six blocks away.

"My father's homecoming was not peaceful," he recalled. "When I was twenty-four, Saleem called me in New York, yelling, 'Dad remarried!' I was stunned. My father had left Kashmir a well-off man but came back after the partition a less prosperous, lowly clerk in the family business. The world had moved on without him."

The family was shocked when, in his late fifties, Ameen took a new young wife, Zareena, a well-off widow in her thirties with two little children. Raheem cited his father's ego in choosing her as "arm candy." But he added that Ameen feared being alone and wanted someone to care for him since Maryam was often "out of it." Raheem's parents never shared a bed again. Ameen moved into a house across the street with Zareena and her kids. "This is not right!" Maryam yelled. "You have a home. Don't leave me. Bring them here."

"As you get older, sexual desire doesn't decrease," Raheem said in a soft voice, leaning in closer to me. "You need intimacy more and miss it." Was he talking about himself? "The new wife was horrible for me and my mom. It was another calamity that exacerbated her condition."

At twenty-eight, he flew to Kashmir to confront Ameen. As he unleashed his anger, his dad listened while his mother scolded, "Don't talk to your father like that." Raheem described it as "surreal." Ameen and his new wife did move back. They created their own partition, dividing the house into different wings with separate kitchenettes for each wife. Ameen had two rooms in the attic fixed up for Maryam. The study was converted to a bedroom for what Raheem called the "ready-made kids." When visiting, he stayed in an attic room near his mother's.

"I'm still the head of this home," Raheem's mom told him, clenching her teeth at every mention of Zareena.

"Islam permits me to take a second wife," his father insisted. "Just like the Prophet, Peace be Upon Him."

"It's very convenient to invoke Islam only when it serves your purpose," his mother hissed.

After this Raheem "forgot" to run his dad's errands. He used to sit next to him at dinner, but switched to his mother's side, worried she was mistreated and misdiagnosed. He saw Maryam's schizophrenia as depression caused by traumatic events: She'd lost her parents young, was stuck in an arranged marriage at fourteen and had six kids during a war that divided her family. She was forced to leave her two eldest kids when she went to Pakistan. Then she was displaced in her home by a woman the age of her daughter. Raheem felt the ECT treatments had made her worse.

"Did you know if she was delusional?" I asked.

"At first we didn't believe she heard voices," he said. "We followed my father's example of ignoring her. Then, if her husband and kids wouldn't listen, she decided the world's leaders would. She dictated her yearnings to my older brother in Pakistan, then to me, in Kashmir. I'd bring lined white paper, my fountain pen, a bottle of ink, and the Oxford Dictionary of Queens English to the dining room. It was a delicate process putting ink in the pen. I'd stain my fingertips. She said ink-stained fingertips were the marks of a prolific writer."

That was how his poetry book *My Mother's Scribe* was born. I recalled how, before I was three, I'd recited Robert Louis Stevenson's poem *I Had a Little Shadow* to my father in his den. He'd turned off his X-ray machine, put down his medical text, kissed my forehead, and told me how smart I was. After that, I'd always felt, the die was cast.

"Why did your mom need you to write for her?" I asked, eating the black olives from my salad.

"She mostly spoke Kashmiri and Urdu. She'd sent me to a nearby school that imported Jesuits from Ireland to teach proper English. So I helped her tell all to President Eisenhower, Prime Minister Gandhi, to long-deceased leaders. At first I thought she was better than other mothers. All they did was cook and get fat. My mom exchanged letters with prime ministers of the world. I was her proud scribe and mailer. I admired that she was an activist who spoke out against what she considered unjust. I found it difficult to say no to her."

One letter was to her idol, Mustafa Kemal Atatürk, the Turkish Ambassador in New Delhi, who became Turkey's first president. She expressed admiration for "the father of modern Turkey" who "drafted Turkey screaming and kicking into the 21st Century" by creating a democratic, secular state. After he sent the letter, she received a black and white portrait of Atatürk. Raheem had it framed and hung it on the wall of her room in the attic.

On a Saturday night when his father, stepmother, and the "ready-mades" were visiting her parents for the weekend, Raheem's mother asked him to write a letter to Prime Minister Indira Gandhi. He assumed his mom wanted to again express admiration. "The idea of writing to Indira Gandhi seemed important," Raheem told me. "I put on my school uniform: gray shorts, white shirt, dark blue tie. My gray cap had the school crest embroidered on it in gold thread: *In All Things Be Men.*"

He waited downstairs in the dining room, worried what his mother would say to the mahatma. His mom came down the steps with wet, combed hair, her face masked with white talcum powder. She was wearing a white linen sleeveless nightgown that had black teddy bears prancing across the front and dark blue slippers. Her toenails were painted red. Her black pupils stood out against the whiteness. Her lips had a natural rosy hue. "Unlike my stepmother, my mom disdained lipstick."

"Mother, you have too much powder," he'd told her. "You look like a ghost."

She rubbed the powder into her face. Her gold bracelets jangled. "No one is to know about this letter," she said in a hushed tone. "If you make mistakes, correct them. Remember, it's to the Prime Minister. You know what's happening."

He recalled his teachers saying that Gandhi had declared a "State of Emergency" and become a dictator. "She's in love with a swami," rumors had it. "It's a love emergency," the kids joked at school. Raheem's mother said she believed in "human rights," but he didn't know what that meant.

His mom dictated: "My dear Indira, How are you? Why is India despairing in your State of Emergency? The newspapers are saying: Nation's star is fading while you're busy loving some Swami. The servants never listen to me. Only when the new wife nods do they run around like rats to fetch the thermos. My husband lost interest in roses. For years he's been saying Maryam is mad. His new wife is young but plump. Her readymades still call me 'Darling Big Mom.' He says she'll take good care of him. It's tearing me apart Indira, again I'm losing my mind."

"Mother," Raheem said. "You can't send this to Indira Gandhi."

"My mind is wider than the sky," she said. "Indira is a woman who lost her husband too. She'll understand."

"But she'll think you're insane," Raheem implored.

"Noble son, please listen to me," she said. "I'll withdraw one thousand rupees from my bank account so you can buy new Comics." She added, "I harbor no ill will towards your father or little mom."

After twenty-five years, the two women forgave each other. "They were both objects of a paternal society, like they'd shared a domestic war together," Raheem said, describing a dinner where his mother announced that his father would go to heaven "because he loves the big mom in the same way as he does the little mom."

"So it is written," the stepmother seconded, cutting up lamb chops for her kids.

"My mom wouldn't leave my father—even with his second wife— until he died in 1999," Raheem said. "After that she came to the States. For ten years she lived with my brother in Westchester. Then we moved her to the Hebrew Home in Riverdale."

"Funny place for a nice Muslim girl," I said as the waiter took away our plates. "We'll take the check."

"Now when I speak to my stepmom on the phone in Kashmir, she sends regards to my mom in New York," Raheem added. "In some ways, my dad's second wife may have preserved my mom's sanity."

I was surprised they were still in touch. "So you've forgiven your father for having two wives?"

"Polygamy isn't *that* foreign to Westerners," he said, sidestepping my inquiry. "Bertha Mason, the notorious madwoman married to Mr. Rochester, was locked in the attic in Charlotte Bronte's *Jane Eyre*. There's the great novel about Bertha by Jean Rhys, *The Wild Sargasso Sea*. Rhys was obsessed with her." As Raheem cited more examples of polygamy in literature from *Dracula* to *Anna and the King*, it seemed he was still wrestling the madwoman from his own attic.

*   *   *

Curious about the polygamous laws in Islam, I went back to Nora Zaki, Vassar's Muslim Chaplain.

"The Quran does say a man can take up to four wives," Zaki told me. "But Islam is a practical religion. In ancient times, when Muslim men were being killed, allowing the deceased's father, brother, or uncle to marry their widow was a way to protect more women and children.

I believe in cultural custom, to follow the law of the land. Since having more than one wife is outlawed in America, we adhere to that."

"Are you married to a Muslim?" I asked her.

"I'm twenty-seven and single," Zaki told me. "I'd like to settle down with a Muslim man. But when I marry, I will put in the Aqd, the marriage contract, that he can never take a second wife."

"That's a religious document, like a Jewish Ketubah?" I asked her.

"Yes, funny the word *kitab* means book in Arabic and *kataba* means to write. Arabic and Hebrew are trilateral languages based on the same roots," she reminded me. But she questioned why I was connecting Muslims with multiple marriage at all. "I think it just sensationalizes Islam," she added.

Although the topic only came up because of Raheem's past, current-day Saudi princes, who followed Wahhabism (one of numerous Islamic sects), had as many as thirty wives and could even divorce a wife without her knowledge. Then again, Islam wasn't the only polygamous religion. There were instances in the old Testament as Jewish men like Abraham, Jacob, David, and Solomon took multiple brides. In modern times, the practice was still found in Tibet, Nepal, and Africa, justified by the desire to keep women and family land safe. I thought about the fifteen million Mormons worldwide, whose founder Joseph Smith first denounced, then approved of, a polygamist lifestyle.

My student Michelle, who grew up Mormon, once mentioned that her grandfather was a big name in South American Mormonism. When I called to ask more about the religion she'd left, Michelle pointed me to their official website. There I found their longer title, The Church of Jesus Christ of Latter-Day Saints (LDS). They believed "that marriage between one man and one woman is God's standard for marriage, except at specific times when God has declared a different standard," adding that in the past, the practice helped lead to an increase in the number of children born to church members.

"Yes it's a religion of revision," Michelle told me. "And proselytism. We were taught to go door to door to convert people. When I worked at a Chabad House, I was shocked that they didn't want me. The Jews don't look for converts and actually make it hard to join."

I asked her about all the "We must forgive" videos on the LDS website that said Mormons were commanded to offer forgiveness and not hold a grudge, since not forgiving was a sin in itself.

"I prefer Alice Miller, who said, 'Forgiving is always in the interest of the perpetrator,'" Michelle told me.

"Miller was writing about child abuse though, wasn't she?" I asked, recalling the Swiss psychologist's book *The Drama of the Gifted Child*, which I admired.

"Yes she was. And I wasn't sexually abused," Michelle told me. "But for Mormons, there are unforgivable sins. One is murder, another is leaving the fold. So I'm damned to hell."

"What about your parents?" I asked Michelle. "Are they still in the church? Did they accept your leaving?"

"Yes. They forgave me for being a bisexual who left Mormonism," she told me. "My mom said family was more important to her than faith. She had a lot of empathy. She was always trying to understand what would make someone sin. Because of her I was able to see the world in complex ways and embrace the complexities in myself."

The fundamentalist offshoots of Mormons still allowed "plural marriage" in Utah, as depicted on the TV shows *Big Love* and *Sister Wives*. No surprise they needed so much forgiveness! As a monogamous liberal feminist, I found the concept of polygamy unfathomable. Especially after reading that the one-time Mormon leader Warren Jeffs, convicted of sexually assaulting two underage girls, had married more than seventy times.

When I commented on Michelle's dim view of theology, she led me to Kajsa, her old roommate at Brigham Young University in Utah, run under the auspices of The Church of the Latter Day Saints. Kajsa, a married mom who taught Ancient Scriptures and called herself "a mainstream Orthodox Mormon," was upbeat about her faith.

"I see forgiving as a commandment and a blessing," Kajsa said, returning my call on the road with her kids, who I could hear in the background.

"Even when someone commits a crime?" I asked. "Or leaves the religion?"

"Well I'm still friendly with Michelle," she said. "And take church sex abuse scandals, for example. You can apply social and legal justice by denouncing the abuse in public, turn in the criminal to the authorities and create a safe space for yourself, while also praying for their soul and trying to forgive the abuser. You do it for your own liberation. Forgiveness takes back your power. You refuse to let someone else's misdeeds rattle your soul any longer. You trust that God is the better dealer of eternal justice."

That reminded me how, if I ever mentioned wanting revenge against someone, my father used to say "They'll dig their own grave."

"What about polygamy?" I asked Kajsa.

"I see families who do it in Utah but it's underground, not allowed or sanctioned anymore. I'm in a monogamous marriage. If any man tried to take multiple wives now, he'd be excommunicated. I come from two polygamous lines, from both sides of my family," she admitted. "That's my soul work, struggling to accept that it happened, historically and religiously."

Clearly that was also Raheem's struggle.

*   *   *

"So you believe your father owed your mother an apology for taking a second wife?" I'd asked him before we left the diner.

"Not for *taking* a second wife. For not asking the permission of his first wife," Raheem broke it down for me. "I wish he'd told her, 'I'm sorry for not asking you, as I should have.'"

"Really? He only needs forgiveness from *her*, over a technicality?"

"It's not a technicality." Raheem sounded annoyed that I wasn't getting it. "This is about demolishing a woman's dignity, misusing her substantial wealth and stealing her dowry. Remember, according to sharia law, Muslims are allowed to have four legal wives at any one time. But it was mandatory for a Muslim man bringing home a new wife to seek permission from his first wife. Islam permits a man who is dissatisfied with his first wife to marry a second wife, without divorcing his first, *after* he asks the first wife's permission and *if* he provides for both equally. And the Prophet Muhammad married four times to unite disparate tribes of his era, to form an army, an important point in Islamic literature."

"What about you?" I couldn't help but ask. "You over-identified with your mother, ate by her, moved your bedroom next to hers." He'd submerged his voice so much into hers, I thought, that he couldn't even ask for his own apology. "You had to be like a husband to your mom, didn't marry until your forties, and then it was long-distance—until you divorced. Is it all connected?"

"Yes, his two marriages scarred me too," he conceded. "It created an incredible longing for me to take care of my mother. He knew it wasn't fair. If he apologized to her, he'd be saying he was sorry to me and the whole family. But he can't. He's too proud, paternalistic and insecure, as if apologizing diminishes his power as the patriarch."

Raheem drifted into present tense. So, it seemed, he hadn't pardoned his father and Ameen's death hadn't weakened Raheem's desire for him to rectify the rift. It fascinated me to think you could still need an apology, or argue for one, after the person who hurt you had died.

"Luckily, my life was already in New York," Raheem said. "My mom is doing better here. I know she loves me. At eighty-seven, at the Home, she tells her aides that she loves them. But she's never told me."

"Doesn't *she* owe you an apology for that?" I insisted on treating, throwing two twenties on the table.

"No, it wasn't our way." Raheem put on his jacket.

"Do you think she's forgiven your father?" I asked. He helped me on with my parka.

"She told her Nepali caregiver she forgave him in absentia for all his misdeeds: his ego, mismanaging her estate, for taking another wife,"

Raheem said, leading me outside. "But she can't find it in her heart to forgive him for not first seeking her permission."

"Wouldn't she have refused?" I asked as he escorted me home, past the crowded corner and subway stop.

"No, I think she would have agreed," he opined. "She accepted that it was a male-dominated society. Had she been allowed to participate in the final decision, it would have left her with dignity and the illusion of control."

"How is she now?" I asked. "Medicated?"

"Yes. She's doing better." He nodded. "Thank you for dinner."

His mom's restored pride probably would have helped Raheem. Standing in front of my building, I asked about the end of his twelve-year marriage to the beautiful Indian woman I'd met at their wedding. She was a fashion stylist who'd moved to Ireland for work not long after they'd wed. He'd relocated with her, but eventually came back to Manhattan, recreating another partition. He let the long distance divide his marriage completely, until they'd divorced.

"We're still close," he said, hugging me goodbye, adding "But sometimes you marry the wrong person."

I wasn't sure who he was referring to now: his mother, his father's second bride, or himself.

Walking inside, I thought about how every member of Dr. Winters' family had divorced at least once—his difficult mother multiple times. Had these domestic cracks informed his powers of perception? I bet that was how he knew to push me towards Aaron and made sure we ended up together. He'd used his mother's marital mistakes to ensure I wouldn't make any, the way I taught my students to avoid my previous errors.

"You're lucky you were betrayed by your shrink and not your husband," Stargazer's voice reverberated.

My father often told me, "Who you marry changes everything." Desperately wanting to get the love equation right, I'd once asked how he'd stayed so happy with my mom for more than half a century.

"It's a crapshoot," was all he said.

CHAPTER 14
SHOWN NO REMORSE, CAN YOU HEAL YOURSELF?
JANUARY 2011

"One of the keys to happiness is a bad memory."

—Rita Mae Brown

"Sometimes I wish she was dead, so I wouldn't have to see her anymore," Kate said.

"My shrink once said that breakups can be worse than death," I told her. "When a mate passes away, you're left with good memories and sympathy. When a lover dumps you, you're expected to get over it in a month. Then for the rest of your life, you're faced with the risk of seeing your ex-lover happier with someone else."

"Well luckily, she's not with someone else, or happier, from what I hear," Kate commented.

We were sitting on the couch of Kate's sparsely decorated eighth-floor one-bedroom loft in Westbeth, the Greenwich Village artist colony where she'd lived alone since splitting from her girlfriend Slim, six years before. My tall, dark-haired NYU teacher colleague was in jeans and a Keith Haring T-shirt and wore no makeup, looking younger than sixty-two, a bit like Lily Tomlin.

Over green tea, crudités, and hummus, Kate shared her anti-forgiveness approach. Speaking quickly, she described growing up the middle child in a conservative Catholic family in Paterson, New Jersey, home of Allen Ginsberg. She'd go to the Paterson Library to hear Ginsberg read, feeling cool that this famous beatnik poet who lived in the Village was from her hometown. In fact, Kate's father was an English teacher at the same school where Ginsberg's father taught. Her mother was a homemaker, active in their church. Before romancing women, she'd had three boyfriends. Ricky was the handsome boy next door she French kissed. She smiled, relating how she'd lost her virginity to her high school boyfriend Bob on the floor of the literary magazine's office at St. Peter's College, where he went to school.

Then she met Joe at the Jersey Shore in 1968, when her sorority rented a house in the party town of Belmar. He liked her Cream album "Wheels of Fire," while she liked his pot and his motorcycle. He was older, with wire-framed glasses and dark hair, longer than hers. He led her from the repressive climate of Caldwell College, a Catholic women's school with priests, nuns, and tea parties, into 60s counterculture. But she was stunned when Joe broke up with her because he was gay.

"When I came out two years later, I realized why the sex wasn't so great," she said, laughing. "I thought, what a hoot: we're both queer. No wonder!"

In 1975, at twenty-five, Kate followed Ginsberg to downtown Manhattan, where she saw herself as a rebellious, politicized Greenwich Village lesbian. She resented Catholicism's attitude that homosexuality was immoral and an abomination. Her father compared homosexuals to rapists and murderers. At the Oscar Wilde Bookshop she bought him a copy of *Now That You Know*, a parent's guide to accepting a queer child. But not wanting to fight, she never gave it to him. She often saw Ginsberg around the Village but regretfully they never officially met.

Kate dated three women in a row who all broke her heart. She was thirty, teaching high school, when she went to a Gay Teacher's Association event. There she met a special education teacher, Slim, a stately Jewish beauty from Brooklyn. Slim was the first of three kids and five years Kate's junior. She was in the process of divorcing her high school sweetheart. After she and Kate started dating, she pushed her husband to sign the divorce papers. Turned out, he was gay too.

As was Kate's first boyfriend Rick, who moved to California, but his mother kept her up to date. She was heartbroken when he and Joe both died of AIDS in the 80s. Kate reconciled with her dad, who embraced Slim and his daughter's relationship several years before he died. In the early 90s, when I met Slim and Kate, they were a cool, happy downtown artistic couple. Kate taught journalism in the same NYU program I did. Slim was a photographer. She'd once taken my picture for an article in *The Daily News*.

"You know, I never liked those photos she took of me," I remarked.

I'd sold the newspaper a piece on Barbie's thirtieth anniversary, mentioning my old Barbie doll collection. It seemed like a funny coincidence when Slim was assigned to photograph me. But coming over to my apartment, she'd insisted on posing me sitting on a chair at a weird angle, dolls from my collection perched at my shoulder. "I told Slim, 'This is going to look bad.' She said, 'No, you'll look great, trust me.' And the picture in the paper was horrific. The worst photo I'd ever taken."

"She didn't get to pick which picture they used. At that point, she'd hand in the roll to the editor," Kate said. "This was before digital." I noted: she was still defending her ex.

Perhaps reading my mind, Kate said, "Oh yeah, Slim could be stubborn and incapable of listening to anyone else's opinion."

Bad photo aside, I'd liked Slim. She seemed smart, talented, and chic in leather jackets, minis, boots and caps, like the actress Judy Carne, who was the Sock-It-To-Me girl on *Laugh In*.

At the time, Kate and Slim were renting a one-bedroom East Village apartment together. Slim was a vegetarian chef who did the cooking. Kate was a busy journalist reviewing concerts for the *Village Voice*. At one show, she couldn't take notes and pictures at the same time. She handed her camera to Slim, asking her to take a few shots. The *Voice* printed those amateur photos with Slim's byline. Fired up by the success, she went to School of Visual Arts to take photography classes and set up a darkroom in their kitchen. Kate later helped Slim put together her website and pick which photos to send out, suggesting captions. On their anniversary, Slim wrote Kate a card that said, "My career as a photographer is forever dedicated to you," a tribute that made Kate cry. While Kate's freelance assignments went up and down, Slim became a workaholic, selling photos to *Vanity Fair* and *Rolling Stone* and winning Pulitzer Prize nominations. As Slim made more money, she started their retirement fund, promising to take care of Kate in their old age.

Kate's position reminded me of cousin Cindy, who'd worked at a low-paying job, helping her husband through medical school. But Slim and Kate couldn't wed since same-sex marriage wasn't yet legal. Instead they became domestic partners by registering at New York's Municipal Building in 1993. The partnership offered few legal benefits. But to Kate, it felt sometimes like a marriage license would have represented their commitment.

After twenty-six years of monogamy, Kate was shocked to realize she'd become a cliché, the loyal wife whose spouse was bored with her and wanted more excitement. Slim refused to go to counseling.

"At first, I assumed she was having a midlife crisis. She hadn't had other girlfriends, so I thought she needed to experiment a little. I went along when she needed to watch gay male porn videos and use sex toys to get off. She even wanted a vibrator for her fiftieth birthday."

"It's funny you were jealous of her porn and fake penis," I said.

"You're confusing a vibrator with a strap-on dildo," Kate snapped, making me feel like a straight married idiot.

I told my writing students, "God is in the details." In Kate's case, it seemed she'd clung to the provocative particulars as evidence, the way a crime victim remembered specifics so they might later help put the perpetrator away. Still, looking around her home, sun poured in from three long windows. Her double bed in the corner had a splashy Indian spread, with orange and red hues that lit up the original artwork on her walls. It did not look like the home of someone depressed or angry.

Earlier, in the 1980s, as broke artists who'd quit teaching, Kate and Slim had put their names on a list to get government subsidized artistic housing at Westbeth. But to qualify, a couple had to earn less than $50,000 combined. By the time their names came up, Slim made more than that. Kate re-registered on her own, with her lower journalist's salary. When a small studio became available for $349 a month in 1997, Slim pushed her to take it alone. Kate did, viewing it as her private work space, and a way to give Slim more room. Seeing each other less spiced up their love life.

But one day in 2006, Slim said she was bored and wanted her freedom. "What do you think you're missing?" Kate asked.

"Probably nothing," Slim answered. "But I have to find out. I don't want to die wondering. Cutting you off is the only way I can move on." Not wanting Kate in their shared East Village apartment anymore, Slim dropped off Kate's clothes and art deco lamps in the Westbeth lobby.

Kate was devastated. At fifty-seven, she felt completely erased. At least she already had her own place and a good therapist who worried the breakup left her with post-traumatic stress disorder. She consulted a lawyer, explaining that she'd helped launch Slim's thriving photography career, that Slim made more money and had promised to fund their joint retirement. The attorney suggested she write Slim a letter stating her case for a "good-faith" settlement, pointing out the sacrifices Kate had made over the years as the supportive partner to a successful artist-wife. Slim responded by emailing, "Leave me alone."

Had they been able to wed, Kate could have argued for equitable distribution of Slim's IRA accounts, she told me. But while Kate's name remained listed as beneficiary, she had no legal claims unless Slim died. As an anti-materialistic Greenwich Village hippie freelancer, Kate hadn't thought to protect herself by making Slim sign a financial contract. Now, she had no rights to any compensation and Slim's refusal was perfectly legal. More than hurt, Kate was enraged. Aside from the monetary remuneration, an official divorce would have provided a public marker, a clear statement and bigger acknowledgment of their demise.

For the next year, Kate had trouble sleeping and eating. She woke up sweating in the middle of the night, afraid she would wind up penniless on the street, like a bag lady. She had a vivid dream where Slim had just come from the bathtub in her robe and they were about to make love. "I knew I was dreaming, but I willed her embrace to continue a bit longer because it felt so comforting," Kate confessed. "When I woke up, I felt so bereft without her."

She told friends and colleagues what Slim had done, calling her "a selfish bitch."

In 2010, Kate had a mammogram with inconclusive results. The doctor ordered more tests. With all her stress and depression, Kate worried that being infuriated with Slim for so long could make her sick. Kate had so many things she still wanted to do: live part-time on the beach, see her beloved grand nieces and nephews grow up, finish the book she'd been trying to complete for years. Mostly she wanted her good health back.

On the advice of a spiritual advisor, Kate considered forgiving Slim. But she did not believe Slim deserved a pardon. After all, she'd coldly left Kate in a fragile economic state without even an apology. Kate decided to shift emotionally, so her resentment wouldn't make her sick, or harder to heal if she was.

After her tests turned out to be fine, Kate embarked on a breakup journey to heal her heart and mind, becoming what she called a "self-help junkie." She did yoga. Meditation. Chanting. She consulted new-age gurus. An astrologer. A psychotherapist. A Tarot card reader. She researched the Law of Attraction. She went to the Omega Institute, an upstate New York retreat. Kate was surprised that what really helped her was the religion she'd felt rejected by—with a twist. She discovered Middle Collegiate Church, a hip multiethnic house of worship with a black female Protestant pastor, Dr. Jacqueline J. Lewis, a "Senior Minister for Public Theology and Transformation."

"After coming out as a lesbian, I couldn't deal with the Catholic church's homophobia and sexism," Kate told me. "The biggest departure is that Middle Collegiate is welcoming and embraces LGBTQ members. Rev.

Jacqui is an active supporter of gay marriage, the church even has a float in the pride parade. Their motto is: 'Love. Period.' The services resemble performance art with great choirs, Broadway singers, and dancing in the aisles. Reverend Jacqui is a charismatic preacher who radiates love and joy."

Indeed, when I called Reverend Lewis, she projected warmth while speaking about her past and her own issues with religious non-inclusivity. Growing up in the Baptist church in Chicago, she was told that women were not allowed to be ordained, and her conservative male pastor over-focused on sin. "While I loved the joyful music, I was afraid I could be bad enough so God wouldn't love me," she admitted. "In the Roman Catholic church, the pope didn't seem interested in female ordination and there were no women preachers in Greek Orthodox Christianity." She studied at the Princeton Theological Seminary, the Presbyterian School of Theology where Reverend Liz Maxwell also went. "As Presbyterian, I was told I could be a child of God and a light in the world. That's where I found grace."

Her current parish was under the auspices of the more liberal United Church of Christ and the Reform Church of America and she was married to a Methodist Minister. All the denominations confused me. I assumed Reverend Jacqui was aiming for an inclusive house of worship relevant for modern day, the way my friend Rabbi Jen Kaluzny said that Reform Judaism embraced the evolving nature of our faith. Yet would the old chestnuts about forgiveness still apply?

"So if someone hurt you badly but won't explain or apologize, why should you even consider forgiving?" I inquired on behalf of Kate, myself, and stubborn grudge-holders everywhere.

"Listen, forgiveness is very hard. Anyone who says they don't think so has never really been hurt or wounded. But forgiveness isn't for the other person, it's mostly for you," Reverend Jacqui said. "It's a spiritual discipline, a cleansing. When a disciple asked Jesus 'How many times do I have to forgive someone? Seven?' Jesus answered, 'Seventy times seven times,' according to Matthew 18:22. That number symbolizes boundlessness."

"Kate said you invited a rabbi, imam and a Sikh clergy to speak for a 9/11 anniversary. Was that about forgiveness?"

"Our interfaith service was a way for New Yorkers to unite and combat all forms of violence, hatred, and religious bigotry," she told me.

"Do certain branches of Christianity offer more unconditional forgiveness than Islam or Judaism?" I asked.

"Well, remember, Jesus was a Jew," the Reverend said. "He was clarifying beliefs for a new religion. In the Lord's Prayer we say forgive us our sins, our debts, our trespassing. In Luke, when Jesus says 'Father forgive them, for they do not know what they are doing,' he was asking God to forgive his killers *while* he was being crucified. Jesus was offering an immediate, unconditional forgiveness that was transformative."

"But in modern day, if someone is abusing you, isn't it smart and self-protective to not forgive?"

"You can forgive someone abusive and get out of there. You no longer have to drag it around or let it define you. It doesn't mean you ever have to see the person again or stay in pain. Forgiving can get you out of pain."

I was curious how Kate unlocked herself from a painful breakup with no forgiveness. She finally published her memoir *Looking for a Kiss*, about her romance, breakup, and recovery, dedicated to "all the women who've been dumped after twenty-five years." One critic called it "the queer, low-budget *Eat Pray Love*." When gay marriage finally became legal in New York, Kate stood cheering in front of the historic Stonewall Inn, but for her the victory was bittersweet. "I felt like the dyke version of a desperate housewife who was dumped and alone," she said.

"What happened to Slim?" I asked.

"I saw her everywhere. The first time I bumped into her in the neighborhood, six months after we split, she was pale and didn't look good. She said she'd had shingles."

"How did you feel?"

"It was hard. Honestly, I felt a little vindicated, because I looked good. And it seemed like the bad karma from the way she treated me caught up with her," Kate confessed. Kate's shrink, her Tarot reader, her astrologer—and a whole chorus of advisors—pushed her to meet some-one new. Even I tried fixing her up, but she didn't take to the former student I thought she'd fall for.

Kate tried speed dating and went on Match.com, which she found challenging in her sixties. While her "gaydar" was intact, she was so critical of all the women she met, her shrink told her to get rid of her "baddar," where she looked for qualities to dislike as a defense mechanism that kept her from getting close to anyone else. It didn't help that the local lesbian community was so tight-knit. She kept running into women who had dated Slim and came up to her saying, "Oh, so you're her ex." Kate's lowest moment was when she stumbled across Slim's picture on a Sapphic dating site.

"Reading her profile, I started cursing," Kate recalled. "How dare she lead off her blurb with 'Looking for Lasting Love.' What a crock from the woman who would not go to one counseling session after ending our twenty-six year relationship!"

Kate's attempt at forgiveness after the cancer scare disintegrated when she read how Slim described herself: "honest, caring, compassionate, and comfortable with myself."

"Isn't it bizarre that a self-identified photographer didn't post a profile picture?" Kate said.

She decided to stop looking for Princess Charming online. She'd enjoy being on her own and stay open to meeting the right woman in person. But she kept bumping into Slim. At a close friend's memorial service at St. Mark's Church, Kate was surprised when Slim waved and patted the chair next to her. Kate joined her. They asked about each other's family and work. It was the first civilized conversation they'd had since their breakup.

"Slim said I looked good, complimenting my pink jeans," Kate recalled, smiling. "I was tan, I'd been at the beach. I told her, 'Just came back from Ocean Grove. I bought these in the thrift shop we used to go to.' Slim said, 'I discovered that store.' Like she had to take credit." By the end of the service, crying over the loss of their friend, they hugged goodbye.

For the first time in years, Kate felt fine to be single. She was better off without Slim. "It was a series of realizations coming together. After the way she treated me and screwed me financially, why would I want to be with her anymore?" she reflected.

In 2011, after fourteen years in a tiny Westbeth studio she associated with Slim, Kate was offered a sunny one bedroom there. She felt she'd won "The New York real estate lottery" since apartments that size in her neighborhood rented for $3,800 a month. "I know it's petty, but it seemed metaphoric: Slim was stuck in our old, cramped rent-stabilized East Village fourth-floor walk-up with no washer or dryer. I was moving into a bigger space in an elevator building in the West Village with a laundry room, art gallery, community area for my artist friends. Slim had never been in this space. I created my own life with different furniture and art, a better view out bigger windows. I felt like the song, 'It's a new dawn, a new day.'"

And yet: Kate still longed for an apology or some kind of acknowledgment of the pain Slim had caused.

"So if she could offer remorse for how she treated you, what should she say?" I asked.

"I actually wrote it down," Kate said, pulling out a notebook. She read aloud: "I made a mistake leaving you. Things have not turned out well for me. I've realized my problems couldn't be fixed by dumping you. I'm sorry I ended our relationship so cruelly ten years ago. Since I reneged on my promise to take care of you in your old age, I'd like to give you $20,000 to start your retirement fund." Kate took a breath from the elaborate apology she'd prepared in advance, spurred by my telling her about my project. Then she added the kicker, the line every dumped person dreamt of hearing: "I'm still single, have not found anyone better, and really miss you."

After she read it, we both laughed.

She received neither an apology nor financial reparation. Nor had she herself found anyone special to replace Slim in her heart or her bed. But I took note: despite not forgiving her ex-girlfriend, Kate managed to move on.

"Since Slim split, my mother and I got closer. I was upgraded to my fabulous new living space. I landed a full-time secure teaching job and took control of my finances, so I no longer have to worry about money every day. And I published my first book at sixty-six, which felt like a triumph." Kate listed her accomplishments as if (like in my family) achievement really was redemption. But then she backtracked.

"Look, my recovery took much longer than I expected. It would have been a lot easier with a divorce settlement or a new girlfriend. But I was able to recover alone." She sounded proud of herself. "I hope to fall in love again. But even if I don't, I'm much better off single than getting old with the wrong person."

It turned out that living well really was the best revenge. Manny had fueled his rage by spiting Hitler. Yet he had a wife, children, and grandchildren to ease his burden. My brother's friend David, cousin Cindy, and my student Sharisse all focused on raising their kids. Kenan and Cliff were single and childless, like Kate. Maybe because they were younger, with money worries, they couldn't yet put away their past anger enough to flourish.

I pondered if the support system provided by Kate's continual therapy and her many friendships allowed her to do well. I also considered how much being well-employed and financially solvent was soothing her pain. Surely, poverty and failure would have made everything worse. But I had stability in my career, real estate and even love—while still feeling tormented by the fallout with Dr. Winters.

It was compelling that Kate remained angry at her ex, yet also managed to thrive. Sitting here, in this room of her own, she was vibrant. The aura was bright and upbeat: this was someone who loved her life.

"I still can't forgive her without acknowledgment of what she did to me," Kate admitted. "Many people stay friends with their old lovers. I resent that she couldn't be kinder about leaving me. I still feel wronged. My Tarot reader said, 'One day you'll get an apology, when you're in a new relationship.'"

Like Manny, Kate seemed to have done well almost out of spite. But unlike him, she'd received no public admission of wrong-doing or restitution, and still believed hearing the words "I'm sorry" would make a difference. There was a saying about writing and love: "You can do anything as long as it works." Was that also true of hate? Either way, when Kate escorted me to the elevator, I felt buoyed by what she'd taught me: You could live well without forgetting you were wronged, hearing regret, or receiving reparations. You never had to offer any forgiveness if you didn't sincerely feel it.

I still wanted to, though.

CHAPTER 15
FORGIVING A CRITICAL RELATIVE YOU CAN'T LEAVE
FEBRUARY 2011

"I wondered if that was how forgiveness budded: not with the fanfare of epiphany, but with pain gathering its things, packing up, and slipping away unnoticed in the middle of the night."

—author Khaled Hosseini

"I think my husband's mother owes me an apology for not loving me," said Alison.

"Really?" I finished signing my last paperback, then stared at her, already hooked by her naked honesty.

After contemplating the agonies of heartbreak, incest and ethnic cleansing, I'd hoped the West Coast's warm weather and Alison, my favorite new colleague, would lighten me up. At the end of the Wednesday night Barnes & Noble reading we'd just given, I'd praised the Amy Tan quote on her book cover. "She's a literary friend and inspiration," Alison said. Jealous of her well-known guru, I'd confessed that falling out with mine had led to my obsessive quest, asking everyone I knew who they deserved an apology from and why.

"Definitely my mother-in-law," Alison answered immediately. "What a piece of work."

"I'll buy you dinner to thank you for setting up such a great event," I offered, with an ulterior motive: I wanted to hear all the dirt. "So why doesn't Ajay's mom love you?" I asked as we walked to a Thai café on the promenade across from the bookstore.

"That's a good question," she said. Seated in a dimly lit booth in the middle of the crowded eatery, under fake palm trees, we ordered a bunch of appetizers. "Nobody has hurt me more," she added quietly.

A former a student of mine who'd moved to Los Angeles and taken her class called Alison "the California Sue." But Alison's background was more international and political than mine. A tough Chinese-American journalist born on the West Coast, she'd won international awards for reporting on Southeast Asian child trafficking. She didn't seem like someone who'd let a monster-in-law get to her. Two protégées of hers who'd been at our reading walked up to say hi, interrupting Alison's engrossing multicultural soap opera. I smiled politely, wishing they'd leave so I could hear the rest. By the time the food came, I was starving, quickly dipping my chicken satay in peanut sauce.

"Tell me what happened," I said as they finally left.

"Oh, when I brought my baby daughter all the way to India to meet my husband's mom, she stared at her and said, 'I'm disappointed she looks Chinese like you and not at all like my son.'"

"Oh god." I dropped my chicken-on-a-stick. "So sorry."

"Can you imagine hearing this about my only child?" Alison looked teary. "It was devastating."

So much for L.A. lightness. Having your husband's mother reject your ethnicity *and* criticize your daughter's looks was beyond reproach. I couldn't imagine forgiving that. I'd just met her tall, slim husband at the reading with their tall, slim fifteen-year-old.

"And your girl is so gorgeous."

"She is!" Alison was pretty too. We shared the same age, height, and long dark hair, though she was thinner and more stylish in her blue dress, heels, and turquoise jewelry. I wore a black skirt, tee, and casual sandals, what Aaron called my "summer black."

"Isn't Indian considered Asian?" I asked.

"Yes. People from India and China have a longstanding respect and alliance. And the dumbest thing is, my daughter Anais now looks very Indian. But when she was younger she looked more Chinese," she said. "You've been married a long time. You know how bad in-laws can be."

"I'm actually close with my husband's mom," I admitted. "When a study showed most women would prefer root canal than seeing their mother-in-law, an editor friend called to ask me for a piece, saying, 'Since you love yours, will you be the anomaly?'"

"I'm jealous you have a mother-in-law who likes you," she said, finishing her shrimp soup, keeping her eyes down.

"Well my former mentor and sister-in-law both can't stand me," I commiserated. I'd read Alison's book about being swept up by the gentle, handsome Ajay when they were in their thirties, both working in Hong Kong. He was from high-class Hindu royalty.

"Did his family like you at first?"

"No. I'm not Indian like they are, I'm not in their caste." She sipped her wine. "To them, I'm not from any caste. I don't even belong to a low one. They have no idea how to classify me. Who I am in their social hierarchy doesn't compute. They just couldn't wrap their heads around this strange, well-educated Chinese-American professional woman."

She described Ajay's father as landed gentry and his mother as a frosty aristocrat who grew up in a 100-room palace in a village called Mokimpur. They were Hindu while she'd grown up "agnostic with Confucian ideals and Buddhist underpinnings."

When she went to the ladies room, I googled Confucianism so as not to appear stupid. Aside from the Confucius sayings I equated with fortune cookies, I knew little about it. According to Wikipedia, it was also called Ruism and was described as a religion, philosophy, tradition, and way of life founded by the ancient Chinese philosopher Confucius. Their holy books rested on the beliefs that humans were fundamentally good, reachable, improvable, and perfectible. From quick reading and typing in "Confucianism" and "forgive," I gathered that forgiveness didn't appear to be idealized in Confucian thought. Yet the poetic sayings that popped up in this general area seemed to encourage a change of heart: "The more people know, the more they forgive." "I could see peace instead of this." "Forget injuries, never forget kindness."

"So it turned out I married a Hindu prince of sorts," Alison said when she returned.

"Doesn't that make you a princess?" I asked, realizing I also needed a refresher course on Buddhism and Hinduism asap.

"Yeah, royalty doing the celebrity journalism hustle and teaching UCLA extension courses," she laughed. "Ajay's more of a lord than a bona fide prince. He's modest. I didn't even know about the palace until after six months of dating, when I overheard him telling my mom. I was stunned; I thought he was a fellow struggling journalist. Then I pictured an exotic palace with marble floors, gilt-framed portraits of maharajas. He owned a part of the residence, but it turned into a nightmare." She signaled the waiter for another white wine. "Sure you won't join me?"

I shook my head. "I'm a decade sober. Why was it a nightmare?" I leaned closer, sipping water.

"The palace was built in 1911, no electricity or hot water. Seventy of their crazy cousins live in different wings. By 1997, when I was there, it was crumbling. It was Jackson Pollacked with mold."

I gathered they were land-rich, but cash poor. "They couldn't sell the palace?"

"No, where would they all live? It's in the middle of nowhere and there's a fair amount of crime."

I knew nothing of foreign real estate, though Aaron and I had put all the money we had—and borrowed—into combining two Manhattan apartments as a home/office, our version of a post-modern palace. Aaron initially said no, but Dr. Winters encouraged buying the one-bedroom next door and assisted me with the complex transaction. When I excitedly told him, during a session, that the value had tripled, Dr. Winters counseled me not to spend more money—and to be careful.

"It's a money pit, not a windfall. The mortgage and maintenance will keep rising. Selling for a profit, you'd owe capital gains tax and need another home," he warned. "You won't increase your investment unless you down-size or leave the city." Based on his advice, I'd learned to better handle finances, easing the stress in my marriage. It felt like Dr. Winters was always with me, all the help he'd offered resounding, even during my tour to get over him.

"Ajay's brother had brought home a traditional Brahmin girl he'd married before I was on the scene," she said. "My evil sister-in-law was not happy to see a Chinese-American girl reporter swanning around *her* palace garden."

"They didn't like you compared to his brother's wife? Just because of your ethnicity?"

"Maybe also because they assumed a Chinese woman could cook. I can't. I was a double disappointment." She chuckled. "For Indians, a woman's cooking skills contribute to her status."

"Funny, for Jewish women too," I said. "I burn water."

"Me too! Before we married, I tried to cook *saag paneer* for Ajay's parents, with *halwa*—carrot pudding—for dessert, since Ajay's mom has a sweet tooth. Every bloody Indian dish has twenty ingredients in it. It took me all day. Then when Ajay's mom came into her kitchen to inspect the meal, she told me, 'We only eat *halwa* in cold winter months, but I'll try to make an exception.'"

"'Taste it, Mrs. Singh,' I said, grabbing the spoon she'd dipped in the *saag paneer* to scoop pudding. She yelled, lunging at my hand and said, 'We never dip a spoiled spoon in a pot of food. Hindus believe this contaminates the entire dish. Now we can't eat this.' She gave it to the servants." Alison was mortified.

As if getting rejected by editors wasn't enough for a writer to deal with. I couldn't imagine also being trashed by a haughty aristocratic mother over a cultural bias. "What did you say?"

"Nothing. I was embarrassed. My mother had warned me, 'If you learn to cook, you'll get stuck in the kitchen,'" she recalled. "I really tried, on a Christmas visit, after we married. Though the holiday meant nothing to the residents in Ajay's village; few had heard of Jesus or Santa Claus. Ajay joked that with three million gods swirling about in the Hindu universe, they had plenty of religious figures without worrying about Christian ones. To make up for my first food disaster, I wanted to blow these royal Indian in-laws away with a yuletide feast. I prepared mashed sweet potatoes with pears, stuffing with sausage and duck. I didn't realize I couldn't make the meal with their primitive electrical system. Everything ended up half-cooked, in sad cold heaps in the silver serving dishes."

Alison loved Ajay, but this culinary humiliation was a thorn in their union, and in her heart. "You couldn't win. Why didn't your husband stand up for you?" I asked, hooked on her dilemma. "What's wrong with his mother?"

"Along with my Chinese looks, Mrs. Singh didn't like my American accent. She doesn't understand my English. I try to sound British with her, adding *bloody*, like Dick Van Dyke in *Mary Poppins*. Ajay translates my English to her Indian English. Another micro aggression," she said. "Ajay's brother and his wife already had an Indian grandchild in Delhi. A Chinese-American feminist in L.A. who couldn't cook or speak their language couldn't compete," she said. "As busy journalists, we couldn't fly to India often. When we get there, Ajay doesn't want to fight with his parents. He grew up isolated, in a British boarding school, so he tunes out emotionally. Even if he hates how they're treating me."

"Your in-laws weren't impressed you're a popular, award-winning author?" I asked. "I loved *Where the Peacocks Sing*." I showed her the extra copy of her paperback in my bag.

"Thanks," she said. "They don't really understand it."

"My own parents don't get what I do. I once flew to see them the day my memoir was optioned by Paramount Pictures. My dad said, 'You can still go to law school.' I was forty-five at the time. My mother said, 'That's great, dear,' and spent the dinner talking about my nephew scoring in the ninetieth percentile on his third-grade math test."

"I'm close with my mother," she said. "I'm one of six, the youngest of four daughters, her favorite."

"Oh I didn't know you came from such a big family," I said. "That must have been hell growing up."

"Why do you say that?" she asked.

"With three younger brothers close in age, I couldn't wait to live alone in Manhattan."

"That's why I moved to Hong Kong after college. Your dad was a doctor who helped you out, right?"

I nodded. But feeling self-conscious about my privilege, I added, "My folks grew up poor on New York's Lower East Side. Mom was an orphan. My grandfather owned a window-shade store. Dad going to medical school was his dream." Aaron's father was the first in his family to go to college. He became a lawyer, then a justice on the Westchester Supreme and Appellate Courts. If Jews had a caste system, I thought, doctor and judge would be at the top. "What did your father do?"

"He was an engineer with a law degree," she said. "Then he became a realtor and an appraiser. But he never quite made it. As he got older, he struggled with mental illness. He was from a rich family. My dad's father was the mayor of Chinatown, who seemed like this icon of benevolence. But my grandfather refused to give him any money for me or my sisters' inheritance. He just wrote off the girls."

"Boy, it sounds like you need apologies for sexism all over the place."

"I know," she agreed. "In some ways, Ajay and my family both moved through the world with a sense of noblesse oblige, fooling ourselves, since our social status was far removed from our lofty ancestors."

I nodded. Growing up with dads who were a judge and doctor, Aaron and I had been blanketed by their success. Later we each felt inferior since we couldn't make a decent living in Manhattan until we were in our forties.

"My mother-in-law galls me most," she said. "I had high expectations since the mother of my British boyfriend in Hong Kong loved me."

"In my case, four parents were happy we'd married fellow Jews," I said. "But then we couldn't have children."

"Yes, I was sorry to read about your infertility," Alison told me.

"Sometimes I think I should apologize to my family for not continuing our lineage," I threw out.

"You'd think with a beautiful granddaughter, my in-laws would give me credit," she said. "I thought I'd get a warm funny Indian version of the mom-in-law Diane Keaton played in *Something's Gotta Give*," she said. "Making six figures, I was helping his parents fix the plumbing and structural problems on their estate."

"You're helping them?" I asked. Her puzzle, from just the first piece I'd seen, was more fascinating than a bitchy mother-in-law. It was a multicultural murder mystery where the dying body was the rickety palace. "So he wasn't the catch he seemed."

"Not financially. When we moved back to America from Hong Kong, he didn't adjust well or get a full-time job for four years. He started teaching, but I still have lingering anger that I had to pay 95 percent of my prince's bills and help his family." She put her spoon down. "He's a great guy and a great father, but honestly, his mother should have been thankful I was female, had two legs, and didn't care about his money. And that I was a hard worker who wanted a career, not a royal title. I brought so much to their family."

"So much more than the other sister-in-law," I commented.

"His sister-in-law hated me more than his mother did. On a trip to India, I asked my cute six-year-old niece, 'So what do you guys do when we're not here?' She said, 'We make fun of you.' She wasn't joking."

"Was your husband upset?"

"Not about that. He's more grounded than I am. One night in Hong Kong after a fancy dinner party, I felt bad about being a Have Not. He said, 'When you're trying to determine where you stand in life, don't look upward at the rich, look downward at people begging on the street. Only by looking down can you understand the cosmic order.' His insight is the emotional center of my life."

"Did the financial struggle make you more of a career woman?" I wondered.

"I never wanted to be a housewife. But I had to face my fears and become a warrior," she said.

I understood. My life had also improved when I stopped expecting my husband to support me and learned to manage money on my own.

Walking outside, I felt a cool breeze as we strolled the boulevard of lit-up stores and eateries, punctuated by real palm trees. Passing the movie theatre, I thought of a funny British comedy I'd seen about a run-down Indian hotel and said, "The plot sounds like the *Best Exotic Marigold Hotel*."

"That's filled with clichés, a rom-com made for a mainstream audience," she said. "In my version, my sister-in-law sued my in-laws, trying to screw Ajay, me, and my daughter out of our family inheritance. My only consolation is that his parents now hate her worse than me. Ha. My happy ending is that I became the better daughter-in-law because I didn't sue anyone. Weirdly, I won by losing."

"Did the lawsuit and their falling out improve things for you?"

"It did!" she said. "The next time we came to India, Mrs. Singh looked at Anais and said, 'I'm surprised how much Mokimpur is in her.' Then a relative commented on Anais's Indian nose. Something changed. I asked her, 'How do you feel now when you look at Anais?' She said, 'Like I am looking at my own child.'"

"Even though those comments are still kind of offensive, she did try to apologize?"

"Mrs. Singh won't ever say she's sorry."

"What exactly would you want her to tell you?" I asked.

Alison paused, then said "I'm sorry for not appreciating all you bring to our son and family, for putting you through Hindu hazing during your first trips to India and for ruining your golden life."

"When did the cold war thaw out?"

"I realized not all communication has to be explicit. Some people are nonverbal and won't ever be able to say what you want to hear," she said. "When Ajay was four, his mother left him at the boarding school by saying, 'I'll be right back,' and took off. He cried every night for months, worried she was lost or hurt. He later asked, 'How could you do that?' She said she couldn't handle two little boys running around. She felt guilty and finally, years later, told him that leaving him there broke her heart. That's why he has so much trouble expressing emotions, though I know how much he loves me and our daughter."

"She really sounds like a frigid fish," I said, thinking that Mrs. Singh also owed her son an apology.

"I know," Alison said. "But I watched her play hide and seek with Anais when we were there last time. She gave her jewelry and Indian clothing. She learned to Skype so she could see Anais's face more. Though she never told me she was sorry for treating me like a second-class citizen compared to her Indian daughter-in-law, watching her be joyful with my daughter, I feel like she's begrudgingly loving part of me."

"So you forgive her even without the apology you deserve?"

"I have worked hard to forgive her." She looked ready to be finished with the whole rollercoaster ride.

"I really wanted to have another child," Alison said. "After rough infertility treatments, I finally got pregnant a second time. But then I lost the baby. The last time we visited India three years ago, after the miscarriage, I saw the sadness in Mrs. Singh's eyes. She's not American, she doesn't have the language we do to express herself. Sometimes you can't get the words you want but it didn't matter. It became clear she desperately hoped I'd give her another grandchild. And she shared my sorrow that I couldn't. Seeing how upset she was really touched me. Although she was silent, I let her sad feelings be her apology."

It was intriguing to see that another fast-talking author and writing teacher I admired—whose context for everything was words—could let empathy stand in for speech.

"I decided my next book will be *Cooking for the Maharani*," she said. "I'll take classes from top international chefs. Then I'll go to India to cook Mrs. Singh seven nights of seasonal feasts."

My father's friend Manny had a simple Freudian theory, that having your parents' love as a child could help you overcome anything. But maybe sharing your mother and father with a lot of siblings could leave you hungry. That could be why Alison and I were still fighting for the approval of impossible parental figures.

As she went home to her husband and daughter, I contemplated her generosity of spirit, impressed she could accept the silent sweetness her mother-in-law now offered. Gradually, over the years, she decided to transform her hurt into a new adventure. Did her attitude stem from her mix of faiths?

According to the Buddhist Centre, that major global religion—with 470 million followers—was founded by Siddhartha Gautama in Nepal around 2,500 years ago. His title *Buddha* meant "one who is awake," which is the source of the current term for calling someone enlightened "woke." He was born a normal person and preached a religion without an authority figure. Buddhists didn't believe in a personal God; they didn't have to repent or pray to Allah, Jesus, or the Jewish supreme being Adonai, who could grant mercy. Instead they meditated and sought truth. Their belief in karma (shared with Hinduism) referred to action based on intention—not transactions, but patterns of behavior that led to future consequences. Good actions like generosity and righteousness brought about happiness in the long run, whereas bad actions like lying or killing ultimately caused unhappiness. I was soothed to read that nothing was fixed or permanent and change was always possible.

These four noble truths basically said: suffering exists. It has a cause. It has an end. And it has a cause to bring about its end. I contemplated the line, "As we are the ultimate cause of our difficulties, we are also the solution."

I'd originally sought out Dr. Winters to make me healthier and happier, and he came through, for the fifteen years that he was my guru, as Buddhists, Hindus and others called their spiritual teachers. I liked the Sanskrit definition of guru as *Remover of darkness, bestower of light.* But maybe my increasing over-reliance on him as a godlike figure was making me suffer now. I thought of Freud's critique of religion as the pathological search for a father. I was still pathologically searching for a father stand-in who liked me more than the real one did.

Swept up in Alison's wisdom, I wished I could break my dependence on Dr. Winters and get past his transgressions without needing an apology. If he would just be empathetic, I told myself, I could try to let him slide by without the words. But he wasn't. And I couldn't force an inauthentic conclusion; I was still angry. Alison's mother-in-law's iciness had melted. My case was the reverse and more mystifying, since the person who was once kind to me had turned cold and stayed that way.

When a colleague who taught at Loyola Marymount University mentioned a Buddhism professor, I asked for an introduction and ambushed Dermott J. Walsh with my big question: "From a Buddhist standpoint, what would you say about forgiving someone who wronged you but refuses to apologize?"

"It shouldn't matter," Professor Walsh said, after thinking for a while. "You can still choose to forgive. Their refusal to repent comes from the same origin as our refusal to forgive without the requisite apology—a sense of self. One might, in a philosophical sense, call it 'self-entitlement,' a feeling that we are entitled to an apology. The person who refuses to say 'I'm sorry' should not be our concern. They are causing themselves harm. By forgiving, even if someone is incapable of apologizing, we are actually helping them and ourselves."

I did feel entitled to an apology, yet I could mend myself, even if Dr. Winters couldn't actually say the words.

"They harm themselves because of the bad karma?" I asked.

He nodded. "Buddha said that all suffering comes from ignorance of the way the world works. In Buddhism the essence of forgiveness is similar to how Jesus saw it on the cross when he said, 'Forgive them Lord, for they know not what they do.' For Buddhists, too, there is a sense that if we only realized all negative actions stemmed from ignorance, we would have an easier time forgiving."

"So you think I need to forgive him anyway?" I asked. "How?"

"It can be very difficult, especially when the wrong done to us has been extreme and unjust. But the chain of one person hurting another, refusing to apologize and then causing hurt must be changed by radical forgiveness or repentance," he said. "They are seen as courageous expressions that relieve pain and suffering in the world."

Dr. Winters once agreed with my theory that most therapists chose their field in order to, on some level, cure themselves. "If you do good, you are good," was the idea. Now I imagined we'd switched roles. With everything I'd learned, what if I could become the more enlightened, stronger healer? And he was the lost, confused follower whose pain I could alleviate, even if he never knew that, through the air waves, I was redeeming us both.

CHAPTER 16
WHEN TRAGEDY OFFERS A SECOND CHANCE

"Tout comprendre, c'est tout pardonner."
— Leo Tolstoy, *War and Peace*

"If I wasn't robbed and beaten up, I may not have reconciled with my mother," Emillio said.

"What? You were mugged? When?" I asked, immediately gripped by another forgiveness tale I wasn't expecting. We were at the Dresden, a hotspot near the Los Angeles Press Club panel I'd moderated on the Thursday night of my West Coast jaunt. Surely the sun and three literary events in a row would lift me out of my funk. I felt cooler just being there, in a white leather booth I recognized from the movie *Swingers*.

My colleague Emillio was a six-foot-tall, handsome, slim thirty-five-year-old Latino San Francisco event planner with the hint of an accent. Moonlighting as a journalist, he'd flown to L.A. to interview me for a new magazine. He'd alluded to having a rough time coming out as gay, reminding me of a relative who'd also stayed closeted to his family. After hours answering his in-depth questions about the addiction therapy that my book chronicled, I was curious to know more about him. "So where are you originally from?"

"The Dominican Republic. My grandfather was a Sephardic Jew. My grandma was Catholic." Twirling his linguine around the fork, he added, "I didn't really know my mom until I was six years old."

"Why not?" I asked.

As Emillio sipped white wine, he described his mother Carmen, a Latin beauty, with light skin, dark hair, and almond eyes, an only child from a big family. At nineteen, she married his father, Luis, an older civil engineer. "She grew up lonely, wanting lots of kids, happy to get pregnant. My father was sexist, not letting her go to college or work. When I was one, they divorced. She went to New York, to make enough money to support us, leaving me with my grandparents in the Caribbean," he said, speaking quickly. "She thought she was doing it for me, to make all of our lives better, but I just wanted to be with my parents."

"That must have been so hard," I said, feeling like he was a kid brother, maybe projecting my own feelings of abandonment.

He was confused by Carmen's photos and letters ending, "Always thinking of you, your mami." His father rarely visited. Emillio developed a weird OCD tic, turning his head to the left, over and over. Then everything got worse when he was five years old. He was sexually abused by his grandmother's fifteen-year-old godchild.

"I'm so sorry," I said. "Did you tell your grandma?"

He shook his head. "No. She had a heart condition. I wanted to please her, not upset her. Anything sexual between boys was frowned upon. I told nobody."

"Not even your mother, when she returned?" I asked.

"By the time Mom came back to get me at six, I hardly knew her. I hated being torn from Grandma's arms and put into a car heading to the airport," he said. "It was a double loss. I was traumatized again."

Sleeping between his grandparents had made Emillio feel safe and special. He was angry his mother dragged him where he didn't know anyone or speak the language. "Obsessed with a Space Voltron cartoon, I thought the skyscrapers were robots," he said. "Eeeen-glish was weird, like the sound of crumpling paper."

At six, everything felt strange to him. His mom kissed and hugged him, then left for work as a seamstress in a factory. His dad visited New York, but they hardly knew each other. Emillio wet the bed. He liked the bilingual classes at school, but they switched him to an English-only class, where he was isolated. At home, nobody spoke Spanish in the hope that he'd learn English faster. He shared his mother with her new husband and their son Wesley, four years younger. Emillio resented his half-brother. "I cried every night for six months. She'd pick up my brother and me from the babysitter and take us to the Bronx Zoo and McDonald's for 'the Happy Family Meal,' saying 'I'm so lucky to finally have both my boys with me,'" Emillio recalled, avoiding my gaze. "We shared a bedroom, slept in bunk beds, but I wasn't close to my half-brother. Everyone at home shared the language I couldn't speak."

Emillio hated his stepfather. When Carmen discovered his shady business dealings, she divorced him and went to college. She brought home fabric. Sitting at the table with Emillio's notebook and her sewing machine, they did homework together. By fifth grade he'd learned English and was an honor roll student. His mother went to every spelling bee and recital.

"I bet academic accolades was your way to get her attention?" I speculated, thinking of my hard-to-please father and our family motto, "as if achievement were redemption." I was competitive with my brothers, too.

"Exactly." Emillio signaled the waiter for more wine. "Wesley was my rival. He had ADHD, needing lots of attention. So the way to my mom's heart was to do well in school. That's why I excelled."

I nodded. I'd been jealous of my brother, a breech birth who was dyslexic. My parents hired tutors and doctors for him starting in nursery school which, I'd reckoned, helped him be more confident and successful later on. I'd needed early intervention too but, like Emillio's, my problems weren't as externally visible.

When she took a garment district job, Emillio's mother met a new man named Alfred. At their wedding, Emillio told stepfather #2, "Mommy is still mine." Instead of understanding a nine-year-old's abandonment issues, Alfred repeated to friends how difficult his stepson was.

As a teenager, Emillio had a secret boyfriend he called his "best friend" or "project partner." He hated living with his mom, her second son, and husband #3 in the Bronx. At seventeen, he took an advertising job and rented his own apartment nearby. She cosigned his lease. His Manhattan friends knew he was queer. But he was haunted by a Dominican teacher who'd beat and disowned her gay son. When Carmen heard what the teacher said, she told Emillio, "It breaks my heart, but God forbid one of my kids turns out like that."

When she moved to Mexico to start a fabric business, Emillio only saw her at Christmas. He didn't tell her he was gay until he was twenty-one, over lunch at an uptown café. "I was afraid. The Latino culture is homophobic. My real father said, 'Any boy who grows up without his father is doomed to be a faggot.' He insulted me publicly. At thirteen, when I gained weight, he grabbed my stomach in front of his friends and said, 'Lose this or you'll ruin yourself,'" Emillio recalled. "I stopped contact with him when I graduated college. I haven't seen him in fifteen years."

Emotional abuse was a good reason to hold a grudge. Divorcing a toxic parent could be healing, Dr. Winters once told me, referring to his own mother. "Were you nervous about her reaction?" I asked Emillio.

"Yes. But she surprised me. 'Don't cut me out, I know you're gay,' she said. You don't need to hide it. I'll fight to defend you. It's the way God made you, now I understand,'" he repeated, his voice cracking.

She'd grown up too. Feeling closer to her, he admitted that he'd been sexually abused as a kid. His mother was upset and sympathetic. "Why did you tell her?" I asked.

"It was right after 9/11, a vulnerable time for us," he said, his leg fidgeting under the table. At forty-one, his mother had found out her third husband had a mistress and love child. She left him. Meanwhile Emillio was scared being an immigrant; some people assumed they were Arab and the World Trade Center bombings ignited prejudices. "I was at a restaurant after the attacks and a guy told me, 'You're probably happy now that your people are destroying everything.' I punched him."

I was startled. Emillio seemed like such a gentle soul. "Had you hit anyone before?"

"Only my brother," he admitted. "The bouncers said to leave in case the racist came back. He didn't. But my family was in emotional turmoil. Maybe that's why my mother apologized."

"When?" I asked, hungry for more specifics. "At your lunch together after 9/11? What exactly did she say?"

"She said 'Forgive me for everything I might have done.'" He rolled his eyes at the memory.

Clearly that was too vague. He needed a fuller, more specific apology: a confession of her error, a sincere recounting of her mistakes, ways to mend his hurt, and proof she saw his side. Her inadequate concession to what "she might have done" only reopened old wounds, exacerbating his original pain. She barely admitted she'd done anything wrong and didn't try to fix it. After divorcing husband #3, she soon had a new boyfriend in the Bronx, another jarring change for Emillio. Why the string of men? Carmen seemed afraid to be alone. It sounded like she'd made bad choices with multiple husbands without caring how much it damaged her son. I felt lucky my parents had stayed together and that Dr. Winters encouraged me to be with Aaron.

"Did you blame your mom for making it harder on you, with all those loser husbands?" I asked.

"Yes, I was upset with her," Emillio confirmed.

At twenty-two, he took a job at a hotel he enjoyed. But he'd get panic attacks when families needed his help. "I'd see Mr. and Mrs. Smith and their cute kids who wanted Broadway tickets and directions to toy stores. I felt overwhelmed. I'd lock myself in the bathroom, sweating and shaking. I thought I was crazy. I told my doctor." The physician referred Emillio to a therapist he saw for two years, covered by insurance. "She delved into my unresolved hurt from my mom's desertion. She was Jewish, warm, open. You remind me of her," he said.

I was flattered, and awed by his therapist's insight: She felt Emillio's panic attacks happened when he saw the happy family he'd wanted. He had to witness and service what he longed for but couldn't get.

Bringing it out in the open helped him. When Emillio was twenty-five, his mom wed husband #4. She invited her sons to Sunday dinner. Wesley, who married at twenty-one, brought his wife. Emillio came with his German boyfriend Arndt. Everyone was welcoming and kind. Yet Arndt and Emillio soon broke up. Wesley and his spouse had four kids. Watching his mother become a terrific grandma to his nephews and nieces rekindled lingering resentment.

Until one fall night, when he was thirty, and had just seen *Memphis* on Broadway with a friend. He took the subway to visit Carmen. Walking down her Bronx street, he felt a blow to his head. A guy in a red hoodie punched him in the face. Another pinned him down and searched his pockets. "I heard the intro to *Law & Order* in my head: 'Dun, dun,'" he joked.

"Oh god," I put my hand on his. "What happened?"

"I crawled to my mother's door. Seeing my bloody, battered face, she burst into tears. Shaking, she dialed an ambulance and called Wesley. They stayed with me as I was wheeled into the ER," he said, in a quieter tone. "She demanded a plastic surgeon stitch my wounds. Wesley challenged the dentist, who wanted to just file my broken teeth down. A detective asked questions. I mumbled answers. Mom got close to my mouth to hear. What she couldn't understand, I scribbled on paper. She didn't leave my side."

"The next day I was released, too weak to return to my apartment. She took me home to her place, tucking me into the guest room in the basement. I had a concussion, my nose and teeth broken, my lip stitched together in two places. I couldn't eat or sleep because of the pain. When I closed my eyes, I relived the assault. I couldn't start the new hotel job I'd committed to, the bruises and scars made it impossible. I laid in her basement, thinking of everything I'd lost. That night my *mami* lay next to me in bed, telling me stories in Spanish about how cute I was as a little *bebecito*," he said. "How she'd sent me a top-of-the-line modern blue stroller from New York. She caressed my forehead until I fell asleep."

The first week, his mom woke up three times a night to change his bandages. He couldn't walk or go to the bathroom without help. She cleaned him with a cloth, fed him Cream of Wheat and berries with a tiny spoon, the last food she'd given him as a baby, before she left. She paid his bills. As he recovered, she took him to the police station. Emillio thought he was the victim of a gay hate crime, but it turned out his attackers were part of a robbery gang. It bothered him to learn the perpetrators were blacks and Latino—local young men of color, like him—who targeted well-dressed people coming from work. He tried to identify his attackers in a lineup, but couldn't.

Insisting he stay with her until he healed, Emillio's mom gave him a weekly allowance. With no social life, he joined his mother, stepfather, and stepbrother for meals. She now had four foster kids living with her. He helped care for them, as well as the toddlers from her new daycare business.

"Was it hard to watch her take care of all these children when she hadn't taken care of you?" I asked.

"At first it hurt," he admitted. "But I wound up very close to Wesley and his wife and kids."

"Did you stay in contact after you moved to San Francisco?" I asked.

"We did, all the time. But sadly, Wesley died recently. At thirty, way too young," Emillio said.

My mouth fell open. This sweet guy couldn't catch a break. "I'm sorry."

"Heart attack. His ten-year-old son called 911, but they couldn't save him." Emillio looked like he was near tears. "I flew to New York to plan the funeral. Mom was distraught. She supports his family now."

"Sounds like Wesley never had an easy time of it either," I said.

Emillio now saw that his years with his grandparents were stable, while Wesley's happy façade hid deeper problems. "In those days they didn't diagnose or treat ADHD well. Wesley self-medicated with food, cigarettes, alcohol. They think he might have been bipolar," Emillio said.

"Do you blame your mom's past for both you and your brother's problems?" I asked.

"No. I stopped being mad at her," he told me. "After my accident, she held my hand at the hospital and police station. She nursed me back to health. Later, going to the Bronx Zoo and Yankee Stadium, eating home-cooked Dominican meals and painting a mural for her daycare kids helped me recover from my past. She completed a course for a government program in LGBT youth for her daycare, the first caregiver to do this in the Bronx. She never said it was for me, but I knew. I was touched. She wanted to make sure no other gay kid was hurt the way I was. I wasn't a single, childless, queer, lapsed Catholic misfit to her, or a disappointment. As an adult I saw that I was her first son who she adored and never meant to hurt."

"Could it be possible that she just had lousy taste in men?"

"She wanted a husband, kids, college, money and career in the U.S., everything all at once, too fast."

"Were you hoping to hear real remorse from her, for deserting you for those six years?" I asked.

"Yes. And she finally did apologize." He signaled the waiter for the check.

"Wait. When?" I asked, captivated. "You buried the lede! What did she say?"

"One night, changing my bandages in the basement, she said, 'I'm sorry I left you so young and couldn't protect you the way I wanted. I racked my brains to figure out what to do. Please forgive me.'"

Moved by her apology he said, "Don't worry, you're here now, that's what matters." They embraced.

"Did those words help?" I asked, amazed that even twenty-five years late, a sincere apology worked.

"Yes. But also the fourteen months she took care of me," he said. "After getting what I'd craved, the past stopped haunting me. It was resolved, like a crash course on getting my mother's love. It gave me closure."

That was the fix most people could never get: not just an apology, but a replacement for what was lost. Again, the reparation mattered as much as the apologizing. Unlike the case of Sharisse's mother moving in with her, Emillio's situation was accidental. A dark coincidence led to an unplanned form of immersion therapy. He became helpless, like the infant he'd been when she'd deserted him. At last she came through—with actions and words.

As we paid the bill, I heard my dad's voice echo: "If you don't have your mother's love, you have nothing." Manny overcame the horrors of the Holocaust because his mom was by his side. Emillio had the love of his mother, lost her, then found her again twenty-five years later. Some psychologists believed it impossible to get over traumatic events that occurred before you were three. Yet Emillio getting mugged turned into a blessing. His mother, helping him recover at thirty, healed the earlier trauma caused by her absence.

"Have you heard the line, 'It's never too late to have a happy childhood?'" I asked Emillio.

"Yes, it was like that," he said, as we walked outside. "We made up for the time we'd lost."

Hugging goodbye, I felt hopeful, as if anything could be repaired.

CHAPTER 17
GIVING THE APOLOGY YOU WANT TO GET

"I have always found that mercy bears richer fruit than strict justice."—Abraham Lincoln

Back at my hotel late I couldn't sleep, so I opened the sliding doors to the balcony. Staring at the ocean, I realized why Emillio's poignant tale had stayed with me. I'd heard it before, in my own family. My Grandpa Harry had a similar immigrant narrative. His mother came to America, leaving him behind with his grandmother, like Emillio's mom. Harry grew up to be a bitter old man. I'd spent decades outraged at how mean he was to my father.

Curious and lonely, I picked up the landline on the desk to dial my childhood house in Michigan. Dad, my fellow midnighter, picked up. "How old was Grandpa when his mom left him in Russia?" I asked.

"He was about six when she took off," Dad said, sounding strangely unsurprised that I'd phoned him so late with this odd question.

"So what really happened with Harry and his mom?" I needed to know now, from a different time zone.

"Well, Pauline married and had two kids, an infant girl who died, and my father," Dad told me. "In World War I, men were drafted into the Russian army for twenty-year stretches. Not wanting to go, her husband cut off two fingers, which a lot of men did. But he bled to death."

"That's horrific." I sat on the wicker chair, half outside.

Typical of my dad—who used to dissect calves' esophagi with my brothers in the kitchen sink before dinner—to share gruesome details. If you caught him in the right mood, he was a great storyteller, with an Isaac B. Singer eye for the dark Jewish twist.

When I was growing up, he was a busy hospital chief of medicine. During my college and grad school years, he'd hand the telephone to Mom when I called. Since he'd retired, he could get downright chatty. Now was my chance to keep him talking, to delve into our background, hoping to excavate the reason for our lifelong emotional distance.

"So what did your Grandma Pauline do after she lost her husband and daughter?" I asked.

"She left my father with her mother in Russia to go to New York," Dad continued in his telling-a-Yiddish-yarn voice. "There she met a man named Shapiro, remarried, and had another kid. But she never told her new husband about her first son. When he learned the truth, he sent money to the Hebrew Immigration Society to get Harry and his grandmother out of Russia. The pair ended up in Amsterdam, where a rabbi took Harry in and gave him an early bar mitzvah at twelve. But then the rabbi fell sick and died."

Hearing the Shapiro's family folklore brought me closer to my father. Since I'd fallen out with my paternal substitute, I was ping-ponging back to the original source.

"Tell me more," I begged.

"At Ellis Island, the immigration officer asked Harry's name. He said 'Harry Serota,'" Dad told me. "They wrote it down as his last name. The word *sierota* meant 'orphan' in Polish. He was mad at his mom for leaving him. So I think Harry was making a statement, declaring he had no family. In New York, Harry slept on the subway and streets."

Was that why my grandpa stayed so sour? One Hanukah, when he was visiting us, my brothers and I shopped at the mall for hours to find him a special audio tape of "My Yiddish Mama." Harry sang along with the whole song, then looked at his four grandkids and said, "Nu. The other version was better." When my dad saved Harry's life at his Midwest hospital, Grandpa growled, "You're no good. You're trying to kill me."

Harry had wanted his son to go into business with him, so they would be partners in Shapiro's Window Shades on Delancey Street. He was the only Jewish parent in history unhappy that his kid became a doctor. I was enraged at the way he'd treated my father; I skipped Harry's funeral, though the rest of our relatives were there. I was in grad school at the time. It was a way to make my own statement.

"So did Grandpa hate his mother for abandoning him in Poland?" I asked, assuming that resentment stayed with him, making him unpleasant and snarly for the rest of his life.

"It was love/hate," Dad said. "Harry wound up working for two brothers who taught him carpentry. They liked him and introduced them to their sister Yetta."

"Grandma Yetta," I smiled. This part of our family tree I knew. "And they fell in love and eloped."

"Yeah, but they lied and told Harry that Yetta was eighteen, like he was. She was really twenty-seven," Dad added.

I'd forgotten the rumors she was much older, focusing on the regal Lower East Side picture I'd had scanned of my late aunt, my dad, and their parents, who'd stayed married until Yetta died.

"So did Grandpa ever forgive his mother?"

"Yeah. Pauline lived to be ninety-nine, just enough time to reconcile," he chuckled. "When I was little, every week Dad would take my sister and me to visit his mother. We invited her for Passover and Hanukah."

I was captivated that Grandpa forgave his mom and stayed close until the end, like Emillio's recent fence mending. These stories gave me hope. It proved that what you did in the present could atone for the past.

"What was your grandma like?" I asked, watching the foamy waves smash against the shoreline outside my hotel room. I flashed to playing in the ocean in Florida as a kid when we'd visited Harry. My brothers had Mom's red hair and pale skin so they avoided the sun. I'd lucked out with Dad's olive coloring; we were the only Shapiros splashing around the water for hours. Swimming every summer recalled those rare moments of joy with my father.

"Pauline was nice to me. She outlived four husbands. I knew her as a heavy old Jewish lady. A little gruff," said the Prince of Gruff, who'd passed his bluntness down to me. My mom called the Shapiro personality "*Tuchos oyfn tish*"—literally "rear end on the table."

"It's amazing that Grandpa and his mother ultimately made up," I said, overjoyed to think my Great Grandma Pauline had the same happy ending as Emillio's mom, reconnecting with the son she'd left.

"Well, it wasn't perfect. When she was really old, she moved in with my father. But by then my mother was sick too," Dad said. "Harry tried to take care of them both."

It was unfair that she expected Grandpa to be her caretaker at the end, when she hadn't been there for him. Yet I guessed that a true reconciliation with a negligent parent, however rocky, was worth the struggle.

"I heard Pauline was a beauty in her day. She looked like my sister," Dad added. "And you."

That melted me. I'd been so intent on getting a mea culpa from Dr. Winters, but I was starting to see it was more important to untangle my estrangement from my dad. He'd been a workaholic, emotionally elsewhere, focusing only on our achievements, washing away everything else. But he'd never respected what I'd accomplished, and had criticized my work in hurtful ways, insisting I stop humiliating him by "spilling my guts in public." If he apologized, I might be able to tell him how much I'd hated the idea that doing what I loved in life had disappointed him. That was why I'd become an escape artist who'd fled his home and insults at sixteen.

In my twenties, visiting my parents when Harry moved into their house, I'd seen how antagonistic he was. I blamed him for my father's nastiness. I'd secretly skipped Harry's Michigan funeral to protest the awful way Harry had treated him, which somehow gave Dad permission to emulate that behavior with me. Since he had my mother and brothers nearby, I didn't think my father needed me to fly in from New York to be by his side. In retrospect, I should have been there. It was on my growing list of regrets.

Before I could say anything else, Dad jokingly yelled, "Don't write about this!" knowing I would.

I laughed, feeling jazzed up, alive and inspired for the first time in six months, as if it were possible to heal my heart sideways. I bet I wouldn't need Dr. Winters if I could have my father back. Paraphrasing Dad himself, I hoped that if you felt your father's love—even a few decades late—you could get over anything.

"I'm sorry I skipped Grandpa's funeral," I said quietly. "I didn't go because I was so pissed off at him for how he treated you. But I should have flown to Michigan to go. For you."

"Your grandpa never really forgave me for leaving New York," Dad told me. "He expected me to stay around and care for him and my mother as they aged, like they did in the old country."

Was he ignoring my apology? Or connecting his father's hurt with his own, when I'd moved East, away from him?

"He refused welfare and food stamps," Dad continued. "He'd rather work two or three jobs at the same time. He didn't have much, but he supported me until I could make a living. He gave me my work ethic."

"So the workaholic gene I inherited came from Grandpa?"

"You remember him at the end, when he was eighty-three and came to live with us for six months," he said. "With kidney failure, his world collapsed. He was thrown into an unfamiliar scary environment, dependent on me because he was ill. He struck out at everyone around him. Finally he refused to go on dialysis and died twenty-four hours later. It made me very sad. He was a great father to me when I was little. I loved him."

He'd never told me any of this. At eighty, ailing from his inherited heart and kidney problems, my dad seemed to be revising his assessment of his father. Hearing the emotion in his tone choked me up. Then I recalled how shocked I'd been to learn that my grandpa's will had left his money and possessions to my mother, not to his only son. Harry obviously knew my parents shared everything, but he had to get in one last zinger from the grave. I didn't mention that now. I suspected our talk had little to do with Harry, who'd been in the ground almost thirty years. I was just grateful my father's husky voice was still echoing through the long-distance receiver I held to my ear.

"Love you Daddy," I told him, my voice cracking.

"Me too," he said quickly before getting off the phone.

Staring at the pull of the slow waves in the water below, I was struck by what apologizing to my father had uncovered. Although I'd always wanted him to tell me *he* was sorry, I now regretted that I hadn't been the one to say it sooner.

CHAPTER 18
WHAT YOU CAN'T SEE CAN BLIND YOU

"Forgive and remember."—Barbara Kingsolver

In a cherished photograph of my father and me when I was three, I'm wearing a carrot-colored dress with tights and patent leather shoes. He's handsome and disheveled, a bespectacled thirty-year-old medical resident in blue scrubs, with dark wavy hair the exact shade as mine. I'm looking up at him adoringly as he holds my little hand, leading me across the street to the Candy Cone ice cream parlor. Between his fingers is an unfiltered Chesterfield. My mother—who probably took the photo—isn't visible. Just Dad, holding my grip while teaching me the poem game, where he'd say one line and I'd jump in with the next.

". . . beauties that I loved/Are in my memory," he crooned. "I spit into the face of time . . . "

"That has transfigured me!" I shouted, like he taught me. "Let's sing it again, Daddy."

According to family legend, I was an early talker who was memorizing entire poems before I'd turned two, marching around our house reciting Robert Louis Stevenson's *I Had a Little Shadow*. For him.

Although my father and I soon stopped sharing poetry, a Chesterfield stolen from his pack was the first cigarette that touched my thirteen-year-old lips. I couldn't quit until I was forty, around the time he, too, kicked the habit. I thought of that picture during the years my dashing, dark-haired therapist metaphorically held my hand through the haze of nicotine withdrawal. It was as if I'd regressed to three, trusting another mad male doctor reciting lyrical lines, this time walking me away from the smoke. I would have followed him anywhere.

"You're so vulnerable now, like you have no skin. So when you go outside even the air hurts," Winters had recited, like a haiku in 2001, the year I stopped smoking. His poignant words both fired me up and soothed my mind as my father's poems had. My shrink became my shield. So during our rift, I felt unprotected again, as if he'd left me alone in the middle of rush-hour traffic on a treacherous strip of highway.

"Why doesn't he care that his desertion gave me weird nightmares?" I emailed Stargazer, annoyed I was still shell shocked, five months after our fight.

"He acted insanely. Stop looking for a rational motive," Stargazer replied.

Was that coming from the Jungian or the astrologer in him? I scrawled "he's insane" in my notebook. What happens when you lose your voice of reason? I'd felt frenzied, as if I were still withdrawing from a substance, one big naked nerve ending needing a fix. Instead of inhaling nicotine or pot, sipping alcohol or sniffing cocaine, I craved the intensity of fatherly wisdom to pull me out of my pain.

"Sue, what do you want?" Stargazer asked.

That one was easy. "I want my good father back."

"You have your good father back," he said. "Winters was just a fake you hired to fill in for a while."

Was that true? I no longer felt in conflict with my dad. I phoned him often and saw him a few times a year, loving him distantly, defensively, the closest I could get to someone who could pierce my calm at any second with ugly, unsolicited commentary on my opinion or work.

"I love your work," Winters had told me after reading my first drafts, offering me the praise I'd wanted most from my father. Lately, Stargazer was a kind of Winters substitute, as I latched onto the next captain in a train of paternal surrogates.

"Why can't I see you every week?" I asked Stargazer.

"The planets don't move as quickly as you do," he insisted. "Bimonthly is enough."

In the children's book *Are You My Mother?*, a baby bird asks everyone he meets that question. As Winters spent more time in Arizona and less in the East, I'd embarked on the "Are You My Therapist?" version, seeing eight shrinks in eight days to find his substitute. His presence in my life was so magical that my 2009 debut novel parodied my pathetic quest for his replacement. To celebrate, I'd thrown wildly popular *Speed Shrinking* parties, enlisting a diverse array of top head doctors I knew to participate—including Dr. Winters himself, before we fell out. But now I saw Stargazer was right. I'd had enough therapy to know I was really asking: "Are You My Daddy?" And to see I was still unresolved.

"Thanks for the speed-shrink experience. Breathtakingly innovative," Dr. Vatsal Thakkar emailed after he'd taken part in an AIDS charity event I'd hosted at Housing Works in Soho. Vatsal was younger, with an eclectic Eastern aura; he was more exotic than Winters the WASP. An Indian-born psychiatrist, he had a higher degree than Winters's PhD in clinical psychology. He'd finished a doctor of medicine, internship, and residency, like my father. Perhaps he could help me finish the Winters puzzle?

"I need a new shrink in real life so I can sort through a problem. Do you have any time?" I called Vatsal to ask.

"I mostly do two-hour medical consultations," he said.

I talked him into one forty-five-minute talk therapy session at his midtown office for $200, what Winters used to charge, and took Vatsal's first opening, two weeks away. I received an email from Winters that night. It felt like male radar, the way an estranged ex would call right before you undressed for a new beau. "As your therapist I would never have wanted to do anything but help you," he wrote. His tone wasn't combative anymore. I scrolled down to see that his email was responding to a question I'd sent back in September: "Don't head doctors take the Hippocratic oath to do no harm?" Still, I wished he'd taken it farther and said, "I'm sorry you felt harmed by my actions."

I didn't know what I was "seeing" wrong. He could have simply quieted my fears by saying "I had my reasons. I'll explain later." I imagined him rereading my old emails to discover why I'd disappeared. I hoped deleting him would heal me faster. But it was like my blood was still knotted inside my veins.

"Why would Dr. Winters lie to me about seeing my student Haley after he'd promised not to?" I asked Vatsal at our session, after I'd filled him in.

"It sounds like he made boundary mistakes," Vatsal said. "But if you build up a man inappropriately, he has to fall."

"Is that an Indian saying? Sounds Yiddish. Do you mean that Winters is just human?" I liked that Vatsal didn't trash my ex-shrink. He seemed respectful of Winters as a fellow professional, clearly recognizing how much I'd revered him.

"When he helped you quit your addictions, you imbued him with supernatural power." Vatsal spoke slowly. He was eloquent and paternal, though we were the same age.

"I did. It felt like magic," I conceded. I hoped this new doctor could unravel the estrangement that had ruined my serenity. But Winters's comfortable office in my neighborhood—filled with embroidered pillows and paintings—had spoiled me. I didn't like schlepping through midtown traffic. Vatsal's space was smaller and more sterile than Dr. Winters'. No artwork, and instead of soft light, he had a bright fluorescent overhead. "You need a lamp with a dimmer switch," I suggested. Then I shared my recent nightmare of riding erratically in an orange Cadillac, Winters at the wheel. I couldn't get out of the car.

"Even your dreams have been in therapy," Vatsal told me.

I took out my notebook to jot that down. "My first car was an orange Cutlass my dad got me for my sixteenth birthday. I bumped into two guys I was in love with at a party. Freaked, I totaled it on the way home."

"Were you okay?" Vatsal asked.

"Not a scratch. My dad saw the car first. All he said was 'Thank God you're not hurt.'"

"I read the essay about Dr. Winters you published last year in the *Times*," Vatsal said.

"You googled me?" I was flattered. Maybe I could get used to Vatsal's bright light and midtown office. "Think it's a pattern? In Freudian dream analysis, driving is supposed to represent your sexuality. Did I tell you Winters was born in August, a Leo like my father? Are you into astrology?"

"You sure you don't have ADD?" Vatsal asked.

"I don't."

"I was joking. You speak so quickly," he explained.

"You speak so slowly." I laughed.

Good, he was chilling me out. I just wanted the Winters saga to go back to being a swashbuckling fable about the heroic Addiction Doctor healing me. I needed it to be funny again, not scary and tragic.

Vatsal was married with two kids, but, like Dr. Winters, there were no pictures. I knew that shrinks intentionally kept their personal life blank so patients could project their own craziness.

"Listen, you've lived through more emotional cycles with Dr. Winters than anybody," Vatsal said. "You trusted him, loved him, idolized him, felt betrayed, hated him, killed him off. Now you're in mourning."

I nodded, scrawling down what he said.

"It will be intriguing to learn the last chapter," Vatsal added, seeming truly curious.

"What if, after fifteen years, we never speak again?" I asked.

"This is not the ending," Vatsal told me, sounding sure. "Here's a metaphor: a commuter was enraged when a woman in an SUV stopped abruptly to get something in the backseat, almost causing an accident. He didn't know the driver's infant was choking. Similarly, there is something you don't know about Dr. Winters' life that will shed light on why he hurt you."

I'd never thought of that angle. "What religion are you?" I asked, not knowing if he'd divulge personal facts, like Dr. Winters did.

"My family is Hindu."

"Is that view Hinduistic?" Had I just made up a word?

"Well." He paused. "I was an immigrant who came to America as a baby. When my parents settled in Tennessee, there wasn't even a Hindu temple there. So my outlook is informed by being an outsider. In Western medicine, there's often one established paradigm. With an Eastern bent, we're open to more possibilities, to seeing a bigger picture."

"Do you think that's what Winters meant by emailing 'Things are not how you see them?'" I wanted to know, frustrated to not be able to see what I was missing. "Do you think he could tell me something that would fix us?"

"Is that what you want?"

"I want him to understand why I'm so upset, explain the reasons he lied to me and saw Haley, dump her forever, and offer to return to being my shrink. And then I'll say no."

"That would be the Rolls-Royce of endings," Vatsal said. I noted that he'd let me stay ninety minutes.

Two weeks later, at our next appointment, I arrived to find an Art Deco lamp with a dimmer switch in his office. "You've been enlightened!" I told him.

"It's not symbolic. I just needed better lighting in here." He grinned.

Glancing around, I noticed my first book on his top shelf. Had I missed it last time? Now that had to be a good omen. "You could be my new shrink," I proposed.

"I barely do talk therapy. I focus on medical disorders," he said. "Being a diagnostician is what interests me."

"I could feign having narcolepsy?"

Perhaps pitying me, Vatsal offered to be a temporary consultant for six sessions. Over the next month and a half, when I wasn't sharing my pathetic hurt over Dr. Winters, I asked about Hinduism. He said some scholars called it the world's oldest faith. With 900 million followers, it was the third-largest religion, behind Christianity and Islam, though 95 percent of Hindus lived in India, where Vatsal was from. Their holy writings were called the Veda, meaning "wisdom," and comprised of ancient scriptures. Hindus were both monotheistic (like followers of Judaism, Christianity, and Islam) and henotheistic, holding the belief in one god without denying many equal gods. Indeed, there were thirty-three million Hindu gods and goddesses. Their dramatic names, such as Shiva the Destroyer and Vishnu the Preserver, were like little poems. Of the twelve classical world religions, Baha'i, Buddhism, Confucianism, Jainism, Shinto, Sikhism, Taoism, Zoroastrianism and Hinduism had many different deities.

I was intrigued that, in the Hindu view, the worship of one god didn't deny the existence of others. It reminded me of how Stargazer preferred astrology to psychology because astrological theories encompassed all mythologies, unlike Freud's intense focus on the Oedipal complex. Astrology was actually a facet of folk Hinduism. My student Lavanya's essay "Zodiac Hijack: How Astrology Ended My Otherwise-Happy Relationship," was about how she fell for a Hindu guy, only to be dumped because, he informed her, their horoscopes were incompatible for marriage.

Seeing Vatsal was mind-expanding. He was non-judgmental. He asked me questions about the good Dr. Winters had done me, readjusting my focus. He reminded me that many things coexisted: Dr. Winters could be a kind person who helped me for fifteen years, while also hurting me for reasons that I—and he—didn't yet understand. Vatsal explained that forgiveness was a cardinal virtue in Hindu Dharma, a "main truth." Hinduism held that a person who did not forgive carried the baggage of bad memories, anger, and unresolved emotions that would limit their present and their future. Vatsal said his people were big on karma, where harmful actions from the past created more future harm and good deeds perpetuated goodness.

To further understand Hinduism's take on forgiveness, I asked my colleague Puloma, who'd spoken highly of her family's Swami, if she could connect us. After many phone calls, emails and pulling strings through her Hindu mother from a Canadian Vedanta chapter, I felt honored to be granted a fifteen-minute phone conservation with Swami Sarvapriyananda, the middle-aged leader of the New York Vedanta Society.

"I heard that forgiveness is a cardinal virtue for Hindus," I said. "Do you agree?"

"There are many schools of Hinduism," he answered slowly, in a warm voice. "Truth is one, but the wise speak of it differently."

That offered an evocative way to see the varied wisdom that both clergy and laypeople had shared with me through my forgiveness tour. There wasn't a singular interpretation, but there did seem to be a universal remedy.

"If someone offended me but won't apologize or repent, would you advise forgiving him anyway?" I asked.

"For us, God is imminent in everyone—even the person who offended you. Holding resentment against him—and thus God—keeps you stuck in what we call the Veils of *Maya*, which we see as ignorance and delusion, and thus away from enlightenment."

"So is my problem that I can't see the whole picture?" I repeated Vatsal's theory, scrawling notes.

"Yes, we are often mistaken about what we think we are," the Swami told me.

"Are Hindu attitudes towards forgiving similar to the Jews, Christians, or Muslims?"

"You should read Huston Smith's *The World's Religions,*" he recommended.

"I have it right here. I just read the Hindu chapter!" I was proud, like a kid acing a test. "I heard the author was born in China to a white Methodist missionary family."

"He actually helped open our first Vedanta chapter in America, in St. Louis in 1938, where he studied," the Swami told me. "They wouldn't sell a house to a brown man. So he signed the lease for us himself."

Talk about good karma.

"Do Hindus have absolute forgiveness, like Jesus's 'Father, forgive them, for they know not what they do'?"

"Our attitude is similar to a passage from the Gospel of Matthew, after Jesus warns that anger leads to murder," the Swami replied. "It basically says: if you offer a gift at God's altar and remember your brother has something against you, you first reconcile with your brother, then come and offer your gift."

"So you have to mend mortal rifts yourself, because animosity towards your fellow man gets in the way of your spirituality?" I asked.

"I would say, holding onto anger is poison; forgiving is nectar. A person who sins will suffer from their own bad karma. If you dish out retribution, you will suffer too. But you can make the choice to do good instead."

"Even when the anger is justified and self-protective?" I couldn't quite let it go yet.

"An angry grudge is like lighting a fire that destroys the place where it's lit," he said. "It burns your own heart first."

I was moved by his words. My heart was still burning. To fight my ignorance and delusion, I had to douse the internal flames and officially undo the Yiddish curse I'd cast on my doctor. Not by reaching out to Dr. Winters, but by looking into myself and remembering the insights he'd shared. After speaking to the Swami, I lit a salt flower candle, a present from a student, placing it atop *The World's Religions* paperback on my desk, messy with books, spirals, forgiveness folders. Swaying to Macy Gray's *On How Life Is,* I read aloud Eastern karmic principles of ricocheting goodness and Confucius's reminder to hold onto kindness more than wounds. I thought of the Jewish and Christian concept of the Book of Life, where all deeds were recorded, hearing Dr. Winters say, "You can be very right and very alone." I decided his past kindness outweighed his desertion, and deemed our bad blood over.

I willed my memories back to the best of my one-time advisor while whispering goodbye. I didn't need him—or my anger towards him—anymore. Regardless of whether I'd ever see him again, I forgave, surpassed, and left him to move on.

The Veils of *Maya* were lifted. Or maybe male radar struck again, letting him know I was totally out the door, because right after my forgiveness dance and last Vatsal session in March, I received another email from Dr. Winters. It had an entirely different tone.

"I'm sorry, Sue," he wrote. "I never meant to hurt you."

Tears stormed my eyes as I read his remarkable apology: "Obviously I screwed up. But I would welcome the chance to meet with you one more time to share important thoughts."

My heart pounded as if demanding pain be released from the prison of my chest. The good Winters was back in real life. Like an addict glimpsing free heroin, I had a manic urge to see him and spill the hurt I'd felt and share all the astute religious philosophies I'd found. But I was afraid, not quite trusting my instincts. Before I succumbed to his spell and ceremoniously forgave him to his face, I double checked with my shrink chorus.

"Listen to what he has to say, then you can decide," Vatsal suggested.

"Different tone, much more contrite," Judy texted. "Something shifted."

"The huge 'importance' of his thoughts feels familiar," Stargazer sniffed. "But hear the guy out."

When Aaron came home, I showed him the email I'd printed and read eighty times.

"I'll come with you," my husband offered. "Or I'll wait outside if you want."

That night we watched *Damages*, a legal thriller on TV, holding each other for an hour on the couch without speaking, as Winters once mandated we do to calm me during withdrawal symptoms from nicotine. After a gut-wrenching scene where a terminally ill father doesn't get to say goodbye to his son, Aaron turned to me and whispered, "You have to forgive him in person."

"For closure?"

"Because he was kind to you for many years." He kissed my forehead. "We probably wouldn't be together without him." I looked in his eyes. Something about the father's farewell on television had moved him. Aaron had never recovered from losing his dad five years earlier. Compared to the enormity of that loss, forgiving an apologetic, still-living paternal figure was a no-brainer.

"I'll go see him alone," I told my husband. Then I had second thoughts.

"What if he argues why it's important for him to treat Haley and wounds me all over again?" I asked Vatsal.

"At the least his words will unlock the mystery," Vatsal answered. "And you hate mysteries."

I did. I was the type who read the last page of a thriller first, to get rid of the agony of not knowing. I'd even scan reviews of TV and film whodunits before deciding if I'd watch, which drove Aaron insane. Vatsal implied that truth equaled healing. I was petrified it would be the opposite.

"Is it real forgiveness if I only tell him I forgive him *after* he says he's sorry?" I called to ask Stargazer.

"Sue, forgiveness is overrated," he repeated. "Holding grudges can be smart and self-protective."

I knew what he meant. "If it's a fake or confusing apology, it could undo all the progress I've made. I've been fine without him for six months."

"You haven't been without him," Stargazer argued. "You punched him when you kickboxed, injuring yourself. You scrawled about him in your journal, fought with him in your head, and analyzed him with other shrinks, priests, rabbis, and gurus. You were with him more than you were before."

Damn. I'd almost convinced myself that living without Winters for 180 days meant I was over him. Seeing him again could be risky. It might be impossible to get what I craved: an apology that would make sense of it all. I heard Vatsal's voice reminding me there was something I didn't know, an essential puzzle piece missing. I waited several days to answer the email—an eternity for a recovering addict. I'd finally learned impulse control. Only quitting Winters could teach me how to manage my fierce addiction to him.

I refused to meet at his office, where he'd be in control. I counter-offered a phone talk. He proposed an in-person meeting wherever I wanted, with Aaron or Stargazer or anybody else I needed there. I knew he worked as late as I did on his visits to New York. So I suggested a drink at Arté, a café between my home and his office, on Tuesday at 10 p.m.

When the seminar I ran at my apartment ended at nine, I was edgy, not knowing what to do for an hour. I took a shower, shampooing my hair, though I'd already washed and conditioned that morning, as if to cleanse away six months of sadness. I feared I'd be early, pathetically waiting an hour, since he was always late. Six months was the longest I'd gone without seeing him in fifteen years.

"With all that Pluto, just thank God you were only betrayed by your shrink," Stargazer kept telling me, "and not your husband, mother, or banker." I didn't feel thankful as I slowly blew my hair dry, the heat soothing. I was as unstrung as I'd felt the night I'd caught him with Haley. I repainted my face and put on a black sweater, black boots, and black pants, funeral attire. The upside to my severed link with Winters was that I hadn't regained the thirteen pounds I'd lost. But what I used to call "the breakup diet" seemed less cute at this age, accompanied by a breakdown.

Walking to the restaurant, I rehearsed telling him how his deception had hurt me and infiltrated my nightmares. I hated how much I still wished he would mend me though I'd already sort of mended myself. I kept checking my watch, paranoia lurking. Vatsal implied I wouldn't get the Rolls-Royce of endings. What would be the most defective lemon on the lot? I envisioned arriving to find Dr. Winters sitting at a table with Haley, who'd be all dressed up and flirty, running her fingers through her long, fiery red hair.

CHAPTER 19
WHY YOU SHOULD LEAD THE LEAST SECRETIVE LIFE
MARCH 2011

"To forgive is to set a prisoner free and discover that the prisoner was you."—theology professor Lewis B. Smedes

Turning the corner on West 9th Street, I caught his silhouette. No longer "Dr." in my mind, he'd become "Winters," demoted from authority figure. He was waiting outside, typing on his BlackBerry. For the first time ever, he was early. By himself. I was nervous, not sure which version of Winters to expect. He was wearing a brown bomber jacket that reminded me of a favorite picture of my father as a teenager on the Lower East Side, in *his* dusty leather jacket, looking like an old-time gangster. Tonight Winters seemed thinner, almost gaunt. His hair was shorter. I slipped my hands in my pockets. When he saw me, he clicked off his device, nodding. He seemed anxious, too.

We headed wordlessly inside the Italian bistro I frequented. Martino, the charming owner, double kissed me. I didn't introduce them. Who would I say Winters was? He wasn't my friend. "Former therapist" would sting, like saying "ex-husband" fresh from signing divorce papers. I asked for a table in the back room, which was empty. I was edgy and guarded,

Ingrid Bergman in an old spy movie. This public meeting with him felt illicit, like something terrible could happen any second. I flashed to all the mobsters who'd shot each other in restaurants.

We sat down, took off our jackets as the waiter brought menus and little glasses of water. I sipped slowly, simmering. In therapy, I'd spill everything the second I sat down, to beat the clock. When I interviewed people about the apologies they'd never received, I made immediate eye contact and launched right into my intrusive questions. But sitting in front of the person I wanted remorse from, I was reluctant to meet his gaze or speak. In successful business negotiations, Aaron advised, you let the other party begin talking and throw out the initial offer before you give anything away. I stayed silent.

"I'm sorry I hurt you." He fidgeted with his napkin. His tone was genuine, regretful.

Gripping my glass, I took another sip. "Traumatized me," I corrected, crunching ice.

"I didn't mean to." He drank his water.

If there were four parts to a good apology, he'd hit a double: #1 acknowledging the offense and #3 expressing remorse. I longed for #2, the explanation. I looked up to scan his eyes. What couldn't I see?

"I've felt more emotions with you than anyone in my life," I confessed, stealing Vatsal's line. "I loved you, idolized you, hated you, killed you off, mourned you, and now you're resurrecting."

"How Catholic of us," he said.

Especially for a Jew and a WASP, I thought, suppressing the urge to pull my notebook from my purse and scrawl that down, the way I used to record incisive jokes and adages he'd share during our sessions.

"So what's going on with you?" I crossed my legs to appear casual, pretending my sanity hadn't been at stake.

"I'm seeing my mother next month. At a nursing home in Texas. She had a stroke."

That totally threw me. I recalled the poem he'd written about his eighty-year-old alcoholic mom who'd wished him dead. He hadn't seen her in thirty-eight years. Now he looked vulnerable, a battered little boy. Was it a ploy for sympathy? It was working. At least he wasn't small-talking me.

"You must have mixed feelings about that reunion," I said, sounding like him.

"That's the understatement of the century." He smiled.

Sinatra's version of *I've Got You Under My Skin* played. Winters ordered a Diet Coke. I craved a vodka tonic, joint, and a More Menthol Light, my old brand. I chose Chamomile tea with honey.

"Can you turn the music down?" I asked the waiter.

"You're such a New Yorker," Winters commented.

What did that mean, that in Arizona they tolerated loud music getting in the way of an important conversation? When the waiter brought our drinks, I spooned honey into my mug.

Winters watched me, then commented, "You're using too much."

How rude. Then I realized we'd never been in a restaurant together. In fifteen years, we'd discussed all his substance abuse theories in his office, while analyzing my smoking, eating and drinking habits ad nauseam. Yet he'd never actually seen me smoke, eat, or drink.

"How's Aaron?" he asked.

Enraged at you, I didn't say. *He had to save me from you.* "Good. How's your wife?"

I'd never met Claudia, a therapist for cancer patients. She ran a charity in Arizona, where they'd relocated after their Battery Park brownstone was ruined on 9/11. I'd been impressed with his description of her as a fearless crusader and selfless mother. A year ago he'd mentioned, in passing, that she'd needed minor surgery to remove a benign tumor. When I'd asked over the summer, he'd said she was expected to make a full recovery.

"She's not well," he said now, his voice cracking.

I leaned forward. "What happened?"

"It was malignant. She needed neurosurgery. There was nerve damage."

I didn't know it was in her brain. "What does that mean?" I was alarmed. "Is she in the hospital?"

"No, she's recovering at home. But she's half-deaf, can't drive, work, fly, or walk without a cane. They don't know if she'll improve."

"Oh no. I had no idea."

This was what I couldn't see! I suddenly saw it all from Vatsal's clinical viewpoint: a caring doctor of fifteen years abruptly slips off the rails. Of course, there had to be an external catalyst for Daniel's complete turn-about. Hearing the sadness in his voice erased my anger, his eyes no longer menacing, just agonized.

"They sent me a $50,000 hospital bill the insurance didn't cover," he added.

"But why the hell didn't you just tell me your wife was sick?" He'd shared so much else: escaping his abusive mother, testifying at his parents' trial for the custody of his kid sister, his past addictions. If he'd said he was treating Haley and any patient who called him to pay medical bills, I would have understood. And recommended him to others. It was his continued deception that unnerved me.

"It was hard for me tell anyone for a while." He looked more stressed than I'd ever seen him. "She's private. And maybe I was in denial that I couldn't keep working the way I always did."

What I hadn't known was that behind his healing façade, his life was falling apart. Here was #2, the explanation for his behavior. If Aaron was seriously ill, I doubted I would be able to keep working. Still, a spouse's illness didn't immediately exonerate everything. If so, caretakers every-where would be quitting their long-term commitments to go on crime sprees. A doctor in charge of a patient should have handled it better. I wished he would have trusted me with the truth.

"Why not email me that you had medical issues? Or personal prob-lems?" I asked. After fifteen years, didn't he owe me that?

"They said she was dying and there was nothing we could do. I regressed back into the nightmare of my childhood, shattering the illu-sion that the world was safe," he said. "I lost my home, my sanctuary, my city. I was scared I'd lose my wife. I couldn't fix her or protect my family."

The Jewish guilt towards my Protestant shrink ricocheted as I revised my overview: How unfair he'd had to leave his native city in the aftermath of the World Trade Center catastrophe, only to have his Arizona life upended too. I irrationally worried he'd given me all of his wisdom and magical powers but didn't keep enough for himself.

I drank my tea, resisting the urge to add more spoonfuls of honey. "The cancer didn't spread?"

"No. The surgeon who operated said it was a miracle they were able to get the whole tumor. But she may not recover any further."

"How's your daughter handling it?" I recalled his only girl was thirteen.

"Kathy was diagnosed with chronic lung disease. She needs treatment too."

His entire family was sick. How horrible. He was like Job. "I'm so sorry," I told him.

The way he'd acted had nothing to do with me. He morphed from mean monster into a healer who couldn't cure his wife and daughter, a proud man too overcome with grief to focus on work. I wanted to apologize for not knowing, to reach for his hand to comfort him. But physical contact was the one boundary we never broke.

I inhaled, taking in his apology and my own. Exchanging the words "I'm sorry" with him made me feel lighter. The unbearable burden of believing he'd intentionally hurt me was lifted from my shoulders, head and heart.

"Hating you screwed up my senses," I said. "It felt like my blood was clogging my veins."

"I'm glad you had Aaron to talk to," he told me.

"It was hard for him to leave you that phone message telling you to stop contacting me," I conceded.

"What message? I never got it."

Of course he had. He'd responded by emailing me, "So your husband speaks for you now?" I'd been so astonished, I'd printed it out for proof. But I saw he'd really forgotten. It was a different kind of heartache, like catching the initial sign of a parent's dementia. For the first time, I felt older, stronger, and clearer than him.

"You've been through hell." I mirrored his feelings, like I was *his* therapist, recalling that he once warned, "Unhappy people have nothing to give. They need all their energy to function. You'd get more from a happy person you barely know."

"I feel like I lost the whole year," he said, staring at me, dazed.

In the months without him, I'd transferred our intense bond to my husband, now my closest confidant. Yet after a decade and a half, changing the guard was agonizing. There were secrets I'd rather share with a therapist, like the details of my insatiable addictions. And how upset I remained that he'd chosen Haley's feelings over mine. His words did not fully erase my distress or make him less accountable for what happened. If this was our last meeting, I didn't want to fake it or leave emotions repressed.

"It still bothers me you're treating my student after I told you she was stalking me," I admitted.

"I'm not treating her anymore."

"Not at all?" I hated that this still mattered so much. I could hear him saying, "Susan, *everything* is too important to you."

"I haven't seen her in five months."

I was confused. I'd pictured them Skyping daily, in harmony and constant touch, the way he and I had been.

"It was a mistake," Winters conceded.

His Haley update seemed game-changing. Because I won the contest I hadn't wanted to play?

"You'll have no contact with Haley?" It came out half-question, half-ultimatum, as if I was negotiating terms to take back a cheating lover. That was #4, the reparation: He was here with me, admitting I was right six months ago, explaining why he'd been amiss, cutting her out of the picture she never belonged in.

"I will not see or speak to Haley again," he said.

I was elated that Haley was out. But wait! I wasn't getting back in. This was the conclusion Vatsal said was too dangerous to hope for. Only now I didn't want a Rolls-Royce ending; I wanted Daniel to stop hurting and his family to heal. He looked so worn down. He needed this debacle to go away as much as I did. But why exactly?

"Are you doing this to shut me up?" I asked.

"Yes! Shut the hell up already!" he said.

We both laughed. But then I feared it was true. "You really just want to quiet me down?"

"Things co-exist," he said. "I don't want you upset anymore. I want this bad blood finished."

It was. It occurred to me that talking about our rift to my husband, Stargazer, Moshe, and others we knew in common—leading the least secret life—probably pushed him towards this apology. We hadn't known his advice would wind up saving me from him.

"Anything else?" the waiter asked. We shook our heads.

But I wasn't ready to bid Daniel goodbye forever. He was the one who'd seen me clearest, the only father figure who'd loved my work. For years we'd ended each talk by confirming the time of our following session. Now everything was altered. Cutting him off while angry kept us entwined; hatred was easier. Letting go of my wrath, I'd have to deal with how much I missed the good Dr. Winters and move on, without him. I felt extremely grateful that he'd given me a complete, mature, flawless apology. How many people could get that? He'd offered valid acknowledgment of the offense. Explanation for why it occurred. Sincere expression of remorse. Reparation ensuring it wouldn't happen again.

Yet mending our broken bond was still complicated. The real problem with forgiving: what comes next?

"How are you feeling now?" he asked, wrestling the shrink reins back.

"My mind is racing. I keep coming up with different subtexts for what happened," I said.

"Like what?"

"You scheduled Haley right before me, then ran late so I'd catch you lying. You felt guilty. So having me see her leave your office was a way to get out of the deception," I tried. "You alienated me, expecting me to cut you off, like your mother did. Then you apologized and wanted a reunion, knowing I'd forgive you."

"But how would I know that?" he asked.

"Because you know me. And unlike your mom, I'm not a raging alcoholic. You fixed my addictions, the way you couldn't fix hers," I said, wishing we could go on talking, start over. Anything but end. "You know, I read over the pages of the addiction book we worked on. It's not bad. Maybe we should finish and publish it."

"We should." His eyes lit up, like it was the best idea anyone ever had.

I felt like we were a married couple, seconds away from getting a divorce, deciding to have a baby instead. Was I being competitive with Haley? She may have seen him too, but if Dr. Winters and I were coauthors, I'd be the one having his metaphorical child. That last bit of over-analysis I kept to myself.

The waiter brought the check. I looked at my watch. Our fifty minutes was up. I let him pay this time.

CHAPTER 20
SEEING THE OTHER SIDE
APRIL 2011

"Before we can forgive one another, we have to understand one another."—activist Emma Goldman

Enveloped in the magic dust of Dr. Winters' mea culpa, I wasn't completely at peace. My six-month hatred of Haley haunted me. I usually championed my students; I'd never not wished a protégé well before. She was a small-town girl estranged from her mother. Even if she'd acted reckless or insatiable, I'd once been a hungry girl devouring the city too. I recalled she was turning thirty next week. I wanted to give her the liberation that my former guru's apology had just given me.

"Dr. Winters and I reconciled; I hope we can too," I emailed her.

"Thanks. I never meant to hurt you," she instantly replied.

Six months of madness melted to memory. I almost said, "Let's take a long walk." Then I caught myself. "Protégés aren't real friends," Dr. Winters had warned. "Mentors have all the power." I recalled the Muslim prophet who told his nemesis, "As much as possible do not come before me," and Gary Weinstein's words, "You can forgive someone you'll never see again, just to move on." There was a difference between forgiving and reconnecting. I shut my laptop.

At 9 the next morning, my phone rang. "Oh Sue, I'm so glad to be back in touch. I just hated fighting with you," Haley said.

I usually resented being interrupted from work but I was drawn in by her soft lilting voice. "Me too. I'm sorry," I echoed.

"The first thing I told Winters was, 'Sue is like a mother to me,'" Haley let me know.

I was moved. Until she added, "His response was 'Get rid of her.'"

I flinched. Man, that was ugly. Another obstacle before forgiveness: to go forward, you had to wade through the mucky past. He'd probably told her to lose me on the same day he'd told me, "This girl is not your friend." Yet if I accepted that his wife and daughter's illness had induced temporary insanity, then everything horrible he'd said had to be relegated to history.

"I saw you're hosting a reading Sunday at the soup kitchen," Haley changed the subject. "Can I come?"

I was flattered; that charity event meant a lot to me. "Sure."

Standing at the podium that night, I saw a shock of red hair slip in the back row. Haley looked lovely in a flowery dress. When she greeted me afterwards, I gave her a birthday present: a crepe Tibetan journal and little silver pen, my favorite gift for fellow scribes and students.

"That's so sweet of you. Let's get together," she said.

I thought *this* was getting together.

"Donald and I split for good and I'm leaving New York soon. But I have time this weekend before I go."

I felt sad for her. "How about coffee after work on Friday? Around 6?"

"Let's have dinner." She upgraded my offer.

Aaron was out of town; I had no plans. "How about I take you out to eat for your big 3-0?"

"Let's see a movie too?"

Familiar red flags flew. We'd never done dinner and a movie. While I hoped Dr. Winters and I would find a healthy way to remain linked, I only wanted to make sure Haley was okay. Then I realized it could be the last time I saw her. So I offered to take her to *Sex and the City: Two*, as if to transform our Felliniesque drama into a romantic comedy, just a couple of gal-pals on the town. She met me at the café next to the theatre, already seated, wearing a light pink sweater.

"Happy thirtieth!" I told her.

"Thanks for the beautiful notebook and pen. And for meeting me. Sue, can I ask you something?"

"Anything."

"What would you say if Donald ordered me out of our penthouse the day Ann told me she's staying with him at his place in Paris next week?"

I thought *I* was incapable of small talk. I saw why we'd bonded. But she was still stuck in an endless breakup cycle. Done with my Oedipal triangle, she'd already found another. Ann was a fifty-five-year-old sharp redheaded critic from my workshop. I wondered if Haley's mother had red hair like hers, Ann's, and my mom.

"Ann's not seeing him,'" I said. "But you and Donald don't work."

She nodded, moved closer, and conspiratorially asked, "Well, don't you think she's being disloyal?"

"No." I was not re-triangulating. "Ann's only ever said how smart and talented you are. She'd never touch Donald." I sipped water. "Want to share the cheese and fruit platter or a salad?"

"Then why is she at his apartment?"

"Because she's your friend and broke. He'd probably offered her a free place to stay in Paris when you guys were still together," I said. "You know, when I turned thirty, my boyfriend left me and my boss fired me from my book reviewing job. I thought my life was over. Then I met Aaron and decided to be an author, not a critic."

"You think I should start over, get rejected daily, and live in Brooklyn with a bunch of roommates?" she asked sarcastically.

"Yes. You're still young," I told her. "I was forty-three before I was happy in work and love."

"Sue, I want your life," she confessed.

"I do too. But you only want what you think is my life," I told her.

"It took decades of sweat and I'm still struggling. You can't just latch onto rich successful older men to save you."

"Didn't you?"

"No!" I yelled. "How could you think that?" Didn't she know me at all?

Then I softened, remembering I had the love, shrink, agent, and editor she coveted. "I worked eighty-hour weeks. I still do. Aaron didn't have a job when we met. I was a book critic for a major newspaper. He was impressed by my column. He found Dr. Winters."

"Well I hoped he'd help me and Donald the way he helped you," she said quietly. I actually wished Winters could have put them back together.

"It seems like he tried," I said.

"He traumatized me," she jumped in.

"How?" I didn't know what had actually transpired between them—from her side.

"I had three appointments with him, for $400 a session, which Donald paid for," she said. "Then Winters went to Arizona and was never available. He didn't return my calls. I was chasing a ghost. In March, I get a message saying he was referring me to another therapist."

I was thrilled to hear he'd charged her his new high rate, quit her because of me, and they'd never clicked, as if a woman who'd slept with my husband was revealing he couldn't get it up with her. Then I felt embarrassed, falling back into an immature rivalry I had to get out of.

"I know he's really sorry. So am I," I said, reaching for the teapot.

"So you just forgave him?" she asked, seeming flabbergasted at the idea.

I thought of everyone who'd shared with me the horrific offenses they'd forgiven, reconciled, or learned to live with. Our quarrel wasn't worth spilling one more ounce of angst over.

"Haley, Dr. Winters saved my life for fifteen years. That buys him one mistake." As soon as the food came, I ate grapes and a chunk of cheddar, my appetite returning. "Listen, I met with . . . " Instead of "this Indian psychiatrist Vatsal," I said, "a new doctor."

"You're not seeing Winters anymore?" she asked.

I shook my head and shared Vatsal's story about the driver honking his horn at the SVU driver, not knowing her infant was choking. Haley didn't seem as enthralled by the badly paraphrased parable as I'd been. She wasn't eating. I pushed a slice of brie her way.

"You're saying that justifies his obnoxious behavior?" she asked, taking a tiny bite.

"If I thought Aaron was very ill, I'd lose it too." I took a long inhale. "Winters and I had years of good will to build on. You two had a bad start. He made an error of judgment, then probably felt guilty, knowing your connection upset me."

"But you wrote about him in your memoir," she said. "It was obvious who he was. His number is listed. Anybody could have called him."

"You weren't just anybody. You were my student coming to my private workshop who took a job I recommended and saw my old female therapist. We over-connected. It was a crazy Freudian storm." I wanted her to know how threatened I was, like I'd been erased. "You had 100 of my friends at your party. It was spooky."

"I knew them too," she said.

"Through me," I pointed out. "For three years I was your guru. Then I get an email you're quitting your job, me, my workshop, and find out you've been lying for months." I still wanted to figure out why.

I treated for dinner. She bought the movie tickets. I wanted to reclaim my role as the magnanimous mentor, sure this final night of repair should be on me. "I'll get popcorn."

Post-movie, we strolled downtown, deciding I was career-crazed Carrie; she was marriage-minded Charlotte, analyzing how bad the script was and if in real life "Mr. Big" would return. After six years off and on, mine had. Haley's didn't. The next day she was leaving her penthouse to bunk with a friend in midtown. Recalling how it felt to be up in the air at thirty, I walked her back to the regal home she was losing.

"So why were you mad at me last May?" I had to ask. "I came to your twenty-ninth birthday party and . . . "

"Yeah and what a present you gave me—the book where you trashed me!"

"What?"

"After the party, I stayed up late reading your novel. Lori was obviously me, your redheaded yogi student, a raging alcoholic and food addict with a rich fiancé who dumped her." Tears fell from her green eyes.

"Wait." I stopped. "You mean the AA and OA meetings I went to with Kim? I wasn't talking about you."

"Who's Kim?"

"Another student. She had red hair too. It was a combined character, for dramatic effect. I did use the yoga and your breakup story," I admitted. "But I never thought you were an alcoholic or food addict."

"You didn't?" She turned to me. "I have addiction problems, so I assumed . . . "

"I never saw you drunk or overeating," I said, confused.

"Gosh, I used to go through tons of wine and devour boxes of cookies at 3 in the morning," she said. "I showed you a piece about it."

"I grade stacks of student papers every week." I shrugged.

"It seemed like a mean parody of me," Haley said.

"It wasn't. It's not a memoir, it's a novel. I was fictionalizing, glomming characteristics of a bunch of students together," I admitted. "Why didn't you tell me you hated it? I would have explained."

"I was too upset. I should have," she conceded as we stood outside her building.

Since this was goodbye, I tried to wrap it up better. "Listen, Haley, you're so pretty and sharp and special. You'll figure it all out." I wanted her to heal faster. "Thirty is when everything great starts."

When I hugged her, she held on like she didn't want to let go. We'd had five hours together, the longest I'd spent with a friend since Claire moved away. Haley was leaving her impossible penthouse and losing her love. Suddenly I was thankful I was older, boring, sober, no longer chaotically fighting to find myself. Our ending appeared poetic, unlocking mysteries of our turbulent year. But it wasn't over.

At home, I stayed up late, perplexed, searching my pages for what lines had offended Haley. I found it in a scene where I sarcastically skewed the redheaded yoga teacher's twentieth breakup with her rich ex. Worse, towards the end, lamenting Claire and Dr. Winters both leaving Manhattan the same season, my first-person teacher heroine admitted, "I was using protégés to fill in my emptiness. Yet there was no substitute for important people in your world. They were irreplaceable."

So that was why Haley was furious! She thought I was saying she meant nothing to me—which wasn't true. I solved the paradox of why she'd quit me in May while grasping for my mentor. I'd insulted her without knowing.

At 9 a.m. the next day she called. "Will you look at my book review before it's due?"

Although I had a rule against allowing anyone to email me their work to edit, let alone in the morning, I acquiesced, seeing it as a final reparation I owed her. I carefully went over her pages, wanting to edit myself back into being the good mentor, not a middle-aged monster who'd wished her dead. Maybe she needed one last blessing over her words.

Soon after, Haley returned to her Southern hometown. Months later, on Facebook, I saw she moved in with a river boat captain. Then she unfriended me. While I wished her well, it felt liberating. Scrolling down, I noticed she'd become "friends" with her mother, which seemed a healthy transition.

I hoped our falling out hadn't soured Haley on professors, classes, or publishing in the future. I recalled the section of Janet Malcolm's *The Journalist and The Murder* where she claimed that all journalists were morally indefensible, justifying their treachery, "the more pompous talking about freedom of speech while the least talented talked about Art." In *Slouching Towards Bethlehem*, Joan Didion said, "Writers are always selling someone out." During our overlapping desperate dashes for success, I was afraid I'd sold out my favorite student without meaning to. Trying to publish a novel for decades, I'd had artistic megalomania, treating my literary agenda as more significant than the humans behind it. Yes she'd wanted to metaphorically kill me off, poach my friends, editors, and role models, and assume my identity. Yet by using details of Haley's life, I'd stolen hers first. I was the one who'd needed to be more careful with boundaries. How myopic and selfish I'd been.

Now I had to forgive myself.

CHAPTER 21
FULL-CIRCLE FORGIVENESS
APRIL 2011

"Remember that forgiveness too is a power."—Margaret Atwood

As part of my atonement, I scanned my world for broken relationships. It was time for a tour where I was the one asking forgiveness. Armed with Dr. Winters' humble apology in my head, I set off to make things right with the people I cared about.

During the fall, while drained by my feud, my close family friend Isabelle had asked me to read and edit for free hundreds of pages of her manuscript about surviving breast cancer. "Can't. Too busy," I'd replied. Angry that I didn't help with her project, she'd cut me off, ignoring my emails asking how she was doing. Now I saw that Isabelle was compelled to share her harrowing experiences and I'd selfishly not been able to make time for her.

"I'm sorry I wasn't there when you needed me," I called to say. "I'll make it up to you. Want to take my upcoming class for free and show me pages every week?"

"Susie, I would love to," she said, using my childhood nickname, erasing all the bad juju.

Next up was my surgeon brother Ben, who'd been enraged about my quotes in a magazine interview. I'd insensitively joked that I'd grown up with the "Jewish Doctor God Syndrome," aimed at creating a male physician factory for the next generation. I'd inadvertently insulted him and his children. I emailed Ben and left him a message. He didn't answer. I asked for advice from my sister-in-law's best friend, who suggested I send Ben's wife a real letter. I used actual stationary, writing sincerely, "I'm sorry. I never meant to insult you, Ben, or your kids. I regret opening my big mouth." I promised future discretion.

Ben responded by putting me back on his email list for Libertarian propaganda. I was in again! And so relieved. In a circle of forgiving, they'd all pardoned me. Even when I didn't believe I'd sinned, I'd learned that if I'd offended somebody I cared about, I could still offer authentic remorse to respect their feelings and erase their hurt. By obsessing over Dr. Winters' disloyalty, I'd been small-minded and blind to how lucky I was. The apology he offered felt transformative and powerful, launching me on a manic forgiveness binge.

I had no idea the next person asking me for mercy would be my husband.

"There's something I've been afraid to tell you," Aaron said one night toward the end of the summer.

"What's up?" I asked. Sitting at the desk in the corner of our living room, I'd mentioned my idea for a new project that chronicled all that happened with my chaotic shrink triangle.

"Maybe we should talk about it another time." Aaron looked pale.

"Let's talk about it now," I said, leading him to the black leather sofa, which I called my "therapy couch" since people who parked there tended to confess everything to me. We sat down next to each other and I looked at him, imagining the worst: He was bankrupt. Terminally ill. Having an affair.

"It's about Daniel," he said.

"Dr. Winters?" Now I was captivated. "What about him?"

"Remember his email asking you for forgiveness?"

"Yes, it was beautiful and perfect." I nodded.

"Well, he didn't write it."

"What?" My heart froze. "Who did?"

"I did," Aaron confessed. "Last month, he called me at my office. He was really upset you still weren't speaking to him and asked my advice. I basically told him to throw himself on his sword. But, as you well know, he's not really a writer. So I wound up dictating what he should say. He was trying to take notes but screwing it up. He felt horrible. I knew his feelings were sincere, he just didn't know how to say it right. And I read that book *On Apology* you left on the table, which you'd underlined so I . . . I'm sorry, I wasn't sure whether I should tell you . . . "

I burst out laughing, feeling a little mind-blown, yet taken care of by my husband's *fakakta* Cyrano de Bergerac routine. On my forgiveness tour, I'd been recommending people write the exact apology they wanted to hear but couldn't get. In essence I'd done just that through my husband, the only "core pillar" who knew me better than Winters himself. Weirdly, it didn't matter how the words originated if the sentiments expressed were true. I believed they were.

"You're not mad?" Aaron asked.

I shook my head no, held him close and kissed him. With my six-month grudge against the world disappearing, I was relaxed, reconciled, and drunk on peace.

POSTSCRIPT
HEALING HEART PROBLEMS
AUGUST 2017

"Forgiveness is another chance to make a new beginning."

—Desmond Tutu

"Your dad says you're a best-selling author and generous professor who might help me."

I was surprised by the email from Olaf, my father's kidney doctor, which I read on the plane to Detroit. He wanted help publishing an essay. Floored by the flattery from my cantankerous father, I promised: "You fix my pop, I'll fix your pages."

Dad hated spending his eighty-fifth birthday as a patient at his old hospital. Though we brought cake and balloons, he was gray and listless. Worried, I texted Olaf, offering an editing session if he'd rush to my father's room. I couldn't weigh in on his treatment like my doctor brothers. But Olaf could. Indeed, he discovered my father was being given the wrong dose of medication. He adjusted it as I marked up his work. Dad was tickled when he learned his favorite doc would be publishing his first essay in a magazine edited by one of my former students.

"What did you tell Olaf about me?" I questioned after everyone else had gone.

"How proud I am of my daughter," Dad answered.

"Why don't you ever tell me that?"

"I am now," he said.

I stayed for a few hours: it was rare to get time alone with my dad. Sitting at the edge of his sickbed, I asked "Why did you always say I was just like your sister Shirley? Because I'm not afraid to argue back?"

"Because you're sharp like her," he said. "Shirley mostly fought with your grandfather. He wouldn't pay for her college because she was a girl. It was especially unfair because Shirley was smarter than me. That's why your mother and I swore all our kids—girls and boys—would get a great education. We'd go into debt if we had to."

Despite disparaging my creative ambitions, he'd covered my tuition while I'd studied subjects he'd loathed—so I could find work I felt passionate about, with no financial burdens.

"Shirley's illness and death were so tragic. I thought you were saying I was too."

"Of course you're not tragic," he told me.

Was that because my father had saved me, before I was even born?

"I'm sorry I was a disappointment to you," I said quietly.

"What are you talking about? You stuck to your guns and became a big success."

"I wish I'd given you grandchildren," I confessed.

"I have a lot of regrets myself," he admitted.

"You do?" He'd never said that before.

"I should have kept teaching med school. But I was stubborn and my big mouth got me fired."

"I have your big mouth and stubbornness too," I admitted "Like Shirley."

"It took me too long to make a good living," he conceded. "I felt like a failure, switching jobs and moving your mother around so much before my career was solid, in my forties."

I recalled Kenan's awe that my father, a street kid whose dad wanted him to partner in Shapiro's Window Shades, became a chief of medicine who cared for his relatives, medically and financially. Seeing Dad as a prosperous powerhouse in our family's rags-to-riches mythos, I was shocked that we'd both had a late-in-life inferiority complex.

After nineteen days as a patient, Dad was strong enough to go home. I offered to extend my stay in Michigan, but he needed some time and space to get re-acclimated, he said. Before leaving for the airport, I went to his den. He was sitting at his desk on the phone, wearing the black Nike tracksuit I'd bought him for his birthday, yelling at the insurance company about a bill they hadn't covered. He was back! Overcome with relief, I started to cry.

"Don't be sad for me, Susie," he said. "Look, I'm eighty-five. My wife, kids, and grandkids mean the world to me. I have no regrets."

"But at the hospital you told me all you regretted," I reminded him.

"Oh, don't believe any of that crap. They had me on too many drugs," he insisted. "I got everything I wanted. I've had a great life."

Thanks to my father, I had a great life too. I loved the way he withdrew his regrets as he stood up to give me a hug, not knowing it would be our last.

A few months later, before I had the chance to visit again over the winter holidays, my mother texted me to say Dad had been rushed to intensive care, in heart failure. She told me he'd recited Poe's "The Raven" to the nurses and physicians, delirious from medication. I remembered when he'd first taught me poetry, testing me on stanzas. At three, when I'd repeated an entire poem he'd shared by heart, he'd kissed my forehead and said, "You're so smart," unwittingly sealing my fate.

I thought for sure he'd pull through again. I was shocked when my brother called to tell me we'd lost him.

At his funeral, I flashed to the night we'd attended a cousin's wedding, after I'd finished graduate school. Dad and I both snuck out of the synagogue for a cigarette, our shared method of self-destruction.

"Why are you so against my writing career?" I'd mustered up the courage to ask him.

Buzzed on White Russians, he'd whispered, "You're doing what I was afraid to."

That January, Dr. Winters emailed that he'd be in town for a few days. I asked if I could come by the new East Village office he used during his visits here. We'd stayed in touch over the last six years, publishing the addiction book we'd coauthored, which became a *New York Times* bestseller (for two weeks), proving how fruitful reconciliation could be. Without him, I wouldn't have a great husband, hardcovers I was proud of, or smoke-free sobriety. I'd felt certain I was off the couch forever.

Yet without my father, all the certainties were upended. I quickly spilled everything that had happened at his funeral and shiva, recalling our last words, and showing Dr. Winters my eulogy, which the rabbi had me read first at his memorial. Everyone cracked up when I shared my father's best, hilarious emails, like his advice on my bunion: "Cure is worse than the disease. So your toe ain't going to Hollywood."

"I'm afraid nothing will ever be the same without him," I said, sobbing.

"It won't ever be," Dr. Winters nodded. "But after the grief subsides, you'll be wiser and more powerful, with all the strength he gave you."

"How do you know?" I asked.

"Because you forgave each other."

APPENDIX
WAYS TO FIND THE PERFECT APOLOGY

During my forgiveness journey, I found many ways to extract an explanation from a person who hurt you and make an apology more likely:

1. EXPLORE WHAT WENT DOWN: "Calmly ask questions and gather more information about what really happened, which can sometimes be illuminating," said Manhattan therapist Patricia Gross. "Often times a rupture is caused by miscommunication and misunderstandings that can be clarified and fixed."

2. EXPRESS YOUR HURT ON PAPER AND SAY WHAT YOU WANT: Journalist Deborah Copaken wrote a letter to the man who had raped her thirty years before, reminding him what he did and how hard it's been for her to overcome. He confessed that he'd blacked out that night from excessive drinking and had entered Alcoholics Anonymous. As he kept saying he was sorry, "Thirty years of pain and grief fell out of me," she wrote.

3. DECIDE IF SOMETHING ELSE CAN COMPENSATE: Emanuel Mandel, the D.C. therapist and Holocaust survivor, never accepted the German government's apology on behalf of the Nazis who wiped out his family. Yet the $1,000-a-month war reparations helped his family reestablish themselves in America and have better lives. This is why compensatory damages are

often awarded in legal cases, though money isn't the only way to make amends.

4. CAN ACTIONS SUBSTITUTE FOR WORDS?: San Francisco event planner Emillio Mesa always harbored resentment that his mother had left him with his grandparents in the Dominican Republic for six years when he was a child. Though he joined her in New York, he kept his distance. Decades later, after he was beaten up in a robbery, he moved back into his mother's Bronx house, where she took care of him for six months. He decided to allow the love she showed him as an adult to make up for her early absence, and they were able to get close again. Is there something that might suffice for you?

5. LET THE PERSON KNOW THEY ARE FORGIVEN: Gary Weinstein, the Michigan jeweler who forgave the drunk driver who killed his wife and children, read a statement aloud in court. The driver expressed his deep remorse and the two met in person, which helped Weinstein move on.

6. FIND A FORGIVENESS SURROGATE: Conservative Rabbi Joseph Krakoff asked an estranged father to recite this prayer with his daughter on his death bed: "You are forgiven. I forgive you. Please forgive me. I love you." The father told his child, "I still don't think I did anything wrong, but I'll say the prayer because the rabbi says it's a better way to leave the world." Even the begrudging words helped her. Often rabbis, priests, reverends, imams, swamis, therapists, or teachers will be able to intervene on your behalf.

7. TAKE IT PUBLIC: Kenan Trebincevic, the Muslim Bosnian War survivor, was dismayed that there was never any official apology issued by the Serbian government's genocide against his people during the Balkan War. Chronicling the atrocities he witnessed, he wrote the apology he felt he was deserved and published it. Many young Serbs contacted him to express their remorse. Becoming a spokesperson for a younger generation of Bosnians

was how he met his Sarajevan wife. By confronting his past, he found his future.

8. ASK ADVICE FROM MUTUAL FRIENDS AND COLLEAGUES: In my more common case of estrangement, letting people who my mentor and I knew in common know about our fight upset him because it threatened his reputation. When he eventually wanted to get together to talk about what happened between us, I asked, "Are you doing this to make me shut up?" He said "Yes! Shut up already!" half-joking—or maybe not. I didn't necessarily care what his motives were—I wanted him to acknowledge he'd been wrong, which he did. Seeing the negative reactions of others in the community spurred him to wake up and reach out to discuss it.

9. TRY TO VIEW THE ESTRANGEMENT AS A MYSTERY, NOT MALICE: Remember the metaphor shared by Vatsal G. Thakkar, the Hindu-born doctor in Connecticut: "A commuter was enraged when a woman in an SUV stopped abruptly to get something in the backseat, almost causing an accident. He didn't know the driver's infant was choking. Similarly there is something you don't know about your offender's life that will shed light on his insensitive actions." In my case, it turned out something shocking had happened to my mentor's family. "I'm so sorry, I had no idea," I wound up telling him, apologizing profusely myself. Ask yourself: What is it I can't see?

10. APOLOGIZE YOURSELF FOR SOMETHING YOU DID WRONG: When I was upset with my father for trashing my work, he seemed impenetrable. But in the middle of a conversation about our family history, I told him I regretted missing my grandfather's funeral. That surprised my dad and he wound up sharing other remorse, love, and support before I lost him.

BOOKS I READ WHILE WRITING
THE FORGIVENESS TOUR

The Sunflower: Of the Possibilities and Limits of Forgiveness by Simon Wiesenthal (1969, Schocken)

The World's Religions by Huston Smith (1991, HarperOne)

Fuhrer-Ex: Memoirs of a Former Neo-Nazi, by Tom Reiss and Ingo Hasselbach (1996, Random House)

Forgive for Good by Dr. Fred Luskin (2002, Harper San Francisco)

On Apology by Dr. Aaron Lazare (2004, Oxford University Press)

The Year of Living Biblically: One Man's Humble Quest to Follow the Bible as Literally as Possible by A.J. Jacobs (2008, Simon & Schuster)

The Power of Stories: A Guide for Leading Multi-Racial and Multi-Cultural Congregations by Jacqueline J. Lewis (2008, Abington Press)

Forgiveness: Finding Peace Through Letting Go by Adam Hamilton (2012, Abingdon Press)

Radical Forgiveness by Colin Tipping (2009, Sounds True)

Wounded I Am More Awake: Finding Meaning After Terror by Julia Lieblich and Esad Boskailo (2012, Vanderbilt University Press)

Forgiveness: 21 Days to Forgive Everyone for Everything by Iyanla Vanzant (2013, Smiley Books)

Where the Peacocks Sing: A Palace, a Prince, and the Search for Home by Alison Singh Gee (2014, St. Martin's)

The Book of Forgiving: The Fourfold Path for Healing Ourselves and Our World by Desmond Tutu and Mpho Tutu (2014, HarperOne)

Looking for a Kiss: A Chronicle of Downtown Heartbreak and Healing by Kate Walter (2015, Heliotrope Books)

White Walls: A Memoir About Motherhood, Daughterhood, and the Mess in Between by Judy Batalion (2016, Berkley Books)

Imi: A Lifetime in the Days of the Mandel Family, by Terry Fred Horowitz (2017, Library of the Holocaust)

A Beautiful View: A Friendlier Christianity as a Way of Life, by F. Morgan Roberts (2018, Cascade Books)

Paths of the Prophets by Rabbi Barry L. Schwartz (2018, Jewish Publication Society)

ACKNOWLEDGMENTS

It took ten years to finish *Forgiveness Tour*. Immense gratitude to:

My awesome, intrepid book team: Jay Cassell, Tony Lyons, Brittney Soldano, Kirsten Dalley, Kathleen Schmidt and Julie Ganz, my great agent Samantha Wekstein, brilliant literary advisors Deborah Garrison & Brenda Copeland, book whisperer Tom Reiss, cover artist Eyal Solomon, and IT geniuses who save me daily EB & JT.

Those who shared their powerful stories: Chris Edwards, Alison Singh Gee, Manny Mandel, Emillio Mesa, David Roberts, Sharisse Tracey, Kenan Trebincevic, and Gary Weinstein, as well as Cindy, Cliff, Leah, Kate, and Raheem.

My Gurus: FCW, Patty Gross, Bob Cook, Reverend Elizabeth Maxwell, Rabbis Jennifer Kaluzny, Joseph Krakoff & Moshe Pindrus, and Dr. Vatsal Thakkar.

Kind Editors who took excerpts: Holly Baxter, Sari Botton, Wayne Hoffman, Brett Krutzsch, Tim Herrera & Erin Keane, and especially AJSA, AJPA, Naomi Firestone-Teeter, and the Jewish Book Council, for awards that gave me hope.

Best Critics: Sara-Kate Astrove, Jenny Aurthur, Judy Batalion, Roberta Bernstein, Kimberlee Berlin, Nicole Bokat, Ruth Bonapace, Haig Chahinian, Claire Cannon, Enma Elias, Alice Feiring, Merideth Finn, Frank Flaherty, Francisco Franklin, Aly Gerber, Eleanor Goldberg, Jenny Greenberg, Sarah Herrington, Jim Jennewein, RK, Tyler Kelley, Jakki Keruba, Amy Klein, Lisa Lewis, Aspen Matis, Sharon Messmer,

Puloma Mukherjee, Guy Niccoluchi, Jerry Portwood, Tony Powell, Rich Prior, Suzanne Roth, Jen Rudin, Carlos Saavedra, Sybil Sage, Abby Sher, Stephanie Siu, Gabrielle Selz, David Sobel, Nirvaan Sudan, Elisabeth Turner, Victor Varnado, Jeff Vashista, Kate Walter, Nicole Whitaker, Tallulah Woitach, Amy Wolfe, and Royal Young.

Life-saving Friends & Colleagues: Sherry Amatenstein, Lincoln Anderson, Nancy Bass, Larry Bergreen, Peter Block, Peter Borish, Peter Catapano, Amanda Chan, Eric Copage, Laura Cronk, Joanna Douglas, Tiffanie Drayton, Ian Frazier, David Goodwillie, Ryan Harbage, Barbara Hoffert, Katherine Goldstein, Josh Greenman, Gerry Jonas, Amy Jones, Daniel Jones, Julie Just, Seth Kugel, Deborah Landau, The Landsmans, Julia Lieblich, Phillip Lopate, Laura Mazer, Stan Mieses, Galia Peled, Danielle Perez, Zac Petit, Robert Polito, Saul Pressner, Eli Reyes, Naomi Rosenblatt, Mark Rotella, Jill Rothenberg, Karen Salmansohn, Joseph Salvatore, Grace Schulman, Mike Schwartz, Jessica Seigel, Gary Shapiro, Court Stroud, James Taranto, Jackson Taylor, John Turner, Lori Lynn Turner, Galen Williams, Yael Yisreali Laura Zam, and Michael Zam.

Treasured Midwest Compatriots: Lisa & Marcia Applebaum, Laura Berman, Judy Burdick, Kathleen Chambers, Arlene and Alli Cohen, Tracie Fienman and Miriam Baxter, Cindy Frenkel, Suzanne Gildenberg, The Grants, Michael Hodges, Sally Horvitz, Jon Jordan, E.J. Levy, Howard Lyons, Dr. Olaf Kroneman, Dr. Karl Zakalik, Tim Ness, Emery Pence, Ellen Piligian, Ronit Pinto, The Perchikovskys, Jill Margolick, Maureen McDonald, Andrea Miller, Nancy Newman, Brian O'Connor, The Saffers, Hilary Shaw, Solways, Karen Sosnick and Wendy & Sunny Shanker.

Loyal West Coasters: Linda Friedman, Kathryn Glasgow, Susie Goldsmith, Stacey, Julie and Carlyn Greenwald, Gary Kordan, Michael Narkunski, Jody Podolsky, Lenny Rohrbacher, Anita Rosenberg, Gary Rubin, Allen Salkin, Cliff Schoenberg, Jane Wald, Zell Williams, and Tom Zoellner.

Beloved Extended Family: The Brinns, Brownsteins, Carol and LuLu Rubin, The Wurtzels, Zippers, Sivan Ilan, Molly Jong-Fast. My Eternal Pillars:

Jack, Mickey, Brian, Eric and Michael. And CR, my favorite husband, love of my life, who once again gave me a great punchline and happy ending.

If I missed anyone: I'm sorry. I've been crazed with work, I'll make it up to you next time. Please forgive me.

ABOUT THE AUTHOR

Susan Shapiro, an award-winning writer and professor, freelances for *The New York Times, The Wall Street Journal, New York Magazine, The Washington Post, The Los Angeles Times, Newsweek, Salon, Tablet, The Forward, Elle, Marie Claire, Oprah, Wired* and *The New Yorker* magazine online. She's the national bestselling author/coauthor of thirteen books her family hates, including *Unhooked, Five Men Who Broke My Heart, Lighting Up, The Bosnia List* and *The Byline Bible.* She and her scriptwriter husband, a New York University professor, live in Greenwich Village, where she teaches her popular "instant gratification takes too long" classes at The New School, NYU, Columbia University, and now privately, online. Follow her on Twitter @susanshapironet and Instagram @Profsue123.